USA Travel Guide

United States of America Travel Guide, Geography, History, Culture, Travel Basics, Visas, Traveling, Sightseeing and a Travel Guide for Each State

by Alex Pitt

Table of Contents

Introduction

The United States of America is a large country in North America, often referred to as the "USA", the "US", the "United States", "America", or simply "the States". Home to the world's third-largest population, with over 318 million people, it includes both densely populated cities with sprawling suburbs and vast, uninhabited natural areas.

With its history of mass immigration dating from the 17th century, it is a "melting pot" of cultures from around the world and plays a dominant role in the world's cultural landscape. It's famous for its wide array of popular tourist destinations, ranging from the skyscrapers of Manhattan and Chicago, to the natural wonders of Yellowstone and Alaska, to the warm, sunny beaches of Florida, Hawaii and Southern California.

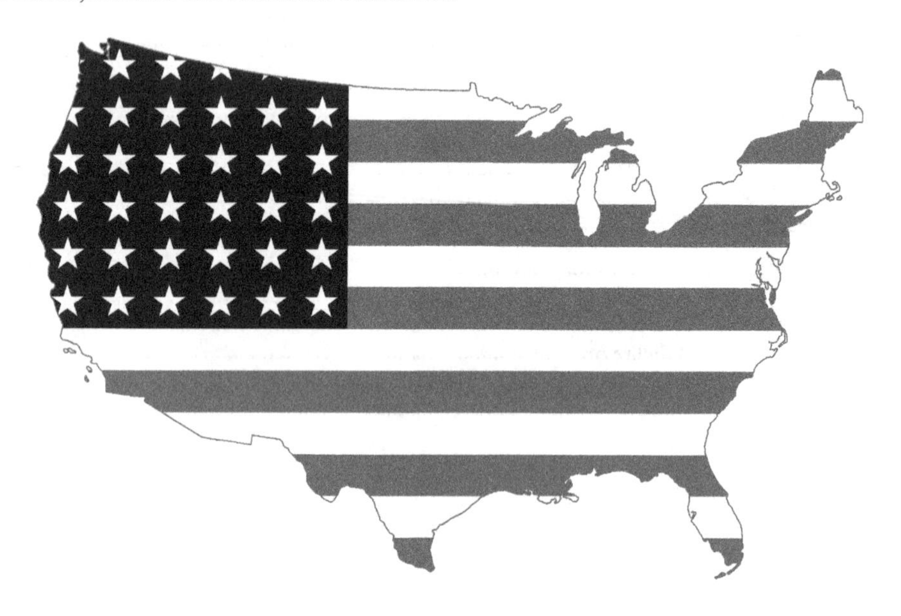

Quick Facts

• Capital: Washington, DC
• Government: Federal presidential constitutional republic
• Currency: US dollar
• Area: 9,826,675km² (water: 664,709km², land: 9,161,966km²)
• Population: 319,309,000(2014 estimate)
• Language: English is the most commonly spoken language. Spanish, Hawaiian, Samoan, Chamorro, Carolinian, Cherokee and many other indigenous languages are recognized at State and Territorial levels
• Religion: Protestant 51.3%, Roman Catholic 23.9%, Mormon 1.7%, other Christian 1.6%, Jewish 1.7%, Buddhist 0.7%, Muslim 0.6%, other or unspecified 2.5%, unaffiliated 12.1%, none 4% (2007 estimate)
• Electricity: 120V, 60Hz (Type "A" plug)
• Country code: +1
• Internet TLD: .us, .edu, .gov, .mil (most sites use .com, .net, .org)
• Time Zone: UTC -4 to UTC -10
• Emergencies: dial 911

The United States is not the America of television and the movies. It is large, complex, and diverse, with several distinct regional identities. Due to the vast distances involved, travelling between regions often means crossing through many different landscapes, climates, and even time zones. Such travel can often be time-consuming and expensive, but often very rewarding.

Geography

The contiguous United States (called conus by US military personnel) or the "Lower 48" (the 48 states other than Alaska and Hawaii) is bounded by the Atlantic Ocean to the east and the Pacific Ocean to the west, with much of the population living on the two coasts. Its land borders are shared with Canada to the north, and Mexico to the south. The US also shares maritime borders with Russia, Cuba, and the Bahamas. If counting the Insular Areas and Minor Outlying Islands, the United Kingdom, Samoa, and Haiti would also share maritime borders.

The country has three major mountain ranges. The Appalachians extend from Canada to the state of Alabama, a few hundred miles west of the Atlantic Ocean. They are the oldest of the three mountain ranges, are covered with a diversity of Subtropical and Temperate flora and fauna, a thick canopy of dense vegetation, and offer spectacular sightseeing and excellent camping spots. The loess lands of the southern Mid-West and the Limestone cliffs and mountains of the south add beauty to the region, with lush vegetation coating the surfaces of cliff faces that border rivers, and mist shrouding beautiful green mountains and gorges. The Rockies are, on average, the highest in North America, extending from Alaska to New Mexico, with many areas protected as national parks. They offer hiking, camping, skiing, and sightseeing opportunities, as well as desert and subtropical getaways in the southern lowlands of the region. The combined Sierra Nevada and Cascade ranges are the youngest. The Sierras extend across the "backbone" of California, with sites such as Lake Tahoe and Yosemite National Park; the Sierras transition at their northern end into the even younger volcanic Cascade Range, with some of the highest points in the country.

The Great Lakes define much of the border between the eastern United States and Canada. More inland seas than lakes, they were formed by the pressure of glaciers retreating north at the end of the last Ice Age. The five lakes span hundreds of miles, bordering the states of Minnesota, Wisconsin, Illinois, Indiana, Michigan, Ohio, Pennsylvania and New York, and their shores vary from pristine wilderness areas to industrial "rust belt" cities. They are the second-largest bodies of freshwater in the world, after the polar ice caps.

The western portions of the USA are rugged and very arid landscapes, complete with wind-shaped desert sand dunes like White Sands New Mexico. Death Valley (282 feet below sea level) is the lowest spot on the USA mainland and one of the hottest areas on Earth. Natural areas include vast areas of desert untouched by humans. Camping and hiking through the majestic landscapes of the Southwest is a big vacation draw for many Americans.

Florida is very low-lying, with long white sand beaches lining both sides of the state. The tropical climate allows many exotic (both native and non-native) plants and animals to flourish. The Florida Everglades are a pristine "river of grass," made up of Tropical jungles and savanna that are home to 20-foot alligators and crocodiles, among many other creatures.

The USA has every biome on earth, in the continental USA alone. From Tropical jungles and subtropical and temperate savannas, to searing deserts and Mediterranean coast lines, from frozen mountain peaks and coniferous forest, to a steamy Subtropical river system, the USA has something for everyone.

The Western United States is mostly mountainous hilly terrain, and has a mostly arid climate with mild to warm winters and hot summers. Parts of Arizona and New Mexico have a monsoon season which lasts from June to September. Frequent training thunderstorms often occur in this area during the summer, which can result in flooding. Dust storms can also occur, caused by downdrafts of a decaying thunderstorm. Coastal California and Oregon, from San Diego to Portland, is considered Mediterranean, and consists of warm winters and warm to hot summers. A cooler variation of the Mediterranean, also known as a maritime climate, can be found in the Pacific Northwest including coastal Washington. Hawaii, most of Florida, and far southern Texas have a tropical climate. Other areas in the south have a substantial amount of tropical microclimates. Central and northern Alaska features a subarctic climate with short mild summers and long very cold winters.

The least variation of climate in the continental United States occurs during the summer, when much of the nation is toasting in 70 to 90-degree (21-32°C) weather. Valleys in the Western United States often see the highest temperatures in the nation, along with many days and sometimes weeks of very dry weather. San Francisco and coastal Washington have the coolest summers in the Western United States excluding alpine regions of eastern California and Colorado. The greatest difference in climate from region to region occurs during the winter season, which is December to March, when temperatures can range from below 0 degrees (-18°C) in the Northern Great Plains, to a much milder 70 or even 80 degrees (21°C) in Florida. Long stretches of below freezing temperatures are common during the winter season across the Northern Midwest and Northern Northeast, getting milder as you travel south. and travelers should prepare to dress accordingly.

History

What is now the United States was initially populated by indigenous peoples who migrated from northeast Asia. Today, their descendants are known as Native Americans, or American Indians. Although Native Americans are often portrayed as having lived a mundane and primitive lifestyle which consisted of day to day survival, the truth is that prior to European contact, the continent was densely populated by many sophisticated societies. For example, the Cherokee are descended from the Mississippian culture which built huge mounds and large towns that covered the landscape, while the Anasazi built elaborate cliff-side towns in the Southwest. As was the case in other nations in the Americas, the primitive existence attributed to Native Americans was generally the result of mass die-offs triggered by Old World diseases such as smallpox which spread like wildfire in the 15th and 16th centuries. By the time most Native American tribes directly encountered Europeans, they were a post-apocalyptic people.

During the late 16th and 17th centuries, multiple European nations began colonizing the North American continent. Spain, France, Great Britain, the Netherlands, Sweden, and Russia established colonies in various parts of present day continental United States. Of those early settlements, it was the original British colonies in Virginia and Massachusetts that formed the cultural, political, legal and economic core of what is now the United States.

Massachusetts was first settled by religious immigrants, known as Puritans, who later spread and founded most of the other New England colonies, creating a highly religious and idealistic region. Its neighbor to the southwest, Rhode Island, was founded by refugees from the religious fanatics of Massachusetts. Other religious groups also founded colonies, including the Quakers in Pennsylvania and Roman Catholics in Maryland.

Virginia, on the other hand, became the most dominant of the southern colonies. Because of a longer growing season, these colonies had richer agricultural prospects, specifically cotton and tobacco. As in Central and South America, African slaves were imported and forced to cultivate in large plantations. Slavery became an important part of the economy in the South, a fact that would cause tremendous upheaval in the years to come.

By the early 18th century, the United Kingdom had established a number of colonies along the Atlantic coast from Georgia north into what is now Canada. On July 4th, 1776, colonists from the Thirteen Colonies, frustrated with excessive taxation and micromanagement by London and encouraged by the ideals of Enlightenment philosophy, declared independence from the UK and established a new sovereign nation, the United States of America. The resulting American Revolutionary War culminated in the surrender of 7,000 British troops at the Battle of Yorktown in 1781. This forced the British government to initiate peace negotiations that led to the Treaty of Paris of 1783, by which the victorious Americans assumed control of all British land south of the Great Lakes between the Atlantic Ocean and the Mississippi River. British loyalists, known as Tories, fled north of the Great Lakes into Canada, which remained stubbornly loyal to the British crown and would not become fully independent until 1982.

Although the Thirteen Colonies had united during the war in support of the common objective of getting rid of British tyranny, most colonists' loyalties at the end of the war lay with their respective colonial governments. In turn, the young country's first attempt at establishing a national government under the Articles of Confederation was a disastrous failure. The Articles tried too hard to protect the colonies from each other by making the national government so weak it could not do anything.

In 1787, a convention of major political leaders (the Founding Fathers of the United States) drafted a new national Constitution in Philadelphia. After ratification by a supermajority of the states, the new Constitution went into effect in 1791 and enabled the establishment of the strong federal government that has governed the United States ever since. George Washington, the commanding general of American forces during the Revolutionary War, was elected as the first President of the United States under the new Constitution. By the turn of the 19th century, a national capital had been established in Washington, D.C.

As American and European settlers pushed farther west, past the Appalachians, the federal government began organizing new territories and then admitting them as new states. This was enabled by the displacement and decimation of the Native American populations through warfare and disease. In what became known as the Trail of Tears, the Cherokee tribe was forcibly relocated from the Southeastern United States to present-day Oklahoma, which was known as "Indian Territory" until the early 20th century. The Louisiana Purchase of 1803 brought French-owned territory extending from the Mississippi River to parts of the present-day Western United States under American control, effectively doubling the country's land area.

The United States fought the War of 1812 with Britain as a reaction to British impressment of American sailors, as well as to attempt to capture parts of Canada. Though dramatic battles were fought, including one that ended with the British Army burning the White House, Capitol, and other public buildings in Washington, D.C., the war ended in a virtual stalemate. Territorial boundaries between the two nations remained nearly the same. Nevertheless, the war had disastrous consequences for the western Native American tribes that had allied with the British, with the United States acquiring more and more of their territory for white settlers.

Florida was purchased in 1813 from Spain after the American military had effectively subjugated the region. The next major territorial acquisition came after American settlers in Texas rebelled against the Mexican government, setting up a short-lived independent republic that was absorbed into the union. The Mexican-American War of 1848 resulted in acquisition of the northern territories of Mexico, including the future states of California, Nevada, Utah, Arizona and New Mexico. After 1850, the borders of the continental United States reached the rough outlines it still has today. Many Native Americans were relegated to reservations by treaty, military force, and by the inadvertent spread of European diseases transmitted by large numbers of settlers moving west along the Oregon Trail and other routes.

Tensions between the US and the British government administering Canada continued to persist because the border west of the Great Lakes was ill-defined.

The Oregon Treaty of 1846 failed to adequately address the complex geography of the region; the boundary dispute remained unsettled until 1871.

Meanwhile, by the late 1850s, many Americans were calling for the abolition of slavery. The rapidly industrializing North, where slavery had been outlawed several decades before, favored national abolition. Southern states, on the other hand, believed that individual states had the right to decide whether slavery should be legal. In 1861, the Southern states, fearing domination by the North and the Republican President Nominee Abraham Lincoln, seceded from the Union and formed the breakaway Confederate States of America. These events sparked the American Civil War. To date, it is the bloodiest conflict on American soil, with over 200,000 killed in combat and an overall death toll exceeding 600,000. In 1865, Union forces prevailed, thereby cementing the federal government's authority over the states. The federal government then launched a complex process of rehabilitation and re-assimilation of the Confederacy, a period known as Reconstruction. Slavery was abolished by constitutional amendment, but the former slaves and their descendants were to remain an economic and social underclass, particularly in the South.

The United States purchased Alaska from Russia in 1867, and the previously independent Hawaii was annexed in 1898 after a brief revolution fomented by American settlers. After decisively defeating Spain in the Spanish-American War, the United States gained its first "colonial" territories: Cuba (granted independence a few years later), the Philippines (granted independence shortly after World War II), Puerto Rico and Guam (which remain American dependencies today). During this "imperialist" phase of US history, the US also assisted Panama in obtaining independence from Colombia, as the need for a Panama Canal had become palpably clear to the US during the Spanish-American War. In 1903, the new country of Panama promptly granted the United States control over a swath of territory known as the Canal Zone. The US constructed the Panama Canal in 1914 and retained control over the Canal Zone until 1979.

In the eastern cities of the United States, Southern and Eastern Europeans, and Russian Jews joined Irish refugees to become a cheap labor force for the country's growing industrialization. Many African-Americans fled rural poverty in the South for industrial jobs in the North, in what is now known as the Great Migration. Other immigrants, including many Scandinavians and Germans, moved to the now-opened territories in the West and Midwest, where land was available for free to anyone who would develop it. A network of railroads was laid across the country, accelerating development.

With its entrance into World War I in 1917, the United States established itself as a world power by helping to defeat Germany and the Central Powers. However, after the war, despite strong support from President Woodrow Wilson, the United States refused to join the newly-formed League of Nations, which substantially hindered that body's effectiveness in preventing future conflicts.

Real wealth grew rapidly in the postwar period. During the Roaring Twenties, stock speculation created an immense "bubble" which, when it burst in October 1929, contributed to a period of economic havoc in the 1930s known as the Great Depression. The Depression was brutal and devastating, with unemployment rising to 25%. On the other hand, it helped forge a culture of sacrifice and hard work that would serve the country well in its next conflict. President Herbert Hoover lost his re-election bid in 1932 as a result of his ineffective response to the Depression. The victor, President Franklin D. Roosevelt ("FDR") pledged himself to a "New Deal" for the American people, which came in the form of a variety of aggressive economic recovery programs. While historians still debate the effectiveness of the various New Deal programs in terms of whether they fulfilled their stated objectives, it is generally undisputed that the New Deal greatly expanded the size and role of the US federal government.

In December 1941, the Empire of Japan attacked Pearl Harbor, a American military base in Hawaii, thus plunging the United States into World War II, which had already been raging in Europe for two years and in Asia since 1937. In alliance with the United Kingdom and the Soviet Union, the United States helped to defeat the Axis powers of Italy, Germany, and Japan. By the end of World War II, with much of Europe and Asia in ruins, the United States had firmly established itself as the dominant economic power in the world; it was then responsible for nearly half of the world's industrial production. The newly developed atomic bomb, whose power was demonstrated in two bombings of Japan in 1945, made the United States the only force capable of challenging the Communist Soviet Union, giving rise to what is now known as the Cold War.

After World War II, America experienced an economic resurgence and growing affluence on a scale not seen since the 1920s. Meanwhile, the racism traditionally espoused in various explicit and implicit forms by the European-American majority against the country's African-American, Asian-American, Hispanic-American, Native American and other minority populations had become impossible to ignore. While the US was attempting to spread democracy and the rule of law abroad to counter the Soviet Union's support of authoritarian Communist governments, it found itself having to confront its own abysmal failure to provide the benefits of democracy and the rule of law to all its citizens. Thus, in the 1960s a civil rights movement emerged which ultimately eliminated most of the institutional discrimination against African-Americans and other ethnic minorities, particularly in the Southern states. A revived women's movement in the 1970s also led to wide-ranging changes in gender roles and perceptions in US society, including to a limited extent views on homosexuality and bisexuality. The more organized present-era US 'gay rights' movement first emerged in the late 1960s and early 70s.

During the same period, in the final quarter of the 20th century, the United States underwent a slow but inexorable transition from an economy based on a mixture of heavy industry and labor-intensive agriculture, to an economy primarily based on advanced technology (the "high-tech" industry), retail, professional services, and other service industries, as well as a highly mechanized, automated agricultural industry.

In the 1970s, 1980s, and 1990s, millions of US manufacturing jobs fell victim to outsourcing. In a phenomenon since labeled "global labor arbitrage," revolutionary improvements in transportation, communications, and logistics technologies made it possible to relocate manufacturing of most goods to foreign factories which did not have to pay US minimum wages, observe US occupational safety standards, or allow the formation of unions. The outsourcing revolution was devastating to many cities, particularly in the Midwest and Northeast, whose economies were overly dependent upon manufacturing, and resulted in a group of hollowed-out, depressed cities now known as the Rust Belt.

The United States also assumed and continues to maintain a position of global leadership in military and aerospace technology through the development of a powerful "military-industrial complex", although as of the turn of the 21st century, its leadership is increasingly being challenged by the European Union and China. US federal investments in military technology also paid off handsomely in the form of the most advanced information technology sector in the world, which is primarily centered on the area of Northern California known as Silicon Valley. US energy firms, especially those based in petroleum and natural gas, have also become global giants, as they expanded worldwide to feed the country's thirst for cheap energy.

The 1950s saw the beginnings of a major shift of population from rural towns and urban cores to the suburbs. These population shifts, along with a changing economic climate, contributed heavily to Urban decay from the 1970s until the late 1990s. The postwar rise of a prosperous middle class able to afford cheap automobiles and cheap gasoline in turn led to the rise of the American car culture and the convenience of fast food restaurants. The Interstate Highway System, constructed primarily from the 1960s to the 1980s, became the most comprehensive freeway system in the world, at over 47,000 miles in length. It was surpassed by China only in 2011, although the US is believed to still have a larger freeway system when non-federal-aid highways are also included.

In the late 20th century, the US was also a leader in the development and deployment of the modern passenger jetliner. This culminated in the development of the popular Boeing 737 and 747 jetliners; the 737 is still the world's most popular airliner today. Cheap air transportation together with cheap cars in turn devastated US passenger rail, although freight rail remained financially viable. In 1970, with the consent of the railroads, who were eager to focus their operations on carrying freight, Congress nationalized their passenger rail operations to form the government-owned corporation now known as Amtrak.

During the 20th century, the US retail sector became the strongest in the world. US retailers were the first to pioneer many innovative concepts that later spread around the world, including self-service supermarkets, inventory bar codes to ease the tedium of accurately tallying purchases, "big box" chain stores, factory outlet stores, warehouse club stores, and modern shopping centers. American consumer culture, as well as Hollywood movies and many forms of popular music, books, and art, all combined to establish the United States as the cultural center of the world. American universities established themselves as the most prestigious academic institutions in the world, thanks to generous assistance from the federal government in the form of the GI Bill, followed by massive research and development investments by the military-industrial complex, and later, the Higher Education Act. Today, US universities are rivaled only by a handful of universities in the UK, mainland Europe, and Asia.

Government and politics

The United States is a federal republic comprising 50 states, the District of Columbia (Washington DC), 16 territories, and numerous Indian Reservations. The federal government derives its power from the Constitution of the United States, the oldest written constitution in the world in continuous use. Although federal law supersedes state law in the event of an express or implied conflict (known in legal jargon as "federal preemption"), each state is considered to be a separate sovereign, maintains its own constitution and government, and retains considerable autonomy within the federation. State citizens enjoy the power to vote for federal representatives, federal senators, and the federal President. The United States has two major political parties, the Republicans and Democrats, that dominate American politics at all levels. Due to the winner-take-all electoral system, smaller "third parties" as they are known to Americans are rarely competitive in any elections at any level, and the Democrats and Republicans have won every single presidential election since 1848. The Republican and Democratic dominant leads to a heavily criticized and frequently corrupt system of "pork-barrel politics" where necessary change is too-often subject to deadlock and bi-partisan point scoring.

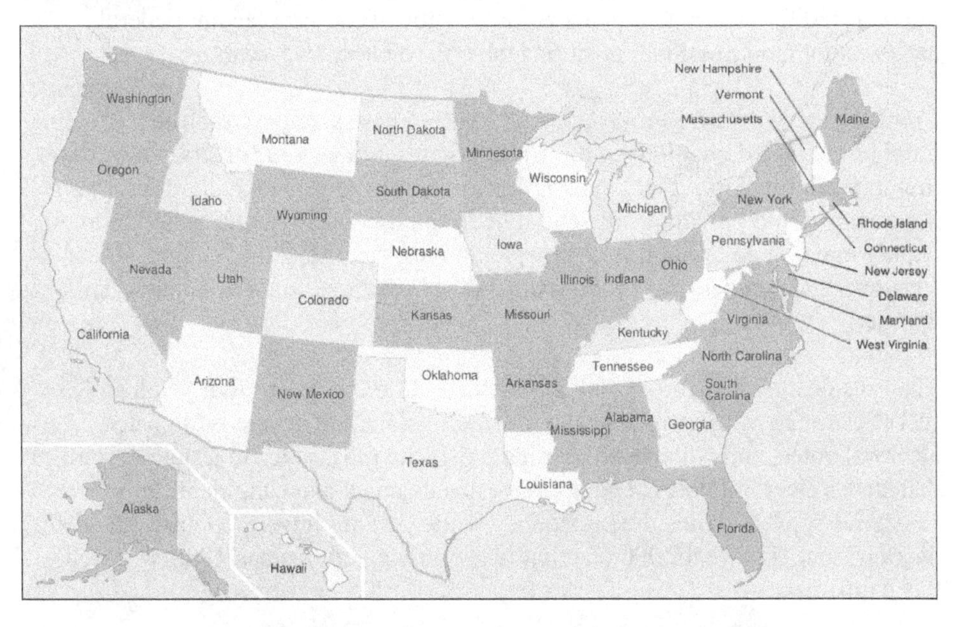

Americans value their rights to political expression strongly, and politics are fiercely debated in American society. In fact, there are many popular web sites and cable channels devoted primarily to political opinion programming. American politics are very complex and change quickly. For example, gay people were not allowed to marry in any US state as recently as 2003, whereas gay marriage is now legal in all 50 states. Many Americans hold and passionately defend strong opinions on a wide range of political issues, many Americans, especially older Americans, are loyal to one party, and political debates often become heated and lead to insults, vulgarities, and personal attacks being exchanged. For these reasons, unless you are intimately familiar with American politics or already know and agree with the political views of the person you are talking to, you are best off not talking about politics at all.

American elections are frequent and lengthy, especially the presidential election. Presidential elections in the United States last nearly two years, so there is a 50% chance that you will be visiting the United States in the midst of one. The November election is preceded by a six-month period from January to June wherein all 50 states, 5 overseas territories, and D.C. each vote one-by-one twice; one time to select the Republican nominee, and the other to select the Democratic nominee. One of these two nominees will be elected President in November. The current president, Barack Obama, first elected in November of 2008 and sworn in on January 20th, 2009, first announced his candidacy in February 2007 - nearly two years before his four-year term began. Federal elections for Congressional positions take place every two years.

Compared to Western European Democracies, there are an extraordinary number of elected positions in the United States. On a single election day, there might be simultaneous elections for dozens of positions. Typically, the average American would be voting for school board members, city councilmen, mayors, deputy mayors, governors, state representatives, state senators, congressmen, senators, the president, and a number of other positions, such as tax assessor or coroner.

The President of the United States is elected indirectly every four years and serves as the head of government and head of state. Each state is allocated electoral votes, and whichever candidate gets the most votes in a state gets all of that state's electoral votes. Though rare, this means that a candidate can win the "electoral vote" and thus the presidency while gaining fewer popular votes than his opponent. The year 2000 election is the only election since 1888 in which this happened.

The Congress is bicameral; the lower House of Representatives has seats assigned to the states proportionally, while the upper house, the Senate, comprises exactly two seats per state.

By way of contrast, the District of Columbia and the overseas territories have limited federal representation, as they can only elect "delegates" to the federal House of Representatives who cannot participate in votes by the Committee of the Whole on the House floor. (D.C. does, however, get three electoral votes with respect to the election of the federal President.) Because they lack state sovereignty, the governments of D.C. and the territories exist at the mercy of the federal government, which theoretically could dissolve them at any time.

The laws and legal systems of the U.S. will be complicated at best to understand and follow. State and territorial laws can vary widely from one jurisdiction to another, meaning that the US actually consists of at least 54 separate legal systems with regard to any area of law not within the purview of federal law. State and territorial laws are quite uniform in some areas (e.g., contracts for sales of goods) and extremely divergent in others (e.g., "real estate," the American term for immovable property). If this was not confusing enough, sovereign Native American tribes are allowed to operate their own legal systems separate from both federal and state law. What's more, the U.S. federal government practices the use of Federal Enclaves. Which are pieces of land or properties owned by the Federal government under an agreement of the state or territory. An example are U.S. national forests. As Federal owned land and property, most state and territorial laws do not apply. Examples are state and territorial anti-discrimination, minimum wage, and criminal laws. While state and territorial laws such as juvenile delinquency, restraining order laws still apply.

The federal government consists of the President of the United States and his administration acting as the executive branch, the United States Congress acting as the legislative branch, and the Supreme Court of the United States and lower federal courts acting as the judicial branch. State government structures are organized similarly, with governors, legislatures, and judiciaries.

Culture

The United States is made up of many diverse ethnic groups and its culture varies greatly across the vast area of the country and even within cities - a city like New York will have dozens, if not hundreds, of different ethnicities represented within a neighborhood. Despite this difference, there exists a strong sense of national identity and certain predominant cultural traits. Generally, Americans tend to believe strongly in personal responsibility and that an individual determines his or her own success or failure, but it is important to note that there are many exceptions and that a nation as diverse as the United States has literally thousands of distinct cultural traditions. One will find South Carolina in the South to be very different culturally from Massachusetts in the North.

Holidays

The United States has a number of holidays — official and/or cultural — of which the traveler should be aware of. Note that holidays observed on Mondays or Fridays are usually treated as weekend-long events. (A weekend consists of a Saturday and a Sunday.) Federal holidays — i.e., holidays observed by the federal government, state and local government and banks — are indicated in bold italics. If a federal holiday with a fixed calendar date (such as Independence Day) falls on a weekend, federal and most state and local government offices will be closed on the nearest non-weekend day. Since the early 1970s, several federal holidays, including Memorial Day and Labor Day, have been observed on a certain Monday rather than on a fixed date for the express purpose of giving federal employees three-day weekends. Foreign embassies & consulates in the U.S. also observe the same federal holidays (in bold italics) in addition to the official holidays of their respective countries. The private sector (besides banks) are usually open for business on most holidays with people working except New Years, Memorial Day, Labor Day, Thanksgiving, the Friday after Thanksgiving and Christmas when a vast number of non-retail businesses do close or open partial hours in observance.

Due to the number of major holidays in close proximity to each other, many Americans refer to the period between Thanksgiving in late November and New Year's Day as simply "the holidays." School and work vacations are commonly taken during this periods:

New Year's Day (1 January) — most non-retail businesses closed; parades; brunches and football parties.

Martin Luther King Day (third Monday in January) — many government offices and banks closed; speeches, especially on African-American history and culture.

Chinese New Year (January/February — varies based on the Chinese lunar calendar) — Chinese cultural celebration. Airfare within the U.S. may be reasonable at this time of the year but if planning to fly from the U.S. to China, Taiwan, Japan, Vietnam, Korea and anywhere in that part of the world the seats may be limited and fares higher so plan accordingly.

Super Bowl Sunday (usually the first Sunday in February) — The Super Bowl is the annual championship game of the NFL (National Football League) American football league and the most-watched sporting event of the year; supermarkets, bars, restaurants and electronics stores are very busy; big football-watching parties everywhere. Those with the extra money to burn DO travel to the host city where the Super Bowl is happening to attend the game live. This makes travel to that city even more hectic with a limited availability of airline seats, hotel rooms, rental cars and parking spaces at much higher than usual prices. The host city varies annually so plan accordingly if planning to be in the host city on Super Bowl Sunday.

Valentine's Day (14 February) — private celebration of romance and love. Most restaurants are crowded; finer restaurants may require reservations made well in advance.

Presidents Day (third Monday in February; officially Washington's Birthday) — many government offices and banks closed; many stores have sales.

St. Patrick's Day (17 March) — Irish-themed parades and parties. Expect bars to be crowded. They will often feature themed drink specials. The wearing of green or a green accessory is common.

Easter (a Sunday in March or April) — Christian religious observances. Depending on location, many restaurants, including franchised outlets of major national chains, may close. Major retailers generally open; smaller shops may or may not close.

Passover (varies based on the Jewish calendar, eight days around Easter) — Jewish religious observance.

Cinco de Mayo (5 May) — A minor holiday in most of Mexico often incorrectly assumed to be Mexican Independence Day which is really September the 16th, but nevertheless a major cultural celebration for Mexican-Americans. As with St. Patrick's Day, expect bars to be crowded, frequently with themed drink specials.

Memorial Day (last Monday in May) — most non-retail businesses closed; some patriotic observances; trips to beaches and parks; beginning of the traditional beginning of summer tourism season which means jacked up summer prices for rooms and airfare to some places.

Independence Day / Fourth of July (4 July) — most non-retail businesses closed; airports and highways crowded; patriotic parades and concerts, cookouts and trips to beaches and parks, fireworks at dusk.

Labor Day (first Monday in September) — most non-retail businesses closed; cookouts and trips to beaches and parks; many stores have sales; last day of the traditional ending of summer tourism season which means a better time to plan for travel to or within the U.S. in many places.

Rosh Hashanah and Yom Kippur (varies based on the Jewish calendar, September or early October) — Jewish religious observances.

Columbus Day (second Monday in October) — many government offices and banks closed; some stores have sales. Columbus Day can be controversial, especially among Native Americans, and is not as widely observed as it was in the past.

Halloween (31 October) — trick-or-treating, parades, and costume parties.

Veterans Day (11 November) — government offices and banks closed; some patriotic observances.

Thanksgiving Day (fourth Thursday in November, date varies annually) — almost all businesses closed, including grocery stores and many restaurants; family dinners. Airports and highways are very crowded. The next day, known as "Black Friday," major Christmas shopping traditionally begins. Many non-retail employees are given Friday off or take it as a holiday. If planning to fly within the U.S. during the week of the Thanksgiving holiday and the weekend after plan accordingly as the airfares are jacked up.

Hanukkah / Chanukah (varies based on the Jewish calendar, eight days usually in December) — Jewish religious observance, often culturally associated with Christmas.

Christmas Eve (24 December) – the evening or day before Christmas Day. The mythical character Santa Claus comes during that night to deliver presents.

Christmas (25 December) — almost all businesses, grocery stores, and many restaurants closed the evening before and all day. Airports and highways are crowded. Families and close friends exchange gifts; Christian religious observances. If planning to fly within the U.S. and internationally around the Christmas holiday and the week between Christmas and New Year's Day plan accordingly as the airfares are jacked up.

Kwanzaa (26 December - 1 January) — African-American cultural observance.

New Year's Eve (31 December) — many restaurants and bars open late; lots of parties, especially in big cities.

From a foreign traveler's point of view, there are two major services affected by federal holidays: visas and mail.

First, if you are a foreigner who needs to apply for a US visa, it is important to note the federal holidays marked in bold italics. All US embassies worldwide close on those days, in addition to the official holidays of the host country and are unable to process applications on those days.

Second, United States Postal Service retail counters are closed on federal holidays, and in high-crime areas, the entire post office stays closed. Self-service kiosks at post offices in relatively safe areas with 24/7 lobby access remain operational through holidays. However, mail deposited at a post office or in a mailbox will not be processed until after the holiday is over.

Other federal services like national parks and airport security operate 365 days a year regardless of federal holidays.

Many state governments also observe official holidays of their own which are not observed in other states or by the federal government.

Units of measure

The United States is the only industrialized country that has still not adopted metric units of measure in daily life (it still uses the customary English units that were in use prior to the revolution, similar to the later British imperial system, but typically with smaller units as one of the major differences), except for scientific, engineering, medical, and military applications.

All road signs and speed limits are posted in miles and miles per hour respectively. Automotive fuel is priced and sold per gallon. Other capacities of liquid products are normally quoted and sold per gallon, quart, or ounce (although liters are often indicated and sometimes exclusively used, as with some soda, wine, and other liquor products). Temperatures are reported in Fahrenheit only; 32 degrees (with units unspecified) is freezing (equivalent to 0 degrees Celsius). The good news is that most cars on the road in the US have both mph and km/h marked on their speedometers (good for trips to Canada and Mexico), and almost all groceries and household items sold in stores are labeled in both systems. The vast majority of Americans, though, have little day-to-day exposure to the metric system (apart from having studied it a little in school) and will assume some understanding of customary measures.

In addition, the US government does not regulate apparel or shoe sizes. Although there are informal standard sizes, they are not strictly enforced. The only thing you can count on is that sizes tend to be consistent within the same brand. If you plan to shop for apparel or shoes, you will have to do some trial-and-error for each brand to determine what fits, because you cannot rely on any brand's sizes as equivalent to another's. Please note that, as the average body size of Americans tends to be larger than that of those living in other countries, a concept known as vanity sizing (the labeling of larger garments with smaller sizes) exists in many clothing retailers, especially those aimed at women. It is very possible for people with smaller body types to have some difficulty finding suitably sized clothing.

Electricity

Electricity in the United States is provided to consumers in the form of 120V, 60Hz alternating current, through wall outlets that take NEMA 1 or NEMA 5 plugs. (NEMA stands for National Electrical Manufacturers Association.) NEMA 1 plugs have two flat, blunt blades (don't worry, they're not sharp), one of which may or may not be polarized (slightly larger than the other), to ensure that the hot and neutral blades are inserted correctly for devices for which that matters. NEMA 5 plugs add a round grounding pin below the blades. All US buildings constructed or renovated after the early 1960s are required to have three-hole outlets that accept the two blades and one pin of NEMA 5 plugs, as well as both polarized and unpolarized NEMA 1 two-blade plugs. The US Virgin Islands uses a slightly lower voltage of 110V. American Samoa uses US plugs, the German Schuko plug, and the Australian standard plug.

All of North America, nearly all of the Caribbean and Central America, Venezuela, and Taiwan follow US standards for electricity and plugs. If you are arriving from outside of those areas, you will need to verify whether your electrical devices are compatible with US electricity and plugs. Japan uses the same plugs as the US, but has a unique standard of 100V with frequency of either 50 or 60Hz depending on region. Most of the rest of the world uses 220-230V at 50Hz, for the simple reason that they began large-scale electrification at much later dates than the US and after wire insulation technology had significantly advanced. This meant they could select a higher voltage and lower frequency, which required less conductor material (meaning less use of expensive metals) but at the expense of more insulation and larger, more heavily insulated plugs. Colombia's voltage is 110V and Ecuador's 120-127V but the frequency is the same as the US.

Most consumer electronics, computers, and shavers are already designed as "dual voltage" devices capable of accepting voltages from 110V up to 230V and between 50-60Hz. For those devices, a plug adapter is sufficient. Purchase your adapter at home before you depart. Most US stores carry adapters designed to adapt NEMA plugs to other countries' outlets, not the other way around.

The differences in voltage and frequency are most frequently an issue for travelers with hair long enough to require the use of a hair dryer for proper hair care. Foreign visitors regularly find their hair dryers to be starved for power in the US; conversely, Americans' hair dryers are regularly burned out and destroyed by high voltages overseas. Apart from doing without or waiting an annoying long time to dry one's hair, the solutions are to either

• buy a high-wattage transformer capable of stepping up 120V to 220V

• buy a hair dryer with a switch that allows it to be switched between 110 and 220V

• buy a cheap US hair dryer for use during your trip; or

• book hotels that cater to international travelers and place hair dryers in the rooms for this reason.

The US federal government sets foreign policy, while the states deal with tourism. As such, the federal government provides the best information about legal requirements for entry, while information about places to visit and see is best provided by state and local tourism bureaus. Contact information is available in the individual state articles. At state borders, highway rest stops sometimes feature visitor centers and often offer travel and tourism information and materials, almost all of which is also available on-line or can be requested in advance by mail. Nearly every rest stop has a posted road map with a clearly indicated "You Are Here" marker. Some also offer free paper road maps to take with you.

Note that government tourism bureaus and their Web sites tend to be rather indiscriminate in their recommendations, since for political reasons they cannot be seen as overly favorable towards any particular area within their jurisdiction.

Regions

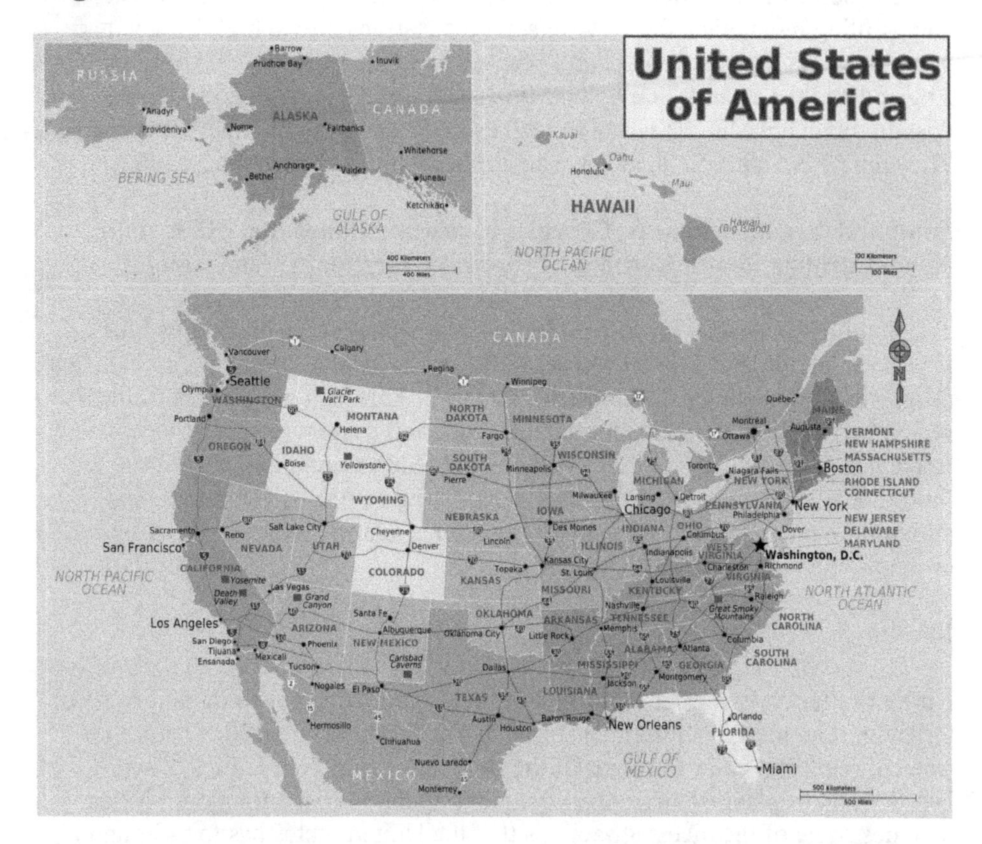

The United States is composed of 50 states, various overseas territories, as well as the city of Washington, D.C., a federal district and the nation's capital. Below is a rough grouping of these states into regions, from the Atlantic to the Pacific:

New England (Connecticut, Maine, Massachusetts, New Hampshire, Rhode Island, Vermont)

Home to gabled churches, rustic antiques, and steeped in American history, New England offers beaches, spectacular seafood, rugged mountains, frequent winter snows, and some of the nation's oldest cities, in a territory small enough to tour (hastily) in a week. The small-town environments have managed to maintain a large degree of autonomy for centuries.

Mid-Atlantic (Delaware, Maryland, New Jersey, New York, Pennsylvania)

Ranging from New York in the north to Washington, D.C., the Mid-Atlantic is home to some of the nation's most densely populated cities, as well as historic sites, rolling mountains, the New Jersey Pine Barrens, the Lehigh Valley, and seaside resorts like the Long Island beaches and the Jersey Shore. Bridging New England and the steamy South, the Mid-Atlantic includes some of the most cosmopolitan areas in the world as well as small enclaves of American history. The climate is Subtropical, albeit with chillier winters than in the South.

South (Alabama, Arkansas, Georgia, Kentucky, Louisiana, Mississippi, North Carolina, South Carolina, Tennessee, Virginia, West Virginia)

The South is celebrated for its hospitality, down-home cooking and its blues, jazz, rock 'n' roll, and country music traditions. A distinct literature, accents, and religiosity help distinguish Southerners as well. This lush, largely subtropical region includes cool, verdant mountains, waterfalls, temperate, subtropical, and tropical forests and jungles, cave systems hidden in vegetation, mist-shrouded limestone cliffs, alligators, ring-tailed cats, flying squirrels, and armadillos, agricultural plantations of cotton and sugarcane, island escapes, vast cypress swamps, and long white sand beaches.

Florida

Northern Florida is similar to the rest of the South, but is not so in the resorts of Orlando, retirement communities, tropical Caribbean-influenced Miami, the tropical rainforests and savannas of the rural areas, and 1,200 miles of sandy beaches and tropical islands. An extremely popular tourist attraction, Florida includes some of the nicest attractions that the United States has to offer and is conveniently located in the Caribbean, facilitating travel to exotic islands.

Midwest (Illinois, Indiana, Iowa, Michigan, Minnesota, Missouri, Ohio, Wisconsin)

The Midwest is home to farmland, forests, picturesque towns, industrial cities, and the Great Lakes, the largest system of freshwater lakes in the world, forming the North Coast of the US. Midwesterners are known for their simplicity and hospitality. The Southern Mid-West is distinct from the Northern portion, with cypress swamps and a Subtropical climate to lend diversity to the region.

Texas

The second biggest state in the nation is like a separate country (and in fact, once was), with strong cultural influences from its Spanish and Mexican past. The state is also a nexus of Southwestern and Southern cultures. The terrain ranges from southeastern subtropical and tropical forests, to the cattle-ranching South Plains, to the sandy beaches and tropical savannas of South Texas, to the mountains and hot deserts of West Texas.

Great Plains (North Dakota, South Dakota, Nebraska, Kansas, Oklahoma)

Travel westward through these supposedly flat states, from the edge of the eastern forests through the prairies and onto the High Plains, an enormous expanse of savannas and steppes (short grass prairies) nearly as desolate as in the frontier days. You can enjoy serenity and a beautiful expanse of subtropical/tropical and temperate savanna that's impossible on the coasts, as well as explore the lunar-like badlands, get comfortable in a wild-west town in the middle of the Black Hills, climb the otherworldly red mountains of Oklahoma, gaze at the bizarre chalk and sandstone formations, discover oddities such as grass covered sand dunes, discover animals such as rattlesnakes, coyotes, prairie dogs, constrictor snakes, and pronghorn antelope, or witness some of the wildest, most dangerous, and most beautiful weather spectacles in the world.

Rocky Mountains (Colorado, Idaho, Montana, Wyoming)

The spectacular snow-covered Rockies offer hiking, rafting, and excellent snow skiing as well as deserts, subtropical lowlands, continental highlands, and some large cities. Tourist cities include some of the nicest amenities for hundreds of miles and some parts of the Rockies are virtually untouched by man.

Southwest (Arizona, New Mexico, Nevada, Utah)

Heavily influenced by Spanish and Mexican culture, this area is home to some of the nation's most spectacular natural attractions and some flourishing artistic communities. Although mostly empty, the region's hot deserts have some of the nation's largest cities. Additionally, a strong Native American influence can be felt throughout as this region includes many large reservations and sovereign territorial lands.

California

Like the Southwest, California has a history under Spanish and Mexican rule and is heavily influenced by Spanish and Mexican culture in addition to massive immigration from around the world. California offers world-class cities, deserts, rainforests, geothermal features, Mediterranean coastlines, snowy mountains, and beautiful beaches. Northern California (above the San Francisco Bay Area) and Southern California (below the San Francisco Bay Area) are culturally distinct.

Pacific Northwest (Washington, Oregon)

The Pacific Northwest offers outdoor pursuits as well as cosmopolitan cities. The terrain ranges from spectacular temperate rain forests to scenic mountains and volcanoes to beautiful coastlines and Mediterranean beaches, to sage-covered steppes and deserts. In minutes, you can travel from a high-tech metropolis to a thick forest or a mountaintop.

Alaska

One-fifth as large as the rest of the United States, Alaska reaches well into the Arctic, and features mountainous wilderness. The state has a rich and diverse tapestry of native cultures including Yupik, Inupiat, Tlingit and others. Around 15% of the residents are of native origin.

Hawaii

A volcanic archipelago in the tropical Pacific, 2,300 miles south west of California (the nearest state), laid-back Hawaii is a vacation paradise. With beautiful cliffs, jungles, waterfalls, and beaches, it's definitely a place to unwind. The indigenous Polynesian population are known for being accommodating and fun-loving.

Politically, the US is a federation of states, each with its own rights and powers (hence the name). The US also administers a motley collection of non-state territories around the world, the largest of which are Puerto Rico (which has the special status of a "commonwealth") and the US Virgin Islands in the Caribbean plus American Samoa, Guam and the Northern Mariana Islands (also has special status of a "commonwealth") in Oceania, along with many others.

Cities

The United States has over 10,000 cities, towns, and villages. The following is a list of just ten of the most notable. Other cities can be found in their corresponding regions.

• Boston - best known for its colonial history, its passion for sports, and its university students

• Chicago - the country's third largest city (though still known as "the Second City"), heart of the Midwest and transportation hub of the nation, with massive skyscrapers and other architectural gems

• Las Vegas - gambling city in the Nevada desert, home to over half of the top 20 biggest hotels in the world; popular for its casinos, shows and extravagant nightlife

• Los Angeles - the country's second largest city, home of the film industry, musicians, artists, and surfers, with beautiful mild weather, great natural beauty from mountains to beaches, and endless stretches of freeways, traffic, and smog

• Miami - attracts sun-seeking northerners and home to a rich, vibrant, Latin-influenced, Caribbean culture

• New Orleans - "The Big Easy" is the birthplace of Jazz, and is known for its quaint French Quarter and annual Mardi Gras celebration

• New York City - the country's largest city, home of the financial services and media industries, with world-class cuisine, arts, architecture, and shopping

• San Francisco - the City by the Bay, featuring the Golden Gate Bridge, vibrant urban neighborhoods, and dramatic fog

• Seattle - rich museums, monuments, and recreational opportunities, and five distinct climates within 200 miles (321km)

• Washington, D.C. - the current national capital, filled with major museums and monuments, along with multi-cultural communities

Other destinations

These are some of the largest and most famous destinations outside of major cities:

• Denali National Park — a remote national park featuring North America's highest peak

• Grand Canyon — the world's longest and most visited canyon

• Mesa Verde National Park — well-preserved Pueblo cliff dwellings

• Mount Rushmore — the iconic memorial of 4 former presidents carved into a cliff face

• Niagara Falls — massive waterfalls straddling the border with Canada

• Great Smoky Mountains National Park — national park in the southern Appalachians

• Walt Disney World — the most popular vacation resort destination in the world

• Yellowstone National Park — the first national park in the US and home of the Old Faithful geyser

• Yosemite National Park — home of El Capitan and the famous Giant Sequoia trees

Get in

The United States has exceptionally onerous and complicated visa requirements. Read up carefully before your visit, especially if you need to apply for a visa, and consult the US State Department's Bureau of Consular Affairs. Travelers have been refused entry for many reasons, often trivial.

There is no airside transit without US entry between international flights. All travelers must disembark and proceed through immigration and customs inspection to enter the United States at first port entry, even if you're only staying for the two to four hours needed to transit between flights. This is most relevant if you're transiting between Asia or Europe to/from Latin America. Therefore, all travelers must be able to enter the United States on the Visa Waiver Program (or other visa exemption) or obtain a visitor's (B1 or B2) or transit (C1) visa.

Law and bureaucracy

The US federal government has five separate agencies with jurisdiction over visitors.

The most important one from a visitor's perspective is Customs and Border Protection (CBP), a bureau of the US Department of Homeland Security (DHS). The CBP's Office of Field Operations operates 20 Field Operations offices which supervise immigration and customs inspection stations at over 320 ports of entry. All travelers entering the United States must undergo immigration and customs inspection to ensure lawful entry. All US citizens and nationals and visitors who can qualify for the Visa Waiver Program (VWP) (as explained further below) generally encounter only CBP officers.

If you cannot enter the US through the VWP, you must visit a US Embassy or Consulate in your home country to apply for and obtain a visa, which will often require a short visa interview with a US consular officer. US Embassies and Consulates are operated by the Bureau of Consular Affairs of the US Department of State.

If you attempt to unlawfully cross a US land border at any other point besides a port of entry, you may encounter the U.S. Border Patrol, which is also part of CBP.

If you attempt to unlawfully come ashore in the US from a body of water at any other point besides a port of entry, you may encounter the U.S. Coast Guard, which is normally part of DHS (but can operate as part of the Department of Defense in wartime).

Finally, if you unlawfully enter the US, commit a severe crime in the US, or overstay your visa, you will likely encounter officers from the division of Enforcement and Removal Operations (ERO) of Immigration and Customs Enforcement (ICE), another DHS bureau. ICE operates a gigantic system of immigration detention facilities. Strict compliance with US law during your stay is strongly recommended. ICE is frequently criticized by human rights organizations like Amnesty International for ongoing problems with substandard healthcare and human rights violations.

Planning and pre-arrival documentation

Visa-free entry

Citizens of the 38 countries within the Visa Waiver Program, as well as Canadians, Mexicans living on the border (holding a Border Crossing Card), Bermudians, Cayman, and Turks and Caicos Islanders (with British Overseas Territories passports) generally do not require advance visas for entry into the

United States. However, the requirements for Guam, the Marianas Islands, and American Samoa are different and are listed below.

For Canadians and Bermudians, the entry period is normally for a maximum of six months. However, entry may still be refused on the basis of a criminal record. Those who have criminal records should seek out a US embassy for advice on whether they need a visa.

For travelers under the Visa Waiver Program, the entry period is strictly limited to 90 days (see additional requirements below).

As of July 2016, the countries participating in the Visa Waiver Program are Andorra, Austria, Australia, Belgium, Brunei, Chile, Czech Republic, Denmark, Estonia, Finland, France, Germany, Greece, Hungary, Iceland, Ireland, Italy, Japan, South Korea, Latvia, Liechtenstein, Lithuania, Luxembourg, Malta, Monaco, the Netherlands, New Zealand, Norway, Portugal, San Marino, Singapore, Slovakia, Slovenia, Spain, Sweden, Switzerland, Taiwan and the United Kingdom.

Citizens of the Federated States of Micronesia, the Marshall Islands, and Palau may enter, reside, study, and work in the US indefinitely with only a valid passport.

Citizens of the Bahamas may apply for visa-free entry only at the US Customs pre-clearance facilities in the Bahamas to the States, Puerto Rico, or the U.S. Virgin Islands, but a valid police certificate may be required for those over the age of 14. Attempting to enter through any other port of entry, whether by land, sea, or air, requires a valid visa. However, Bahamian citizens are not exempted from visa requirements for traveling to American Samoa.

Persons holding a passport from the Cayman Islands, if they intend to travel directly to the US from there, may obtain a single-entry visa waiver for about $25 prior to departure. If traveling by air or cruise ship, a police certificate will be needed to travel to the States, Puerto Rico, Guam, or the Northern Mariana Islands. This is the same for holders of British Virgin Islands or Turks and Caicos Islands passports. However, passport holders of the British Virgin Islands do not need a police certificate to travel to the U.S. Virgin Islands as only a passport will be needed.

Visa Waiver Program requirements

Travel under the Visa Waiver Program is limited to transit, tourism, or business purposes only; neither study, employment, nor journalism is permitted under the

VWP. The 90-day limit cannot be extended nor will travel to Canada, Mexico, or the Caribbean reset the 90-day limit. Take care if transiting through the US on a trip exceeding 90 days to Canada and/or Mexico.

Travelers entering the US under the VWP and arriving by air or sea must apply for Electronic System for Travel Authorization (ESTA) approval on-line before travel, preferably 72 hours before travel. An ESTA approval is valid for two years (unless your passport expires earlier) and costs $14 (payable by credit card). If granted, it allows the traveler to commence their journey to the US but (as with any visa or entry permit) it does not guarantee entry.

Entry under the Visa Waiver Program by air or sea also requires that you are using a signatory carrier. It is a fairly safe assumption that commercial scheduled services to the US will be fine, but if you are on a chartered flight or vessel you should check the status of the carrier, as you may require a visa.

Travelers entering by air or sea must also have a return/onward ticket out of the United States. If the return/onward ticket terminates in Canada, Mexico, Bermuda, or any Caribbean island, the traveler must be a legal resident of that country/territory. If travelling by land, there is a $7.00 fee when crossing the border.

A criminal record, including arrests, will generally make a potential traveler ineligible for visa-free travel with the following exceptions:

• Traffic violations

• Civil infractions (such as littering, noise violations, disorderly conduct)

• A single conviction for possession of marijuana

• Purely political offenses (e.g. non-violent protest in countries where it is not allowed)

• Offenses committed before the age of 16.

The ESTA application contains a questionnaire, which if answered truthfully will direct you to apply to a visa if you are ineligible for the Visa Waiver Program for reasons of criminal history, etc. If you have any concerns, complete the ESTA application well in advance of your departure to allow time to apply for a visa if directed to do so.

Effective as of 2016, any person who is a citizen of both a VWP country and of Iran, Iraq, Sudan, or Syria, or a citizen of a VWP country and who has visited any of those four countries since March 2011 is ineligible to enter the United States under the Visa Waiver Program.

There are disadvantages and restrictions to entering under the Visa Waiver Program. Under normal circumstances, these include the following:

• you can't apply to extend your authorized stay

• you can't apply to change your status

Obtaining a visa

Common US Visa/Residence Statuses

• B1: Business visitor
• B2: Tourist (also includes persons visiting family or friends)
• C1: Transit
• F/M: Student
• H/L: Employment
• I: Journalism/Media
• J1: Exchange program
• K: Prospective spouse
• TN: NAFTA employees from Canada or Mexico
• WB: Visa Waiver Program, Business; not extendable past 90 days
• WT: Visa Waiver Program, Tourist; not extendable past 90 days

For the rest of the world, or for those who don't fit the profile of a Visa Waiver Program entry (e.g., need to stay more than 90 days) the visa application fee is a non-refundable $160 (as of April 2012) for visas that are not issued on the basis of a petition (ex. business, tourist, transit, student, and journalist) and $190 for those that are (employment). This fee is sometimes waived under very limited circumstances, namely for people requesting certain exchange visitor visas.

Under US law, all persons requesting entry as non-immigrants are presumed to be immigrants (that is, trying to permanently migrate) until they overcome that presumption by presenting evidence of "binding ties" to their home country as well as sufficient proof that the visit will be temporary. To obtain a visa, face-to-face interviews at the nearest US embassy or consulate are required for nearly all nationalities. When the US rejects a visa application, it is usually because the applicant did not show enough binding ties to his or her home country to convince the consular officer that they will not try to overstay their visa. Since waits for interview slots and visa processing can add up to several months, you must start researching how to obtain a visa well in advance of your planned departure date. If you do not live close to a US consulate, you will need to set aside a day (or two) to travel to the closest consulate for the visa interview.

For technical and scientific fields of work or study, processing a non-immigrant visa application can take up to 70 days, as it can require eight weeks to receive approval from authorities in Washington. This especially applies to military and dual-purpose fields which are mentioned in a so-called technical alert list.

Note that a visa does not guarantee entry into the US. It only authorizes you to proceed to a port of entry and request admission. Be sure you apply for the right visa for your visit. Applying for the incorrect/inappropriate visa may lead to serious legal problems, as well as a possible indefinite bar from obtaining any US visa.

Travel to US possessions

The territories of Guam, Puerto Rico, the US Virgin Islands and the Northern Mariana Islands all have the same entry requirements as the 50 states. Although, the COFA nations aren't considered part of the U.S. and are independent countries, the U.S. maintains and exercises some extent of jurisdiction over the countries so the countries are somewhat US possessions. Which is why they are included here as US possessions.

Guam-Northern Mariana Islands

Guam and the Northern Marianas Islands allow entry, by air only, for an additional group of foreign nationals under the Guam-CNMI Visa Waiver Program: Brunei, Malaysia, Nauru, Papua New Guinea, Taiwan (only on non-stop flights from Taiwan), and Hong Kong. Citizens of Australia, Japan, New Zealand, South Korea, Singapore, and the United Kingdom are also allowed entry under the Guam-CNMI VWP and may enter either under that or the federal VWP. Entrance under the Guam-CNMI VWP requires a valid, machine-readable passport and evidence of a return airfare, and is limited to a 45-day stay in Guam and the CNMI only. Residents of Hong Kong must present a valid HK permanent identity card and are allowed entry with either a Hong Kong S.A.R. passport or British National (Overseas) passport. Residents of Taiwan must present a valid R.O.C. National Identification Card in addition to an R.O.C. passport. Citizens of Russia are eligible for parole (essentially the same as visa-free travel) to enter the Northern Marianas Islands only. Because of differences in entry requirements, a full immigration check is done when traveling between Guam and the CNMI as well as on flights to the rest of the US (currently, only Guam-Hawaii flights).

Despite not being part of the Guam-CNMI Visa Waiver Program, citizens of Russia can enter both territories Guam-CNMI visa-free under the waiver program, as long as they are in possession of a machine-readable passport, a completed Form I-736 (Guam-CNMI Visa Waiver Information form) and Form I-94 (Arrival-Departure Record) and a non-refundable and non-transferable return ticket.

Citizens of China will need a visa to enter Guam, but not one to enter the Northern Mariana Islands. Citizens will need to be in possession of a machine-readable passport, completed Form I-736 (Guam-CNMI Visa Waiver Information form) and Form I-94 (Arrival-Departure Record) may enter the CNMI only visa-free for up to 45 days (travel to Guam still requires applying for a visa in advance).

US and American Samoan citizens must have a passport as proof of citizenship for entry to Guam and the CNMI. However, US and American Samoan citizens can live, work, and travel freely in both territories.

American Samoa

American Samoa lies outside federal immigration jurisdiction and has separate entry requirements, which even apply to US citizens. Entry is allowed for 30 days (extendable to 60 days) for tourism with a valid passport and proof of onward travel or local employment. Nationals from the following countries can visit American Samoa for tourist purposes only visa-free for up to 30 days; Andorra, Australia, Austria, Belgium, Brunei, Canada, Denmark, Finland, France, Germany, Iceland, Ireland, Italy, Japan, Liechtenstein, Luxembourg, Marshall Islands, Micronesia, Monaco, Netherlands, New Zealand, Norway, Palau, Portugal, San Marino, Singapore, Spain, Sweden, Switzerland and United Kingdom. However, an entry permit will be issued upon arrival. Entry requirements are somewhat different for Americans with US citizenship. US citizens are required to have only a six month valid passport, an entry ticket, and an exit ticket. US citizens can live, work, and travel freely for a unlimited time in American Samoa.

Puerto Rico-US Virgin Islands

Both Puerto Rico and the US Virgin Islands choose to follow the Mainland US entry requirements. As with the Mainland, any non-US citizen who is eligible may enter under the Visa Waiver Program. American and American Samoan citizens don't need a passport nor visa to travel to both Puerto Rico and the US Virgin Islands. Only some form of government ID (example; a driver's license) is needed for proof of citizenship. Any US and American Samoan citizen can live, work and travel freely for a unlimited time in both territories.

COFA nations

US citizens and citizens of countries under the federal Visa Waiver Program plus Palau, the Marshall Islands, and the Federated States of Micronesia are allowed visa-free entry. And can reside and work anywhere in the United States for a unlimited time. All other foreign nationals must contact the American Samoa Attorney General's office to obtain a visa at (684) 633-4163.

US Minor Outlying Islands

All foreign, US and American Samoan citizens must have special travel permits to travel to all uninhabited territories that make up the US Minor Outlying Islands.

Arriving in the United States

Before arrival, if you are not a Canadian or Bermudian, you will receive either a white I-94 (if entering with a visa) or green I-94W (if entering on a visa waiver) form to complete. For visitors travelling under the Visa Waiver Program arriving by air, the I-94W has now been replaced by the electronic ESTA system; therefore, the form is not required. Again, remember that the ESTA approval is in essence, a permit to travel - not a guarantee of entry, hence there is no need to produce a copy of it at passport control - had there been any problems you would have been denied boarding at your origin airport, however most travelers tend to keep a copy of it in their possession anyway, just in case.

I-94 forms are now used primarily at land ports of entry. As October 2013, the I-94 paper form is now optional for virtually all visitors arriving by common carrier at air and sea ports of entry. CBP now has arrangements in place to electronically receive manifest information directly from all major common carriers. From the manifests, CBP's computers create and maintain electronic I-94 records for all passengers who are foreign visitors. CBP operates a Web site where visitors may view their own electronic I-94 record while they are still in the United States.

When you reach a CBP immigration checkpoint, you will undergo a short interview if you are not a citizen or resident of the United States. A CBP officer will attempt to determine if the purpose of your visit is valid. Usually, the determination of admissibility is made in a minute or less.

Otherwise, you may be referred to further questioning in a more private area. At that stage the CBP officers will likely search your possessions, and may read any documents, letters or diaries found in your possession. Do not bring anything that could imply you intend to permanently immigrate or otherwise violate the terms of your visa. For example, you should not be carrying work-related or sales materials if you are entering on a tourist visa. If you are unable to convince the CBP officers that you will abide by the terms of your visa (or VWP ESTA authorization if applicable), it can be cancelled on the spot, and you will be denied entry.

Like immigration and customs officials everywhere, CBP officials are humorless about any kind of security threat. Even the most flippant joke implying that you pose a threat can result in lengthy interrogation at best, and summary expulsion at worst.

For non-residents, your entry forms will need to state the street address of the location where you will be staying for the first night. This should be arranged in advance. The name of your hotel, hostel, university, etc. is not sufficient; you must provide the street name and number.

Once you are admitted, the departure portion of your I-94 or I-94W will be stapled to your passport (if you were required to fill it out). Keep it safe as you will need to give it CBP upon departure from the US. In the alternative, even if you weren't required to fill out a I-94, the CBP officer will place an admission stamp in your passport which shows that you were admitted to the United States under a certain class and until a certain date.

For most travelers entering on visitor status (B1 or B2), you will normally be granted permission to stay for up to six months. Travelers entering under the VWP will receive permission to remain for 90 days only. If you enter under a student (F) or exchange visitor (J) status, your permitted duration of stay will normally be indicated as D/S, which means "permitted to remain provided status as a student/exchange visitor is maintained".

At customs

All travelers entering the US (including US citizens, nationals, and permanent residents) must fill out the Customs Declaration form, CBP Form 6059B, a blue-colored form in the shape of a tall narrow rectangle. It used to be distributed on the plane, but some airlines now hand it out at check-in for flights to the US.

If you are travelling with family members, then only one form per family is required to be filled out. Normally, the head of the family is responsible for ensuring the declaration is accurate.

The Customs Declaration form asks you to declare whether you are bringing with you a variety of heavily regulated items, such as more than USD10,000 in cash. In addition, you must list on the back side all goods that you are permanently bringing into the US and leaving there (such as foreign gifts for US-based friends and family). The Form 6059B is notorious for not having enough space on the back, so ask for and fill out multiple forms if you have many items to declare.

After you are admitted into the US and retrieve your bags from the baggage claim, you will proceed to the secondary inspection area (the customs checkpoint), regardless of whether your journey terminates at this airport or if you are transiting onward via another flight. Hand your customs declaration to the officer. Most of the time, the officer will point you to the exit and that will be it.

Sometimes, the officer may ask you a few routine questions and then let you go. The officer may refer you to an adjacent X-ray machine to have your bags inspected or may refer you for a manual hand search of your bags. Any search more intrusive than a bag search is rare and is usually indicated only if some sort of probable cause has been established through questioning or during the bag search to suggest suspicious activity.

Note that you can't bring meat or raw fruit or vegetables, but you may bring cooked non-meat packaged foods, such as bread, cookies, and other baked goods. See APHIS for details. The US Customs process is straightforward. Most articles that are prohibited or restricted in any other country are prohibited or restricted in the US. One rule that is unique to America is that it is generally prohibited to bring in goods made in countries on which the US has imposed economic sanctions such as Cuba, Iran, North Korea (DPRK) and Syria.

The US possessions of American Samoa, Guam, the Northern Marianas Islands, and the US Virgin Islands are all outside federal customs jurisdiction. Each imposes their own separate requirements. Travel between these regions and the rest of the US requires a customs inspection. There are some differences (mostly larger) in duty exemptions for US citizens returning from these destinations.

After customs

As noted above, all inbound citizens, nationals, and visitors must pass through immigration and customs at their first point of entry, regardless of whether they have onward connections to other destinations inside or outside the US or not. Many major airports have special arrangements for travelers with connecting flights such as a bag drop, check-in counter or security checkpoint just for the use of connecting passengers (you will need to re-clear security because you had access to your bags while passing through customs) upon coming out from customs inspection. Some airports do not, meaning that you will need to proceed to the main check-in desks with other departing passengers.

Closed cities

If you managed to get into the United States visa-free or not, if you plan on visiting rural Nevada, be careful on where you are. There is a closed city in Nevada called Mercury which the town was involved in nuclear testing programs by the U.S. government, something it no longer conducts. This city like many other closed cities are closed off to the public, including foreigners. You will need special permission from the U.S. government in order to enter the town. Attempting to enter without the permission will get you arrested.

Leaving the United States (and re-entering from Canada or Mexico)

Unlike most countries, the US does not provide formal passport control checkpoints for those exiting the country. This used to be a big problem for many tourists who left by air or sea, but is not a major issue any more. Since CBP now receives manifests automatically from all major common carriers, CBP can automatically update their electronic I-94 records to show you timely departed from the United States as long as you leave on a common carrier (like a major airline).

Otherwise, if you are leaving the US for the last time on a particular trip (e.g., not returning from Canada or Mexico), it is ultimately your responsibility to turn over the departure record of your I-94 or I-94(W) to CBP at the Canadian or Mexican borders if leaving by land.

By plane

Most visitors from outside Canada and Mexico arrive in the United States by plane. While many medium-sized inland cities have an international airport, there are limited flights to most of them. Most travelers enter the US at one of the major entry points along the coasts:

• From the east: New York City, Newark, Chicago, Philadelphia, Atlanta, Charlotte, Boston, Washington, D.C., Orlando, and Miami are the primary entry points from Europe and other transatlantic points of departure. All the major East Coast airports have service from a few key European cities. Other cities, such as Dallas, Houston, Los Angeles, San Francisco, and Seattle, while not on the east also have a good number of flights from major European cities flying over northern Greenland and the Hudson Bay or the Arctic Ocean. US immigration and customs can be completed prior to boarding in Shannon and Dublin airports in Ireland.

• From the west: New York City, Los Angeles, San Francisco, Seattle, and Honolulu are the primary points of entry from Asia and other transpacific points of departure. with Chicago, Houston, Dallas, Detroit, Atlanta, Boston and

Washington, D.C. having a few international flight options. Of course, if you arrive in Honolulu, you must take another flight to get to the mainland. Foreign airlines are not allowed to transport passengers to/from Hawaii or Alaska and the other 48 states (except for refueling and in-transit). They may allow a stopover in Hawaii for free or for an extra cost to passengers travelling onwards from the United States. If you are flying into the West Coast to transit to another destination, San Francisco International Airport has a free frequent SkyTrain linking terminals and relatively short security lines, in comparison to Los Angeles where you will be exposed to the weather catching a shuttle bus or walking between terminals and will have to put up with huge security lines. Qantas serves Dallas/Fort Worth non-stop from Sydney, in addition to their daily service to Los Angeles from Sydney, Melbourne and Brisbane and San Francisco from Sydney. Air New Zealand also serves Houston from Auckland as well as Honolulu, Los Angeles, and San Francisco.

• From the north: Chicago, Detroit and Minneapolis feature many flights from major Asian and Canadian cities. Most major US airports receive nonstop flights from most major cities in Canada while others closer to the Canadian border also have direct buses by various companies to/from the nearest Canadian city north of the border (such as Vancouver-Seattle; Toronto-Buffalo; Detroit-Windsor, etc.). In most major Canadian airports, U.S. immigration and/or formalities are completed and approved PRIOR to boarding a U.S. bound flight thus arriving into the U.S. as 'domestic' flight.

• From the south: Miami, Atlanta, Houston, and Dallas are the primary entry points from Latin America, primarily South and Central America and the Caribbean. Also Los Angeles, Chicago, New York, Washington, DC, and Charlotte are major international waypoints. Most major US airports receive nonstop flights from most major cities in Mexico. There are very limited number of direct flights available between the 'west' (China, Japan, Korea, Australia, New Zealand, etc) and 'south' (Central & South America) which can requires a transfer or stopover in the United States. Most travelers travelling between Asia-Pacific and Central and South American destinations usually transfer flights in Los Angeles. Others may arrive into Los Angeles and continue across to Dallas, Houston, or Miami and continue south from there (vice versa) depending on the destinations and the airlines used. From the "east" and "other side of the world" they may arrive in Chicago, Houston, New York, or Miami to make connections for south bound flights).

• From Cuba: Miami is the primary entry/exit points from/to Cuba. Due to the ongoing strict embargo against Cuba, flights are available on a chartered basis through specialized travel agents authorized to sell tickets by OFAC (Office of Foreign Assets Control) and only to those with an OFAC license to spend money in Cuba. As of December 17, 2014 Presidents Barack Obama and Raul Castro announced moves to re-establish diplomatic relations between the two countries as well as to loosen trade and travel restrictions. Implementation plans are underway to normalize trade & travel in the coming months or years and this section is subject to change as the airlines plan regular flights between the US and Cuba and to apply for approval to fly the routes from authorities on both sides of the Florida Strait.

• From the other side of the world: New Delhi, India has non-stop service to New York (via JFK and Newark airports), Chicago, and San Francisco. Mumbai has non-stop flights to New York (JFK and Newark). From Pakistan, Saudi Arabia, Uzbekistan and United Arab Emirates you can also fly to New York (JFK). Qatar, and Saudi Arabian fly to Washington, D.C., and South African Airways goes to New York (JFK) and Washington, DC (Dulles). Los Angeles, Dallas, and Houston both offer non-stop service to Qatar and the United Arab Emirates.

Luggage allowance for flights to or from the US usually operates on a piecewise system in addition to the weight system even for foreign carriers. This means that you are allowed a limited number of bags to check-in where each bag should not exceed certain linear dimensions (computed by adding the length, width and height of the bags). The exact allowances and restrictions on weight, linear dimension and number of baggage allowed are determined by the carrier you are flying with, your origin (if coming to the US) or destination (if leaving the US) and the class of service you are travelling in.

Airport security

International flights bound for the United States tend to feature extremely strict security. Besides going through a regular security search to enter the departure area of the airport terminal, it was standard up until 2015 at many airports to have an additional layer of security around waiting areas for gates for US-bound flights with a secondary security checkpoint of its own. While that kind of security is no longer seen at many airports, all airlines with US-bound flights continue to carefully inspect all documents at time of boarding and often still perform hand searches of carry-on bags on the jet way.

Within the US, airport security procedures continue to evolve. The TSA (Transportation Security Administration) now requires all passengers to remove shoes and outerwear (coats and jackets) and submit those items along with all personal belongings to X-ray screening. Laptops and large cameras must be removed from bags and scanned separately.

Full body scanning x-ray machines are now in use at many US airports, which are capable of detecting many non-metallic threats. Because of early problems with displaying far too much detail at security checkpoints to the embarrassment of travelers, the scanners were subsequently modified so that a fully detailed image is displayed only at a remote analysis center. The off-site screener marks rectangles on a generic diagram corresponding to any portions of a traveler's body that look unusual. Only that marked-up diagram is displayed at the checkpoint, thereby enabling TSA officers to focus any necessary pat-down on those areas. If there is nothing suspicious on the scan, the off-site screener sends an "OK" message authorizing the traveler to proceed.

The full body scanners are optional and passengers have the legal right to "opt out" and request a manual search instead. Furthermore, passengers may also be randomly selected for additional screening, such as an "enhanced pat-down." Do not assume that you are in any sort of trouble or that you are even suspected of causing trouble, simply because you are being subjected to these further screenings.

Pre-clearance

Passengers whose journeys originate in major Canadian airports and involve either US or Canadian carriers will have the advantage of clearing US entry formalities (passport control and customs) at their Canadian port-of-exit. As far as most flights from Canada are concerned, they are treated similarly as US domestic flights but only because clearance has been performed at the Canadian airport. Hence once passengers from Canada arrive at their US port-of-entry, rather than walk through a secluded corridor, they can see the display of restaurants and shops at the domestic terminal on their way to baggage claim. It is worth noting that most Canadian carriers are located in US domestic terminals.

Take note that passengers on US-Canadian flights operated by foreign carriers like Philippine Airlines and Cathay Pacific will still see traditional entry formalities upon arrival at their US port-of-entry; a Canadian transit visa may be required even if passengers are confined to a holding area for the entire transit time.

Some airports in Canada, including Vancouver International Airport, Terminal 1 of Toronto-Pearson Airport, and Montréal-Trudeau Airport generally do not require passengers in transit from abroad to pass through Canadian Customs and Immigration controls before going through US pre-clearance formalities. However, even if you pass through these airports, make sure that your papers are in order to allow you to enter Canada. If you cannot travel to the US on the same day you go through pre-clearance, if you are not cleared for entry to the United States, or if you and/or your luggage is not checked through by your airline to at least your first destination in the United States, you will need to report to Canada Customs, and in that event, a Canadian transit or temporary resident visa may be required.

Pre-clearance facilities are available at most major Canadian airports (Toronto-Pearson, Montreal-Trudeau, Ottawa Macdonald-Cartier, Vancouver, Calgary, etc.), Queen Beatrix International Airport in Aruba, Grand Bahama and Lynden Pindling International Airports in the Bahamas, Bermuda International Airport in Bermuda, and Dublin and Shannon International Airports in Ireland.

Passengers on British Airways flights from London to New York City transiting via either Dublin or Shannon, Ireland can take advantage of US passport control and customs pre-clearance at Dublin or Shannon. Upon arrival at the US, they will arrive as domestic passengers and can transfer immediately to domestic flights.

By car

Visa Restrictions:
All persons wishing to enter the United States by land must possess a valid passport; NEXUS, FAST, or passport card; Laser Visa; or an "enhanced driver's license" (issued by certain US states and Canadian provinces)

Traffic travels on the right-hand side (as it does in Canada and Mexico), except in the US Virgin Islands, due to left-hand driving being common in the smaller Caribbean islands.

If you are entering under the Visa Waiver Program, you will need to pay a $6.00 fee, in cash, at the point of entry. No fee is payable if you are simply re-entering and already have the Visa Waiver slip in your passport.

The US-Canada and US-Mexico borders are two of the most frequently crossed borders in the world, with millions of crossings daily. Average wait times are up to 30 minutes, but some of the most heavily traveled border crossings may have considerable delays—approaching 1-2 hours at peak times (weekends, holidays). Current wait times (updated hourly) are available on the US customs service website. The US-Mexico border is vulnerable to high levels of drug trafficking, so vehicles crossing may be X-rayed or searched by a drug-sniffing dog. If anything about you appears suspicious, you and your vehicle may be searched. Since this is an all-too-common event, expect no patience or sympathy from border agents.

As Canada and Mexico use the metric units of measure but the US uses customary units, bear in mind that after the border, road signs are published in miles and miles per hour. Therefore, if you are driving a car from Canada or Mexico, be mindful that a speed limit of 55mph in the US is 88km/h.

By bus

Greyhound offers many inexpensive cross-border services from both Canada and Mexico throughout their network. Some routes, such as Toronto to Buffalo have hourly service. Megabus US also runs multiple daily trips from Toronto (also a hub for Megabus Canada) to New York City via Buffalo for as low as $1.

Be warned that bus passengers often experience greater scrutiny from US customs officials than car or train passengers.

Onward travel to:

• Mexico is provided by Grupo Estrella Blanca; Grupo Senda or see the specific Wikitravel articles for individual cities and towns near the border between US and Mexico.

• Canada is provided by Greyhound Canada which has a Canada-wide network.

By boat

Entering the U.S. by sea, other than on a registered cruise ship, may be difficult. The most common entry points for private boats are Los Angeles and the surrounding area, Florida, and the Eastern coastal states.

Some passenger ferries exist between Canada and the U.S., mostly between British Columbia and Washington State (from Victoria & Sidney, BC) or Alaska (from Prince Rupert).

Cunard offers transatlantic ship travel between the United Kingdom and New York City.

By train

Amtrak offers international service from the Canadian cities of Vancouver (Amtrak Cascades has two trips per day to Seattle), Toronto (Maple Leaf has a daily trip to New York City), and Montreal (Adirondack has a daily trip to New York City) into the US. Note that cross border rail service is more expensive and less quick than the buses, which are more frequent and serve a larger range of US destinations from both Canada and Mexico.

On international trains from Montreal and Toronto, immigration formalities are conducted at the border.

Those travelling from Vancouver clear U.S. immigration and customs at the Union Pacific Station before they get on the train itself. Be sure to allow enough time before departure to complete the necessary inspections.

Amtrak does NOT offer cross border trains to/from Mexico nor are there any other onward passenger trains going south from the U.S./Mexican border.

Therefore, the nearest train stations to the Mexican border are in San Diego (Pacific Surfliner) and El Paso (Sunset Limited & Texas Eagle). From either train station take local transportation (light rail in San Diego or bus or taxi in El Paso) to get to the actual border crossing.

By foot

There are many border crossings in urban areas which can be crossed by pedestrians. Crossings such as those in or near Niagara Falls, Detroit, Tijuana, Nogales, and El Paso are popular for persons wishing to spend a day on the other side of the border. In some cases, this may be ideal for day-trippers, as crossing by car can be a much longer wait.

Get around

The size of the US and the distance between some major cities make air the dominant mode of travel for short-term travelers over long distances. If you have time, travel by car, bus, or rail can be interesting.

Be Aware: In general, outside of the downtown areas of big cities (especially New York, Boston, Philadelphia, Washington, D.C., Chicago and San Francisco), public transport in the U.S. is not as commonly used, developed, nor reliable as in many European and Asian countries. Due to cheap fuel prices, endless available parking spaces, cheap auto insurance, very cheap car prices and large distances to travel, Americans prefer to drive their own car rather than opt for public transport.

By plane

The quickest and often the most convenient way of long-distance intercity travel in the US is by plane. Coast-to-coast travel takes about six hours from east to west, and five hours from west to east (varying due to winds), compared to the three or four days necessary for land transportation. Most cities in the US are served by one or two airports; many small towns also have some passenger air service, although you may need to detour through a major hub airport to get there. Depending on where you are starting, it may be cheaper to drive to a nearby large city and fly or, conversely, to fly to a large city near your destination and rent a car.

Major carriers compete for business on major routes, and travelers willing to book two or more weeks in advance can get bargains. However most smaller destinations are served by only one or two regional carriers, and prices to destinations outside of the big cities can be very expensive.

Service types

There are several types of airlines flying in the United States today:

Mainline or legacy carriers - Due to numerous bankruptcies and acquisitions, there are only three major and two minor legacy carriers left: Delta Air Lines (Northwest Airlines has merged with Delta), United Airlines (Continental has merged with United), and American Airlines (US Airways has merged with American); plus, Alaska Airlines and Hawaiian Airlines. These carriers used to be "full-service", although because of their chronic financial distress, they are increasingly taking after overseas carriers like Ryanair and transitioning into "no-frills" carriers. On a domestic flight in economy class, expect to pay extra for anything beyond a seat (with very limited recline), 1 or 2 carry-on bags, and soft drinks. In-flight entertainment on mainline carriers' ageing domestic jetliners is generally limited to drop-down LCD screens that show the same programs to all economy passengers. Newer domestic jetliners do not even have LCD screens on the assumption that economy passengers will bring their own phones and tablets, which means flight attendants must pull out a set of props to do the pre-flight safety briefing (as has always been the case on smaller planes). Some flights to/from Hawaii or Alaska still offer a few perks, but check for your particular airline and flight.

Mainline carriers also offer first class service which features a larger seat which can recline farther, free food and drinks, a fully interactive personal entertainment system, and generally better service. Round-trip fares can run over a thousand dollars, even for short flights, making the added cost not worth it for the vast majority of travelers. (Most travelers in first class get their seat as a complimentary frequent flier upgrade or similar perk.) You may also be offered an upgrade at a much lower cost during check in or at the airport if there are open seats available.

Note that on certain premium transcontinental services between New York City and Los Angeles/San Francisco offered by American ("Flagship Service") and United ("United p.s."), first class and business class services are comparable to equivalent international offerings with gourmet meals and lie-flat seats. The same is true of some flights between the East Coast and Hawaii.

Regional airlines come in three varieties.

Regional subsidiaries operate under an umbrella brand such as "American Eagle" or "United Express" and run small regional jets or turboprops to locales where it is not economically or technically feasible to run a full-sized jet. These flights are booked through their parent's reservation system (e.g., Delta Connection through Delta), either as a stand-alone flight or connecting to a mainline itinerary, and any miles earned are recorded in the parent's frequent flier account system. Their operations are supposed to be seamlessly integrated (at least in theory) with their parent brands with respect to things like check-ins, boarding passes, and checked baggage. On-board service is very basic for all classes.

They flourished in the early 1990s when the financially distressed mainline airlines began specializing in running only very large jetliners on lucrative long-distance routes. Their regional allies, specializing in operating smaller planes, would run feeder routes into the parent's hubs that would enable passengers from small towns to connect to the parent's long-distance routes; conversely, the regional airlines would enable passengers coming off the parent's long-distance routes to easily connect to outlying small towns rather than exiting at a hub airport and completing the rest of the journey by car, bus, or train.

Regional airlines tend to have a mediocre safety record. They often hire desperate pilots who are eager to break into a career in commercial aviation but for whatever reason could not qualify for or did not want to earn their flight hours in the US military. Regional pilots thus tend to work for low pay and long hours in the hope of building sufficient flight experience to apply for and get a decent-paying job as the pilot of a full-size jetliner with the regional subsidiary's parent legacy airline. As a result, there have been a number of crashes or near-misses blamed upon low-paid, overworked regional pilots.

They are operated by SkyWest; Mesa Air Group; Republic; and Express Jet as United Express, Delta Connection, American Eagle/Envoy, Alaska Airlines, Frontier, and/or US Airways Express. They operate one or several brands of the bigger 'legacy' parent(s) at the same time. Reservations and ticketing with the "regional (commuter) carriers" are handled through the "legacy" parent carriers instead of these airlines themselves.

Independent regional airlines are not affiliated with a mainline carrier. They are usually found in more out of the way places, as well as near island communities (Cape Cod, Hawaii, Virgin Islands, etc.). The ones operating on their own names and not affiliated with the bigger carriers (as named above) are: Cape Air, Great Lakes Aviation, SeaPort, Silver Airways and Vision.

Commuter airlines primarily serve the business travel market, with 10-30 seat turboprop planes. If you can work with their schedules and choice of airports (usually private aviation airports and municipal airfields) - their consistent fares can be a bargain compared even to low cost carriers. Additionally, since fares are the same whether you buy a month in advance or the day of, tickets are also flexible with no cancellation or change fees.

Low-cost carriers have grown rapidly in the U.S. since the early 1990s. The most famous of these is the ubiquitous Southwest Airlines, a favorite of leisure and business travelers alike; while Frontier, Spirit; Allegiant and others (including the big mainline carriers and hybrid carriers) have been growing into formidable competitors. Amenities vary greatly by carrier. On one end, Southwest is the only airline in the United States that lets passengers check two bags free of charge. They have done away with some of the formality of air travel; they do not take reservations from travel agents (all reservations are through their Web site or call center), and they have no assigned seating or buy-on-board programs (free soft drinks and snacks for all passengers).

At the other end of the spectrum, Spirit Airlines sells seats for as low as $9.00, but charges fees for everything beyond the seat: checked and hand luggage, buying a ticket online (if you want to avoid that fee, you have to buy at the counter), advance seat assignments, checking-in at the airport, printing out documents at the airport, on-board refreshments, etc. European visitors familiar with Ryanair will find Spirit's fee-for-everything business model to be strikingly similar.

Southwest and Allegiant serve destinations nationwide, although they sometimes use smaller or alternative airports such as Chicago Midway instead of the larger O'Hare International Airport, Houston Hobby instead of the Houston Bush Intercontinental or Dallas Love Field instead of Dallas-Fort Worth International Airport.

Other low-cost carriers such as Allegiant and Sun Country focus on "vacation destinations" like Florida, Mexico, the Virgin Islands, etc.

Hybrid carriers offer more amenities than low-cost airlines but with fares lower than the legacies. The most famous of these is JetBlue Airways which has an extensive network covering primarily major airports, one free checked bag, 34 inches between seats (very generous for an American airline) and free satellite TV (DirectTV) in every seat.

A relative newcomer is the trendy brainchild of Sir Richard Branson: Virgin America which offers a relatively low-priced First Class option, as well as mood lighting, relatively comfortable seats, and interactive in-flight entertainment in all classes in its aircraft.

Fees

The FAA has been cracking down on non-disclosed fees for a while, so the good news is that most of the prices that you immediately see when searching for flights already include all taxes and other mandatory fees applicable to all passengers. This is true whether you directly check the carrier's website or an online travel agency like Orbitz. Unlike carriers in other foreign countries, most US carriers do not explicitly impose a fuel surcharge. However, carriers charge for extra services, especially mainline/legacy ones. Here is a run-down of services that may incur additional fees, as well as strategies for avoiding them if they aren't a service you need or want. Even baggage fees can be avoided with careful planning:

Checking in with an agent: A few airlines are charging an additional fee ($3-10) for checking in with an actual human being, and Spirit Airlines also charges you for using the airport kiosk instead of checking in online. Unless you need to check in with an agent (e.g., if you have specialized equipment that qualifies for a baggage fee waiver) you should check in online and print your boarding pass at home to save time and avoid additional charges. Some airlines will let you use your iPhone, Android, or BlackBerry as a boarding pass, either by showing an e-mail with a barcode to security and the gate agent, or through a specialized app, although many smaller and regional airports do not support mobile boarding passes yet.

Checked baggage: Though prices vary by airline, you're generally looking at between $25 and $35 to check a single bag, an additional $50 for a second bag, and up to $100 or more for a third bag. Bags that are oversized or overweight will easily double or triple these fees.
You're allowed to carry on one small suitcase or garment bag and one personal item (like a briefcase, backpack, or purse) free of charge. If you can get everything in your carry-ons, this is the best way to avoid baggage fees. Due to ongoing security restrictions, liquids, gels, shaving creams, and similar items must be under 3.4oz (100mL) and must be removed and presented to security inside a transparent resealable plastic bag for separate examination. Razor blades, electric shavers, scissors, or anything else with a blade or sharp edge can never be placed in your carry-on, and will be confiscated on the spot if discovered.

Ultra-low cost carrier Spirit Airlines charges $20-35 per bag for carry-ons, depending on whether you're a member of their fare club and whether you pay online or at the airport, in many cases it's actually cheaper to check these bags instead of carrying on. As of 2015, no other airline charges for carry-on baggage.

Members of frequent flier rewards programs who have "elite" status may typically check 1 or more bags free of charge, or may receive other perks such as additional weight allowances. Some airlines have a branded credit card that offers similar perks.

Pre-paying baggage charges online may give you a slight discount on some carriers.

Discount carriers JetBlue and Southwest allow all passengers one and two checked bags free of charge, respectively.

Due to these fees, another popular alternative is to ship luggage via UPS, FedEx or the U.S. Postal Service, although this does take some extra planning and preparation.

Curbside check in: $2-10 on top of any bag or check-in fees, plus a tip is usually expected.

Extra legroom seats: the cost depends on the length of the trip but expect to pay anything from 5 to 15% of the standard economy class fare. This is bookable at the time you purchase your ticket. Those in higher tiers can get this at no extra cost.

Food: Most airlines offer some small snacks (e.g., peanuts, potato chips, cookies) free of charge on all flights. On flights longer than 1.5–2 hours, a buy-on-board option may be offered where you can purchase prepackaged sandwiches, snacks, and occasionally hot food at inflated prices. Many legacy airlines used to include in the base ticket price at least one hot meal service for all classes on domestic flights over four hours in length, but due to their financial distress, dramatically cut back on the quality of in-flight meals in the 1980s (which led to an epidemic of jokes in that era about "airline food") and eventually stopped including it altogether by the mid-1990s. Since then, most domestic passengers who did not have the time to stop for a real meal before arriving at the airport usually eat at a post-security airport restaurant before boarding their plane. Flights from the East Coast to Alaska, Hawaii and U.S. Pacific territories (which can be over eight hours in length) and intercontinental flights still feature traditional meal service.

All airlines allow you to bring your own food and non-alcoholic beverages on board. All except the smallest airports have an array of fast food and quick serve options in the terminal — but you can't bring liquids through the security checkpoint (and some airports do not allow food either), so don't purchase anything until after you've cleared security. While airside food outlets will inevitably be more expensive than what's available before security or off-airport, it still costs much less and likely has a larger selection than what's available on board. Some cities, such as Philadelphia, regulate airport food vendors and limit how much air-side restaurants can markup.

Drinks: Beverage service is one thing the airline industry hasn't done away with, and even the shortest regional jet flights still feature complimentary coffee, tea, water, juice and soda - an exception is ultra-low fare carrier Spirit, who charges for anything other than water. If you'd like something stronger, you can pay $5–7 to pick among a decent selection of beer, two or three varieties of wine, and a couple of basic cocktails that can be mixed easily and quickly (e.g. gin and tonic).

In-flight entertainment: Most US carriers offer entertainment of one kind or another on longer domestic routes. Delta, JetBlue, Virgin America, and some of United's fleet offer free satellite TV in every seat, as well as movies on demand for purchase for $3-8. American has overhead screens showing movies and sitcom episodes on most longer routes, while U.S. Airways and Southwest do not have in-flight entertainment of any kind.

In-flight Wi-Fi: Delta, JetBlue and Southwest offer in-flight Wi-Fi on nearly all their domestic fleets - American, U.S. Airways and United offer it on select flights. Prices range from $5-20, depending on the airline, length of flight, and device (tablets and smartphones get a discount as they use less data) but the Internet connection is good for almost the entire flight (at least until told by crew to switch-off your devices). Daily and monthly passes are also available for less than $50/month. Most airlines do not offer power ports in economy, so be sure you're charged up or have extra batteries for your device. Mobile phones are usually permitted to be operated in-flight as long as they have been set to flight mode (which effectively shuts-off the mobile phone signal from your provider) before being airborne.

Pillows and blankets are disappearing rapidly. Some airlines don't have them at all; some will charge you for them (but you get to keep after you pay); and one or two offer them for free (but you have to ask for them). Red-eye and long (>5 hour) flights are more likely to have free pillows and blankets. As always, check with your airline, and bring your own from home if you think you'll need them.

Lounge passes: Each mainline carrier operates a network of lounges, such as Alaska Airline's "Board Rooms" and Delta's "Sky Clubs" - offering a quieter space to relax or work in, business amenities such as free Wi-Fi, fax services and conference rooms, as well as complimentary finger foods, soft drinks, beer and wine. Frequent flyers buy annual memberships to these lounges, but any passenger can buy a day pass during check in or at the club itself, usually around $50, although sometimes less if you buy online. Only you can decide if the fee is worthwhile, but if you're in the upper elite tiers of an airline alliance (One World Sapphire or Emerald, Star Alliance Gold or SkyTeam Elite Plus) you may have access to these lounges for free with your frequent flyer card. For members in the highest tiers, this privilege may be extended to a travelling companion. Additionally international Business and First Class passengers can also access these lounges for free.

First class upgrades: Delta, United, and US Airways sell upgrades on a first come-first served basis at check-in if first class has open seats. This is one to actually consider, especially if you're checking bags - "day of" upgrades can sometimes be as low as $50 each way, less than the cost of two bag fees. You'd may be paying less to check your bags and additionally getting priority security screening, boarding and baggage handling, along with a larger seat and free refreshments on board.

Most mainline carriers feature "cashless cabins" meaning any on-board purchases must be paid with either Visa or MasterCard (Delta also accepts American Express). Regional subsidiaries generally do still accept cash on-board, although flight attendants may not be able break large bills - hence the traditional request "exact change is appreciated." If you paid in advance for first class, checked baggage, meals, and alcoholic beverages are all included with the price of your ticket, as well as priority access to check-in agents, lounge access and boarding.

Ironically, America's discount airlines, such as JetBlue, Southwest, and Virgin America sometimes have more amenities than the legacy carriers, and for many people may be a much better experience. Jet Blue offers over 45 channels of satellite television, non-alcoholic beverages and real snacks for free on every flight; Virgin America also has satellite TV, in addition to on demand dining (even in economy). On Jet Blue your first checked bag is free ($35 for a second bag), and Southwest is the only U.S. carrier to still offer two checked bags per passenger free of charge. Virgin America charges for checked bags, but their fees are considerably lower than the legacies.

Security concerns

Security at US airports is known to be onerous, especially during busy holiday travel periods. Allow plenty of time and pack as lightly as possible. Ensure the amount of liquids you bring does not exceed the prescribed limit and is properly placed in the prescribed containers. Currently those limits are referred to as '311' - 3 ounces or less liquid bottles placed in one single, transparent, resealable plastic bag that is 1 quart (1 liter) or less in size. Please note that you can take as many of the little "travel size" 3-ounce (100 ml) bottles that you can cram into that single bag. The little bottles of shampoo and conditioner provided in the rooms at most decent hotels are perfect for this. Many pharmacies, as well as Wal-Mart, Target, and most major grocery stores have a section for "trial or travel size" bottles of personal care liquids that fall under the three-ounce limit.

By private plane

The cost of chartering the smallest private jet begins at around $4,000 per flight hour, with the cost substantially higher for larger, longer-range aircraft, and cheaper for smaller propeller planes. While private flying is by no means inexpensive, a family of four or more can often fly together at a cost similar to or even favorable to buying first class commercial airline tickets, especially to smaller airports where scheduled commercial flights are at their most expensive, and private flying is at its cheapest. Though you may find it cheaper than flying a family of four first class internationally, it is rarely the case, except when traveling from Western Europe.

Air Charter refers to hiring a private plane for a one time journey. Jet Cards are pre-paid cards entitling the owner to a specific number of flight hours on a specified aircraft. As all expenses are pre-paid on the card, you need not to concern yourself with deadhead time, return flights, landing fees, etc.

By train

Amtrak

Except for certain densely populated corridors (mostly near and between the big cities of the Northeast), passenger trains in the United States can be surprisingly scarce and relatively expensive. The national rail system, Amtrak (1-800-USA-RAIL), provides service to many cities, offering exceptional sightseeing opportunities, but not particularly efficient inter-city travel, and is often just as expensive as a flight. In more urban locations, Amtrak can be very efficient and comfortable, but in rural areas delays are common. Plan ahead to ensure train travel between your destinations is available and/or convenient. They have promotional discounts of 15% for students and seniors, and a 30-day U.S. Rail Pass for international travelers only. If you plan to buy a regular ticket within a week of travelling, it pays to check the website for sometimes significant "weekly specials".

Amtrak offers many amenities and services that are lacking from other modes of transport. Amtrak offers many routes that traverse some of America's most beautiful areas. Travelers with limited time may not find travel by train to be convenient, simply because the country is big, and the "bigness" is particularly evident in many of the scenic areas. For those with ample time, though, train travel offers an unparalleled view of the U.S., without the trouble and long-term discomfort of a rental (hire) car or the hassle of flying.

Trains running on the Washington D.C. to Boston Northeast Corridor (Acela Express and the Regional) and the Philadelphia to Harrisburg Keystone Corridor (Keystone Service and Pennsylvanian) generally run on time or very close to it. These two rail lines are electrified and owned by Amtrak or other commuter railways and are passenger only. Outside these two areas, Amtrak operates on freight lines and as a result must share track with freight trains hosted by host railroads. This means you have about as good a chance of a delay as not. While these delays are usually brief (trains make up time en route), have a contingency plan for being at least three hours late when travelling Amtrak. In fact, six hour or longer delays, especially on long-distance routes, are not uncommon, either.

If you miss an Amtrak connection because your first train is late, Amtrak will book you onto the next available train (or in rare cases a bus) to your final destination. If your destination is on the Northeast Corridor, this isn't a big deal (departures are every hour) but in other parts of the country the next train may not be until tomorrow. If your reservations involved sleeper accommodations (Amtrak's First Class on their long-distance overnight trains) on either your late-arriving train or your missed connection, you will get a hotel voucher for the unplanned overnight stay. For coach class passengers in the same situation, you will not get a hotel voucher; your unplanned lodging arrangements and cost will be your responsibility. However, after your travel is completed, Amtrak's Customer Service will commonly offer travel vouchers of $100 or more off future Amtrak travel to inconvenienced passengers. This is true for all classes of service.

If you plan to board an Amtrak train at a location other than the train's initial place of departure, it's usually a good idea to call ahead before you leave for the station to see if the train is running on time.

A major Amtrak line in regular daily use by Americans is the Acela Express line, running between Boston and Washington, D.C. It stops in New York City, New Haven, Philadelphia and many other cities on the way. Acela Express is electrified, with top speeds of 150 miles per hour (though the average speed is a good deal slower because many track sections have curves too tight to be safely traversed at more than 90mph). The Acela Express features comfortable first class intercity service, but can be quite expensive. Given the difficulty and expense of getting from the center of some of the major Northeastern cities to their respective airports, trains can sometimes be more convenient than air travel. There are also frequent but much slower regional trains covering the same stations along the Northeast Corridor for lower fares.

During usual American vacation times, some long-distance trains (outside the Northeast) can sell out weeks or even months in advance, so it pays to book early if you plan on using the long-distance trains. Booking early also results in generally lower fares for all trains since they tend to increase as trains become fuller. On the other hand, same-day reservations are usually easy, and depending on the rules of the fare you purchased, you can change travel plans on the day itself without fees.

One major scenic long-distance train route, the California Zephyr, runs from Emeryville in the Bay Area of California to Chicago, via Reno, Salt Lake City and Denver. The full trip takes around 60 hours, but has incredible views of the Western deserts, the Rocky Mountains, and the Great Plains, things that you just cannot see if you fly. Many of the sights on this route are simply inaccessible to cars. The trains run only once per day, and they usually sell out well in advance.

Amtrak's single most popular long-distance train is the Chicago-Seattle/Portland "Empire Builder" train via Milwaukee, St. Paul/Minneapolis, Fargo, Minot, Glacier National Park, Whitefish, and Spokane. In the 2007 fiscal year, this train alone carried over 503,000 passengers.

Amtrak also provides reasonably speedy daily round trips between Seattle and Vancouver, Canada and several daily trips between Seattle and Eugene, Oregon on the Amtrak Cascades line.

Passengers travelling long distances on Amtrak may reserve a seat in coach (Economy class) or pay extra for an upgrade to a private sleeping compartment (there are no shared rooms), which also includes all meals in the dining car.

Amtrak trains in the West feature a lounge car with floor to ceiling windows, which are perfect for sightseeing.

Local trains

Separate from Amtrak, many major cities offer very reliable commuter trains that carry passengers to and from the suburbs or other relatively close-by areas. Since most Americans use a car for suburban travel, some commuter train stations have park and ride facilities where you can park your car for the day to use the commuter train to get to a city's downtown core where it may be more difficult to use a car due to traffic and parking concerns. Parking rates at the commuter train stations vary due (some facilities may be operated by third parties). Some commuter train systems and services though do not operate on weekends and holidays so it's best to check the system's website to plan ahead. Please don't forget to buy tickets before you board the train as some systems will have a substantial mark-up on the tickets sold on-board while others won't sell tickets on-board and will subject you to a hefty fine instead.

Some cities also have subway and light rail systems for local travel within a city.

By boat

America has the largest system of inland waterways of any country in the world. It is entirely possible to navigate around within the United States by boat. Your choices of watercraft range from self-propelled canoes and kayaks to elaborate houseboats and riverboat cruises.

Rivers and canals were key to developing the country, and traversing by boat gives you a unique perspective on the nation and some one of a kind scenery. Some examples of waterways open to recreational boating and/or scheduled cruises are:

The Erie Canal System of New York State operates four canal systems consisting of 524 miles of waterway open for recreational and commercial use. The most famous of these canals is the Erie Canal, which starts around Albany and heads west to Buffalo. By navigating up the Hudson River from New York City, it's possible to go all the way to the Great Lakes and beyond via these waterways. Side trips to the Finger Lakes in Western New York or to Lake Champlain and Vermont are possible. Small watercraft, including canoes and kayaks, are welcome on these canals.

International Charter Group. Yacht charter and sailing, one of the world's largest yacht charter companies, can take care of all charter requirements, from bareboat to crewed in Hawaii. Operating from nine offices worldwide (USA, Spain, UK, Germany, Italy, France, Spain, Switzerland, Caribbean, Hong Kong and Dubai).

The St. Lawrence Seaway is now the primary port of entry for large ships into North America. Recreational boaters are welcome, however, the Seaway is designed for very large craft and a minimum boat length of 6m applies. The Seaway starts in eastern Canada and goes to the Great Lakes.

The Mississippi River There are two channels of navigation from the Great Lakes to the Mississippi. The Mississippi affords north-south access through the interior of the U.S. to the Gulf of Mexico and connects with all major interior waterways, including the Missouri River.
Each year, many first time and beginning boaters successfully navigate these waterways. Do remember that any kind of boating requires some preparation and planning. In general, the Coast Guard, Canal and Seaway authorities go out of their way to help recreational boaters. They will also at times give instructions which you are expected to immediately obey. For example, small craft may be asked to give way to larger craft on canals, and weather conditions may require you to stop or change your route.

Several coastal cities, including San Francisco, Seattle and New York City, operate ferry services between local destinations. Some islands, such as Catalina Island or Nantucket are only accessible by ferry.

By car

America's love affair with the automobile is legendary and most Americans use a car when moving within their city, and when travelling to nearby cities in their state or region. However, many Americans can and do travel between the vast regions of their country by auto - often going through different time zones, landscapes, and climates. In the winter months (Dec though March) millions of American nomads travel south to the warm desert and subtropical climates in everything from cars to motor homes (called "RV's").

Generally speaking, the older American cities like New York, Chicago, San Francisco, Boston, Washington, DC, Seattle, and Philadelphia are best to see using public transport or even on foot (at least within their downtown cores). However, the newer sunbelt cities (normally in the West and South) are built for the automobile, so renting or bringing your own car is usually a very good idea. This applies even to very large cities like Los Angeles, Atlanta and Miami, where public transport is very limited and having a car is the most practical way of getting around. In the smaller American cities, everything is very spread out and public transport thin. Taxis are often available, but if you're not at the airport, you may have to phone for one and wait a half-hour or so to be picked up, making similar arrangements to return. Taxis are typically an expensive option to use. While most Americans are happy to give driving directions, don't be surprised if many aren't familiar with the local public transport options available.

Gas stations usually sell regional and national maps. Online maps with directions are available on several websites including MapQuest and Google Maps. Drivers can obtain directions by calling 1-800-Free411, which will provide them via text message. GPS navigation systems can be purchased for around $100, and car rental agencies often rent GPS units for a small additional fee. Many smartphones are now bundled with GPS navigation software that offers turn-by-turn directions. Your mobile phone provider may charge you for data use, since mobile phone GPS navigation is best used with an Internet connection. Several GPS navigation apps can now support "offline maps" features where you can download maps in advance, but without Internet access, the navigation app will not have access to real-time traffic data and may direct you to drive right into the middle of a severe traffic jam. Even states that ban the use of hand-held phones by drivers often allow the use of GPS features, as long as the driver enters no data when in motion (check local laws in the places you will be travelling).

Unlike most of the rest of the world, the United States continues to use a system of measurement based on the old British imperial system for the most part, meaning that road signs are in miles and miles per hour, but fuel is sold in gallons smaller than those used in the UK. If driving a car from Canada or Mexico, make sure you know the conversions from metric to imperial units. In the case of Canadian cars, you should check your owner's manual to see if your speedometer and odometer can be switched from metric to imperial (and back), and if so, how to do so, and make the switch at the border stop. Most cars sold in the US and Canada today can be readily switched between the two sets of units. The vast majority of cars in the United States (and Canada, for that matter) are equipped with automatic transmission - manual (stick shift) cars are very much the exception to the rule and are generally only found on sports cars, so bear that in mind if you do rent a car.

Great American road trip

A romantic appeal is attached to the idea of long-distance car travel; many Americans will tell you that you can't see the "real" America except by car. Given the dearth of public transportation in most American cities, the loss of time travelling between cities by car rather than flying can be made up by the convenience of driving around within cities once you arrive. In addition, many of the country's major natural attractions, such as the Grand Canyon, are in rugged landscapes and environments, and are almost impossible to get to without an automobile. If you have the time, a classic American road trip with a rented car (see below) is very easy to achieve and quite an adventure. Just keep in mind that because of the distances, this kind of travel can mean many hours, days, or even a week behind the wheel, so pay attention to the comfort of the car you use. Some roads go through hazardous environments (hot deserts, dense forests and jungles, harsh steppes and savannas, marshy/wet areas, geothermal areas, rugged mountains,) and through areas with dangerous wildlife (Bobcats, Pumas, Jaguars, constrictors, Pronghorn, poisonous snakes, alligators, Coyotes, bears...etc) and weather (the U.S. can be struck by any manner of disasters, from tornadoes, dust storms, and hurricanes, to earthquakes, volcanic eruptions, and tsunamis,) so be aware of the environment you are travelling through.

Interstate system

The United States is covered with the largest and most modern highway system in the world. Interstates are always freeways—that is, controlled access divided highways with no at-grade crossings, the equivalent of what Europeans call a "motorway". These roads connect all of the major population centers, and they make it easy to cover long distances—or get to the other side of a large city—quickly. These highways cross the entire US mainland from the Atlantic to the Pacific, through several time zones, landscapes, and climates.

Most of these highways have modern and safe state run "Rest Areas" or "Service Plaza" areas. These rest stops normally offer restrooms, vending machines, and phone service. Service Plazas (more likely found on toll roads) may offer fuel, restaurant(s), and simple vehicle repair. Many of these rest stops also offer tourist information and picnic areas. Additional commercial traveler services tend to congregate on the local roads just off popular interstate highway exits. Sometimes you'll find a truck stop, an establishment that caters to long-haul truckers but is open to all travelers. Signs on the highway will indicate the services available at upcoming exits, including gas, food, lodging, and camping, so you can choose a stopping point as you're driving.

Note that in some eastern states, Interstates are called expressways or just highways. Western states as well as US federal law defines expressways as limited access divided highways with reduced at-grade crossings (meaning that you can and will see occasional cross-traffic on western expressways), while freeways are defined as divided highways with full access control and no at-grade crossings. Many eastern states do not follow the same distinction.

Primary Interstates have one- or two-digit numbers, with odd ones running north-south (e.g. I-5) and even ones running east-west (e.g. I-80). Three-digit interstate numbers designate shorter, secondary routes. An odd first digit signifies a "spur" into or away from a city; an even first digit signifies a "loop" around a large city. The second two digits remain the same as the primary Interstate that travels nearby (e.g., I-495 is a loop that connects to I-95).

The vast majority of interstates do not charge tolls. However, the Departments of Transportation of Florida, New Jersey, Ohio, Oklahoma and Pennsylvania operate long-distance, limited-access toll roads called Turnpikes. Tolls are also frequently levied for crossing notably large bridges or tunnels, and some states are even turning to requiring tolls on Federal Interstate highways to defray their maintenance costs (West Virginia is most notable for this). While the majority of entrances and exits for the Turnpike systems of these states collect tolls in cash, states are increasingly turning to electronic tolling by outfitting vehicles with small RFID transponders, or, more recently, photographic recording and recognition of the vehicle's license plate. If you plan on driving in a state that offers toll roads, it is worthwhile to ask your rental car agency about the electronic tolling options available to you, as paying tolls in cash is becoming incrementally more difficult as electronic options and open-road tolling (paying tolls electronically without having to stop), on Florida's Turnpike in particular, are rapidly becoming more widely accepted. Nearly all rental car agencies that operate in Florida offer some form of prepaid tolling plan. Credit cards and travelers' checks are usually not accepted by state-operated toll plazas, but there are some exceptions (for example, the Ohio Turnpike accepts most major credit cards).

Speed limits on Interstate Highways can vary from state to state, and also according to geography (for example, slower on mountain passes and within cities than on long straight rural sections). Posted speed limits can range from as low as 45 miles per hour (70km/h) in densely urban areas to as much as 85mph (135km/h) in certain rural stretches of Texas, but mostly they'll be between 65 and 70mph (105–113km/h) on the east coast and 65 to 75mph (105-120km/h) out west. The speed limits (in miles per hour) are always clearly and frequently posted on Interstates.

American drivers often drive a bit over the posted speed limit, especially on Interstates (5 to 10mph (8–15km/h)). Driving more than 10mph over the posted speed limit greatly increases the chance of receiving a speeding ticket; 15mph or more over the limit when observed by law enforcement will usually earn you a ticket or, depending on the state, result in a license suspension. Driving too slow can actually be dangerous. A good rule of thumb is to avoid driving much faster than all other cars. Highway Patrol officers are usually most concerned with the fastest drivers, so ensuring you are slower than the fastest speeders is one way to avoid their attention. If you are pulled over, be respectful, address the officer as "Officer," and express heartfelt regret at your excessive speed. You may or may not get a ticket, but remain in your car while the officer process your information. The officer will approach the car and you should roll down your window to speak. The officer will ask to see your driver's license and car registration. Such traffic stops are often routine and low key.

Many Interstate Highways, particularly around and through very large cities, will segregate the far left-hand lane or lanes and reserve them for high-occupancy use. These lanes are clearly signed, marked with white diamonds down the center of the lane, have double-white lines on the right, and are limited to vehicles with two or more occupants. High-Occupancy Vehicle lanes, called HOV lanes or carpool lanes, are designed to ease congestion on Interstate freeways around large population centers during the very start and very end of the business day, also known colloquially as Rush Hour. At least 22 U.S. cities have HOV lanes, of which about half enforce them only during rush hour and half enforce them 24 hours. If you do not see specific hours posted for HOV lanes, assume the HOV lane restrictions are in effect at all times.

Off the interstates

A secondary system of federal highways is the US Highway system. US Highways may be divided with multiple lanes in each direction on some sections, but they are often not dual carriageways, sometimes with just one lane in each direction. US Highways, which generally pre-date the Interstate system, tend to be older routes that lead through town centers as local streets (with a local name or number) at slower speeds. In many cases, Interstates were constructed roughly parallel to US Highways to expedite traffic that wishes to bypass the cities and towns. If you don't mind stopping at traffic lights and dealing with pedestrians, US Highways can lead you to some interesting off-the-beaten-path sights.

Each state is responsible for maintenance of the Interstates and US Highways (despite the names), but each one also maintains its own system of State Highways (or State Routes) that form the bulk of the inter-community road network. State Highways are usually undivided but may occasionally be freeways; you can generally count on them being well maintained (and plowed in the winter) and that following one will get you to some form of civilization sooner rather than later.

In most states west of the Mississippi River, the term "freeway" means a divided highway with full access control with maximum speed limits up to 75-80mph (120-128km/h) in Utah and western Texas, while the term "expressway" means a divided highway with partial access control. Expressways in western states can and do have occasional at-grade intersections with cross-traffic (that is, travelling perpendicular to mainline traffic approaching at speeds with speed limits set between 40-65mph (64-104km/h)). Only freeways in those states are guaranteed to have no cross-traffic at grade. In most states east of the Mississippi River, the term expressway always means full access control and the term freeway is either a synonym or is not used.

Driving laws

As with the rest of North America except for most former British Empire colonies, Americans drive on the right in left-hand drive vehicles and pass on the left. The exception to this is the U.S. Virgin Islands which continues to drive on the left-hand side with mostly left-hand vehicles. White lines separate traffic moving in the same direction and yellow lines separate opposing traffic. Right turn on red after coming to a complete stop is legal (unless a sign prohibits it) in some states and cities (New York City is a notable exception to this rule). Red lights and stop signs are always enforced at all hours in nearly all US jurisdictions. Traffic lights and lane lines are strictly enforced, and there is zero tolerance for many traffic maneuvers often seen elsewhere in many countries around the world. Jumping the green, running a red, straddling lanes (especially in a car or truck) or swerving across the double yellow line into opposing traffic on major urban roadways to pass slower, but still moving, traffic will all result in an expensive ticket.

Most American drivers tend to drive calmly and safely in the sprawling residential suburban neighborhoods where the majority of Americans live. However, freeways around the central areas of big cities often become crowded with a significant proportion of "hurried" drivers — who will exceed speed limits, make unsafe lane changes, or follow other cars at unsafe close distances (known as "tailgating"). Enforcement of posted speed limits is somewhat unpredictable and varies widely from state to state. Not exceeding the pace of other drivers will usually avoid a troublesome citation. Beware of small towns along otherwise high-speed rural roads (and medium-speed suburban roads); the reduced speed limits found while going through such towns are strictly enforced.

Another issue in many locations is drivers who linger in left lanes of divided highways — i.e., refuse to move to the right for traffic attempting to pass. While this is seen as extremely discourteous and often dangerous, it is not a violation in most locations unless the driver is travelling well below the speed limit. (This differs, for example, from Germany, where failing to move right to make way for passing drivers and passing on the right are very serious violations and strictly enforced.) One state attempting to address this issue is Georgia, which passed a law in March 2014 making it a violation to fail to move to the right for a passing vehicle, even if the driver being passed is exceeding the posted speed limit.

Driving law is primarily a matter of state law and is enforced by state and local police. Fortunately, widespread adoption of provisions of the Uniform Vehicle Code, and federal regulation of traffic signs under the Highway Safety Act, means that most driving laws do not vary much from one state to the next. All states publish an official driver's handbook which summarizes state driving laws in plain English. These handbooks are usually available both on the Web and at many government offices.

AAA publishes a AAA/CAA Digest of Motor Laws, which is now available online for free. The Digest contains comprehensive summaries in plain English of all major driving laws that typically vary between states. The Digest's coverage includes all US states and all Canadian provinces.

International visitors aged 18 and older can usually drive on their foreign driver's license for up to a year, depending on state law. Licenses that are not in English must be accompanied by an International Driving Permit (IDP) or a certified translation. Persons who will be in the United States for more than a year must obtain a driver's license from the state they are residing in. Written and practical driving tests are required, but they are usually waived for holders of valid Canadian, Mexican, and some European licenses.

Traffic signs often depend on the ability to read English words. Drivers who can read English will find most signs self-explanatory. (Progress toward adopting signs with internationally understood symbols is extremely slow; don't count on seeing any.) Distances and speeds will almost always be given in miles and miles per hour (mph), without these units specified. Some areas near the Canadian and Mexican borders may feature road signs with distances in both miles and kilometers.

Police patrol cars vary in make, model, color, and livery from state to state and even town to town, but all are equipped with red and/or blue flashing lights and a siren. Many police vehicles in the United States are American brand (Ford, Chevrolet, etc). If you see the lights or hear the siren, pull to the right-hand shoulder of the road to let them by. If the patrol car is directly behind you, it's your car the officer is targeting; in that case, pull over as soon as it is practical for you to do so safely, even if this means driving some extra distance. It is extremely important that you pull off the road as soon as you are able. Use your turn signals or your hazard lights to show the officer you are complying. The officer will request to see your driver's license, the registration for the vehicle, and your proof of insurance coverage, and/or rental car documentation. Many traffic stops are recorded by a video camera in the officer's patrol car, as well as a lapel microphone on their person. See the section on police officers in the Stay Safe section below.

There's a chance of coming across a police interior border checkpoint when driving on the highway. The permanent ones are in the states bordering Mexico. But there's a random chance of encountering temporary ones in any state. The purpose is to help prevent illegal immigration. As with crossing into the U.S. from neighboring countries, police will require you to show proof of identification and will check your vehicle for any possible illegal immigrant(s) or other illegals federal or state wise.

Car rental

Generally, you must be 25 or older to rent a car without restrictions or special charges. Rental car agencies in some states may be able to rent a vehicle to drivers as young as 21, but may impose a hefty surcharge. The states of New York and Michigan have laws forcing rental car agencies to rent to drivers as young as 18.

Virtually every car from every rental agency in the U.S. runs on unleaded gasoline and has an automatic transmission. Renting a car usually costs anywhere from $20 and $100 per day for a basic sedan, depending on the type of car and location, with some discounts for week-long rentals.

Major car rental agencies found in nearly all cities are Alamo ☎ +1 877 222-9075; Atlantic choice ☎ +1 800 756 3930; Avis ☎ +1 800 230 4898; Budget (+1 800 527 0700); Dollar (+1 800 800 4000); Enterprise Rent-A-Car (+1 800 RENT-A-CAR); Hertz (+1 800 230 4898); National (+1 877 222 9058); and Thrifty (+1 800 847 4389).

European car rental giant SIXT ☎ +1 888 749-8227 has been expanding into the US in recent years, and is found in a handful of states and but is absent from important states like Hawaii and Illinois. For several years, European car rental company Europcar was allied with National, but in 2013 switched its US alliance partner to Advantage Rent A Car.

There are no large national discount car rental agencies, but in each city there is usually at least one. Some discount car rental companies which operate only in particular regions are Advantage Rent A Car (now owned by Hertz and expanding across the country), E-Z Rent-A-Car (+1 800 277 5171) and Fox Rent A Car. The Internet or the Yellow Pages are the easiest ways to find them. Another well-known discount chain is Rent-A-Wreck (+1 800 944 7501). It rents used cars at significantly lower prices.

Most rental car agencies have downtown offices in major cities as well as offices at major airports. Not all companies allow picking up a car in one city and dropping it off in another (the ones that do almost always charge extra for the privilege); check with the rental agency when making your reservations.

One factor that will strongly influence the price of your car rental will be location. Sometimes renting a car at an airport or near-airport location will cost three or four times as much as renting the same car from the same company at a location far from the airport (but your cost calculations must incorporate the additional time and money it will take to reach the distant off-airport location). In other areas, the airport location may be cheaper. Online travel websites such as Orbitz or Expedia can be useful for comparing prices and making reservations.

Rental agencies accept a valid driver's license from your country, which must be presented with an International Drivers Permit if your license needs to be translated. You may wish to join some kind of auto club before starting a large American road trip, and having a cell phone is a very good idea. Most rental agencies have some kind of emergency road service program, but they can have spotty coverage for remote regions. The largest club in the United States is the American Automobile Association (+1-800-391-4AAA), known as "Triple A". A yearly membership runs about $60. AAA members also get discounts at many hotels, motels, restaurants and attractions; which may make it worth getting a membership even if you don't drive. Note that some non-U.S. automobile clubs have affiliate relationships with AAA, allowing members of the non-U.S. club to take full advantage of AAA road service and discount programs. Among these clubs are the Canadian Automobile Association, The Automobile Association in the UK, and ADAC in Germany.

Alternatively, Better World Club (+1-866-238-1137) offers similar rates and benefits as AAA, but with often more timely service. It is an eco-friendlier choice as 1% of revenue is donated to environmental cleanup programs.

Most Americans renting cars are covered for loss or damage to the rental car either by their credit card or the insurance policy on their primary personal vehicle at home. Without appropriate loss/damage waiver cover, you could be liable for the entire cost of the car should it be written off in an accident. Purchasing loss/damage waiver cover and supplemental liability insurance may add up to $30/day to the price of a rental, in some cases doubling the price of the rental. If you visit the car rental website and identify your country of origin, you may be given a quote which includes the loss/damage waiver and liability insurance for considerably less. Many travel insurance policies include cover for some rental car damage - check your policy against the rental terms and conditions.

Fuel

Gasoline ("gas") is sold by the gallon, at stations that are primarily self-service (you must pump your own gas) with the exception of those in New Jersey and Oregon (where self-service is illegal). The American gallon is smaller than the UK gallon, and equals 3.785 liters. The US octane scale is different from that used in Europe; a regular gallon of U.S. gasoline is rated at 87 octanes, the equivalent of about 92 in Europe. In most states, gas stations offer a choice of three levels of octane: 87 (regular), 89 (midgrade or plus), and 91 (premium). Unless you are renting a luxury vehicle, your vehicle will likely require only 87 regular.

One octane-related detail to watch for—at higher elevations in the mountain west, regular unleaded is often rated at 85 or 86 octanes. This practice began when car engines had carburetors, and lower octane helped those cars run smoothly at altitude. Using 85 or 86 octane in a modern, fuel-injected vehicle rated for 87 octanes or higher for prolonged periods may cause engine damage.

Visitors from countries where self-service is illegal may feel intimidated by the idea of pumping their own gas, but should not be. US self-service gas pumps have clear directions printed on them and are easy to use. The pump will automatically stop when it senses gas backing up into the nozzle (thus indicating the tank is full). When you finish, replace the nozzle in its slot on the pump, reinsert and turn the gas cap until it begins to make clicking noises, and then close the gas cap access door.

Nevertheless, most self-service gas stations will have staff on-hand to pump gas for you if you need assistance. Simply honk your horn quickly a couple of times, or ask for assistance inside the office or adjoining convenience store.

Diesel is not as common, due to heavier federal taxes on it. But it is still widely used and available at most stations, especially those catering to truckers. Untaxed "off-road diesel", sold in rural areas for agricultural use, is dyed red and should not be used in cars, as there are heavy fines if you're caught.

Despite increasing petroleum prices worldwide and some increases in gas taxes, the American consumer-voter's attachment to his automobile, combined with abundant domestic oil reserves and relatively low taxes on gasoline, has kept retail fuel prices much lower than in many parts of the world. Prices fluctuate by region and season. As of December 2014, current prices are averaging near $2.27/gallon (equivalent to $0.59/L) for regular and $3.16/gallon for diesel ($0.83/L). Fuel prices in the United States tend to change every season.

Gas prices vary dramatically from state, territory, and federal district based on a number of variables, primarily state sales tax rates (which are invariably included in the advertised price) and anti-pollution requirements. The highest prices are usually found in Hawaii, Alaska, the West Coast, Illinois, and New York. The lowest prices are generally found in the south-central US and also South Carolina. Prices can also vary by city, town, village, and rural area.

The only truly nationwide gas station chains are Shell and Mobil. Other large chains have achieved almost nationwide coverage but are notably absent from at least one region, like Chevron, Texaco, Exxon, Valero, and Conoco.

Many gas stations have adjoining "mini-marts" or convenience stores where snacks, soda, coffee, and cigarettes are sold, and may or may not offer public bathroom access. In some states, you can also purchase beer. Larger chain stations may also be attached to an "express" version of a fast food chain (McDonald's, Dunkin Donuts, Subway, etc).

By bus

Long distance

Intercity bus travel in the United States is widespread and, while not available everywhere, there are at least three daily routes in every state. Service between nearby major cities is extremely frequent (e.g. as of July 2012 there are 82 daily buses, by seven operators, on an off-peak weekday each way between Boston and New York, an average of nearly one every 10 minutes during daytime hours). Many patrons use bus travel when other modes aren't readily available, as buses often connect many smaller towns with regional cities. The disadvantaged and elderly may use these bus lines, as automobile travel proves arduous or not affordable for some. It's commonly considered a "lower class" way to travel, but is generally dependable, safe, affordable.

Greyhound Bus Lines (First Group) ☎ +1 800-229-9424 and several subsidiaries and affiliated partners (Neon (Toronto & New York); Cruceros USA (US states of Arizona & California and Mexican states of Baja California

Norte & Sonora); Valley Transit (Rio Grande valley in southern Texas); Autobus Americanos (US states of Colorado, New Mexico & Texas and the Mexican states of Coahuila, Chihuahua, Nuevo Leon, Tamaulipus), and Greyhound Canada) have the predominant share of American bus travel. Steep discounts are available to travelers who purchase their tickets 7-14 days in advance of their travel date. Their North American Discovery Pass allows unlimited travel for ranges of 4 to 60 days, but you might want to try riding one or two buses first before locking yourself in to an exclusively-bus American journey. Greyhound buses typically runs in 5-7 hour segments, at which time all passengers must get off the bus so it can be serviced, even if it's the middle of the night. Continuing passengers are boarded before those just getting on. There are no reservations on Greyhound buses. All seating is on a first come, first served basis, with the exception of select cities, where you can pay a $5 fee for priority seating. Greyhound buses are being refurbished with more comfortable seating, wireless Internet, and other improvements.

Stagecoach Group owns & operates Coach USA and Megabus. They offer inexpensive daily bus service departing from curbside bus stops in various parts of the country: the entire East Coast from Maine to Florida and as far west as California and Nebraska (and to Canada) from several hub cities.

Trailways is another provider of intercity bus service. They are not a single company, but a group of individual companies franchised to form a network. Trailways used to have many more routes until most of them were bought by Greyhound in 1987. Today it is still possible to travel to many places by Trailways, but some companies are isolated from the system and you must connect through Greyhound while other Trailways companies operate mainly as a chartered bus and do not offer scheduled services. They do serve many places that Greyhound doesn't and ally with Greyhound against other competitors.

So called Chinatown buses also provide curb-side departures for a standard walk-up cash fare often much lower than other operators' fares. These lines operate through the East Coast down with some further out destinations in the Midwest, the South, and along as along the West Coast. GoToBus.com is the largest online booking agent for these smaller "Chinatown" bus companies. Please note that most Internet-based and Chinatown buses only go to large cities, skipping the smaller towns that many bus travelers ride to. A number of these smaller "Chinatown" companies had also been shut down by the government due to safety violations.

Hispanic bus companies tend to have the most spacious buses in the country. Connections within Texas or from Texas to the Midwest (all the way to Chicago), the Southeast, and/or Mexico are offered by:

• Tornado Bus
• El Expreso
• El Conejo
• Ominbus Mexicanos
• Grupo Senda

Service in and out of Florida to the southeast and with some continuing up along the eastern seaboard to New York & Pennsylvania (I-95 corridor). They are offered by:

• JetSet (Chilean owned)
• Red Coach (Argentinian owned. Travels mainly within Florida)
• Florida Bus (Dutch owned. Travels mainly within Florida)
• La Cubana

In Arizona, California, Colorado, New Mexico and/or western Texas and the northwestern Mexican states of Baja California Norte, Chihuahua, Durando and Sonora include:

• FuturaNet
• TUFESA
• El Paso-Los Angeles Limousine
• InterCalifornias

Onward travel further south of the border can also be booked with Grupo Estrella Blanca through Greyhound as well.

There are numerous other independent operators, many of which are also affiliated with Greyhound or Amtrak through partnership agreements while others are unaffiliated. The below are some of the other independent carriers:

BoltBus competes with Megabus & Chinatown buses on major routes in the Northeast (Baltimore-Washington-Philadelphia-NY-Boston); California (Los Angeles - SF Bay Area and Los Angeles-Las Vegas); and the Pacific Northwest (Vancouver-Seattle-Portland-Eugene, OR).

Concord Coach Lines (Massachusetts, Maine and New Hampshire)

Dartmouth Coaches (Hanover, NH; New York & Boston)

Tripper Bus Daily routes between New York City and the Washington D.C. area suburbs (Arlington, VA & Bethesda, MD stops)

7Bus New York & upper Long Island (formerly a Bolt Bus route)

Indian Trails (Travels from Michigan to Minnesota, Wisconsin, Illinois and Indiana)

Jefferson Lines Midwestern states of Arkansas, Iowa, Kansas, Minnesota, Missouri, Montana, Nebraska, North Dakota, Oklahoma, South Dakota, Texas & Wisconsin.

Michigan Flyer & Indian Trails Primarily in Michigan.

Peter Pan & Bonanza Northeastern states of Connecticut, Massachusetts, Maryland, New Jersey, New York, Pennsylvania, & Rhode Island.

Vamoose New York, Maryland, Virginia

Eastern New York, Maryland, Virginia

The U.S. Department of Transportation's Federal Motor Carrier Safety Administration regulates and certifies all interstate bus operators. FMCSA is notorious for being overworked and underfunded, which means they have a hard time properly regulating the numerous bus operators around the country. The newer curbside bus operators (as in the Chinatown and Internet-based buses) are more dangerous than traditional terminal-based operators like Greyhound, though buses in general are still far safer than driving a private vehicle.

Local travel

Otherwise see the entries for individual U.S. states and/or cities for additional independent companies and transit agencies (operated by local government (local council))

Rural (and even urban) casinos may also offer scheduled shuttle buses between their casinos and nearby cities and towns as a way to draw more customers. Even if you don't gamble you can still take their shuttle bus from 'City A' to the casino where you transfer to another bus to 'City B' for free or for a fare. Check their respective sites.

There are also long distance bus and shuttle services from the airports to various places outside the principal city that airport serves. Same thing from between university towns and the nearest major cities where the majority of the students are from. The university shuttles operate on limited schedules revolving around the university schedules when students go home to their parents on Friday afternoons for the weekend, during the Thanksgiving, Christmas/New Year Break and Spring Break and return to the college town on Sunday afternoons/evenings or at the end of the break period.

In most locations from small towns up to large cites, there are bus systems run by the local government that provide service either along a fixed route, as a deviation from the route or door-to-door. Bus companies are either publicly funded as local public transportation or independently owned & operated companies serving rural and urban areas locally and/or across long distances between cities & towns. In some rural areas these can be the only thing available to get there and around with limited or no Greyhound or Amtrak services. See the article(s) on a specific city, town or state as to what's there. In Alaska, Hawaii and Puerto Rico there are NO Greyhound, Megabus/Coach USA, Chinatown, Boltbus, Trailways and Amtrak services as there are in the Lower 48 or the Mainland. See the respective articles as to what's available there.

By recreational vehicle (RV)

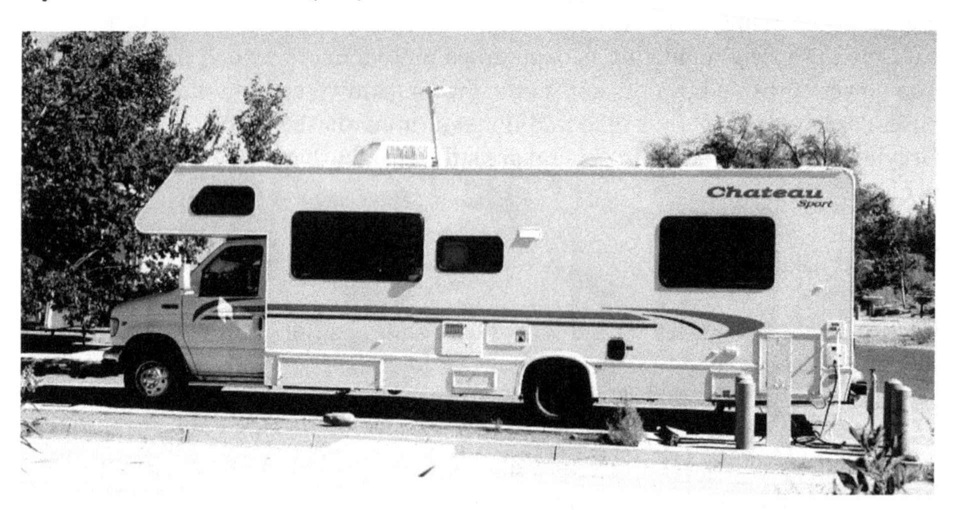

Recreational vehicles – large, sometimes bus sized vehicles that include sleeping and living quarters – are a distinctly American way to cruise the country. Some RVers love the convenience of being able to drive their home anywhere they like and enjoy the camaraderie that RV campgrounds offer. Other people dislike the hassles and maintenance issues that come with RVing.

And don't even think about driving an RV into a huge metropolis such as New York. Still, if you want to drive extensively within the United States and are comfortable handling a big rig, renting an RV is an option you should consider.

By motorcycle

The thrill and exhilaration of cross country travel are magnified when you go by motorcycle. Harley-Davidson is the preeminent American motorcycle brand and Harley operates a motorcycle rental program for those licensed and capable of handling a full weight motorcycle. In some parts of the country, you can also rent other types of motorcycles, such as sport bikes, touring bikes, and dual-sport bikes. For those inexperienced with motorcycles, Harley and other dealerships offer classes for beginners. Wearing a helmet, although not required in all states, is always a good idea. The practice of riding between lanes of slower cars, also known as "lane-sharing" or "lane-splitting," is illegal, except in California where it is tolerated and widespread. Solo motorcyclists can legally use "high-occupancy vehicle" or "carpool" lanes during their hours of operation.

American enthusiasm towards motorcycles has led to a motorcycling subculture. Motorcycle clubs are exclusive clubs for members dedicated to riding a particular brand of motorcycle within a highly structured club hierarchy. Riding clubs may or may not be organized around a specific brand of bikes and offer open membership to anyone interested in riding. Motorcycle rallies, such as the famous one in Sturgis, South Dakota, are huge gatherings of motorcyclists from around the country. Many motorcyclists are not affiliated with any club and opt to ride independently or with friends. In general, motorcycling is seen as a hobby, as opposed to a practical means of transportation; this means, for example, that most American motorcyclists prefer not to ride in inclement weather. However, you choose to ride, and whatever brand of bike you prefer, motorcycling can be a thrilling way to see the country.

By thumb

A long history of hitchhiking comes out of the U.S., with record of automobile hitchhikers as early as 1911. Today, hitchhiking is nowhere near as common, but there are some nevertheless who still attempt short or cross-country trips. The laws related to hitchhiking in the U.S. are most covered by the Uniform Vehicle Code (UVC), adopted with changes in wording by individual states. In general, it is legal to hitchhike throughout the majority of the country, if not standing within the boundaries of a highway (usually marked by a solid white line at the shoulder of the road) and if not on an Interstate highway prohibiting pedestrians.

In many states Interstate highways do not allow foot traffic, so hitchhikers must use the entrance ramps. In a few states it is allowed or tolerated (unless on a toll road). Oklahoma, Texas and Oregon are a few states that do allow pedestrians on the highway shoulder, although not in some metropolitan areas. Oklahoma allows foot traffic on all free interstates, but not toll roads and Texas only bans it on toll roads — and on free Interstates within the city of El Paso. Oregon only bans it in the Portland metro area. Missouri only bans it within Kansas City and St. Louis city limits.

Hitchhiking has become much less popular due to increasing wariness of the possible dangers (fueled in part by sensational stories in the news media). International travelers to the U.S. should avoid this practice unless they have either a particularly strong sense of social adventure or extremely little money. Even many Americans themselves would only feel comfortable "thumbing a ride" if they had a good knowledge of the locale.

Craigslist has a rideshare section that sometimes proves useful for arranging rides in advance. If you are open with your destination it's almost always possible to find a ride on C.L. going somewhere within the U.S.

5-1-1

Some states offer traffic and public transport information by dialing 511 on your phone.

Talk

Most Americans speak English. In many areas, (parts of the South, New England, inner cities, and in the upper Midwest), you'll find some distinctive regional accents and dialects. Nowhere should this pose any problem to a visitor, as Americans often admire foreign accents and most will approximate the standard accent to help you understand them, or try to speak your language if they can.

Even so, visitors are generally expected to speak and understand English. Because of this, the US does not have an official language at the federal (national) level (most states have English as their official language). A growing number of popular tourist sites have signs in other languages, but only English is certain to be available at any given location. There is a wide accent barrier across the U.S., where certain words are spoken or pronounced differently.

Due primarily to immigration from Latin America, the United States has the second-largest Spanish speaking population in the world. Spanish is the primary second language in almost all of the United States, especially California, the Southwest, Texas, Florida, and the metropolitan areas of the Midwest and East Coast. Many of these areas have Spanish-language radio and television stations, with local, national and Mexican programs.

Spanish is the first language of Puerto Rico and a large minority of residents on the mainland, particularly in the western states. Spanish speakers in the United States are primarily Puerto Ricans, or first- and second-generation immigrants from Latin America. As a result, the Spanish spoken is almost invariably a Latin American or Puerto Rican dialect. Although areas where no one speaks English are extremely rare, a good handle on Spanish can make communication easier in some places. Americans are generally taught Spanish in schools from an early age, and therefore many can understand basic phrases while a small but significant population of non-immigrant Americans speaks Spanish fluently. Because many immigrants take service-industry jobs for substandard pay, employees at restaurants, hotels, gas stations, and other such establishments can generally be counted on to understand, speak, and translate Spanish.

French is the primary second language in rural areas near the border with Quebec, in some areas of Louisiana, and among West African immigrants, but is not widespread elsewhere. In southern Florida, Haitian immigrants primarily speak Haitian Creole, a separate language derived from French, as their second language, although a substantial number also speak French.

Thanks to the North American Free Trade Agreement (NAFTA), some products now have trilingual packaging in English, Spanish, and French for sale throughout the entire trade bloc, especially household cleaning products and small electric appliances. In areas with large numbers of Spanish speakers, the major discount stores like Walmart and Target have internal directional signage in their stores in both Spanish and English. However, the vast majority of consumer products are labeled only in English, and most upscale department stores and boutiques have signage only in English, meaning that a rudimentary grasp of English is essential for shopping.

Hawaiian is the native language of Hawaii but is rarely spoken. Japanese is widely spoken. In the various Chinatowns in major cities, Cantonese and Mandarin are common. Smaller immigrant groups also sometimes form their own pockets of shared language, including Russian, Italian, Greek, Arabic, Tagalog, Korean, Vietnamese, and others. Chicago, for instance, is the city with the second largest ethnic Polish population in the world, behind Warsaw. The Amish, who have lived in Pennsylvania and Ohio for generations, speak a dialect of German.

Some Native Americans speak their respective native languages, especially on reservations in the west. However, despite efforts to revive them, many Native American languages are endangered, and people who speak them as their first language are few and far between. Navajo speakers in Arizona and New Mexico are an exception to this, but even a clear majority among them speak and understand English too.

Bottom line: unless you're certain you'll be traveling in an area populated with recent immigrants, don't expect to get by in the United States without some English or Spanish, if you will travel in the southern half of the country.

American Sign Language, or ASL is the dominant sign language in the United States. When events are interpreted, they will be interpreted in ASL. Users of French Sign Language and other related languages may find ASL intelligible, as they share much vocabulary, but users of British Sign Language or Auslan will not. Closed-captioning on television is widespread, but far from ubiquitous. Many theaters offer FM loops or other assistive listening devices, but captioning and interpreters are rarer.

For the blind, many signs and displays include Braille transcriptions of the printed English. Larger restaurant chains, museums, and parks may offer Braille menus and guidebooks, but you'll likely have to ask for them.

See

The United States is extraordinarily diverse in its array of attractions. You will never run out of things to see; even if you think you've exhausted what one place has to offer, the next destination is only a road trip away.

The Great American Road Trip (see above) is the most traditional way to see a variety of sights; just hop in the car and cruise down the Interstates, stopping at the convenient roadside hotels and restaurants as necessary, and stopping at every interesting tourist trap along the way, until you reach your destination.

Heartbreakingly beautiful scenery, history that reads like a screenplay, entertainment options that can last you for days, and some of the world's greatest architecture—no matter what your pleasure, you can find it almost anywhere you look in the United States.

Because the country is so big, it is impossible to truly see it all in one trip. Even the longest available coast-to-coast escorted tour packages (approximately 20 to 45 days in length) only cover about half of the Lower 48 states and do not include Alaska, Hawaii, or the inhabited territories (i.e., Puerto Rico, the U.S. Virgin Islands, and Guam), all of which are also fine tourist destinations in their own right. Thus, as with any large country, you need to do extensive research and prioritize regions and destinations.

Natural scenery

From the spectacular glaciers of Alaska to the steamy and lush, weathered peaks of Appalachia; from the otherworldly desertscapes of the Southwest to the vast waters of the Great Lakes and the perpetually warm jungles of the south; few other countries have as wide a variety of natural scenery as the United States does.

America's National Parks are a great place to start. Yellowstone National Park was the first true National Park in the world, and it remains one of the most famous, but there are 57 others. The Grand Canyon is possibly the world's most spectacular gorge; Sequoia National Park and Yosemite National Park are both home to the world's largest living organisms, the Giant Sequoia; Redwood National park has the tallest, the Coast Redwood; Glacier National Park is home to majestic glacier-carved mountains; Canyonlands National Park could easily be mistaken for Mars; and the Great Smoky Mountains National Park features abundant wildlife among beautiful, verdant waterfalls and mountains. And the national parks aren't just for sightseeing, either; each has plenty of outdoors activities as well.

Still, the National Parks are just the beginning. The National Park Service also operates National Monuments, National Memorials, National Historic Sites, National Seashores, National Heritage Areas... the list goes on (and on). And each state has its own state parks that can be just as good as the federal versions. Most all of these destinations, federal or state, have an admission fee, but it all goes toward maintenance and operations of the parks, and the rewards are well worth it.

Those aren't your only options, though. Many of America's natural treasures can be seen without passing through admission gates. The world-famous Niagara Falls straddle the border between Canada and the U.S.; the American side lets you get right up next to the onrush and feel the power that has shaped the Niagara gorge. The "purple majesty" of the Rocky Mountains can be seen for hundreds of miles in any direction, while the placid coastal areas of the Midwest and the Mid-Atlantic have relaxed Americans for generations. The lush, humid forests of the east, the white sand beaches, the limestone mountains of the south, the red extraterrestrial landscapes of the west... it's a country that has something for everyone.

Historical attractions

Americans often have a misconception of their country as having little history. The US does indeed have a tremendous wealth of historical attractions—more than enough to fill months of history-centric touring.

The prehistory of the continent can be a little hard to uncover, as many pre-contact sites in the Eastern and Midwestern parts of the country have been covered by other structures or farmland. But particularly in the West, you will find magnificent cliff dwellings at sites such as Mesa Verde, as well as near-ubiquitous rock paintings. In the Midwest, the Cahokia Mounds State Historic Site is worth a visit. The Museum of the American Indian in Washington, D.C. is another great place to start learning about America's culture before the arrival of European colonists.

As the first part of the country to be colonized by Europeans, the eastern states of New England, the Mid-Atlantic, and the South have more than their fair share of sites from early American history. The first successful British colony on the continent was at Jamestown, Virginia, although the settlement at Plymouth, Massachusetts, may loom larger in the nation's mind.

In the eighteenth century, major centers of commerce developed in Philadelphia and Boston, and as the colonies grew in size, wealth, and self-confidence, relations with Great Britain became strained, culminating in the Boston Tea Party and the ensuing Revolutionary War...

Monuments and architecture

IN THIS TEMPLE
AS IN THE HEARTS OF THE PEOPLE
FOR WHOM HE SAVED THE UNION
THE MEMORY OF ABRAHAM LINCOLN
IS ENSHRINED FOREVER

Americans have never shied away from heroic feats of engineering, and many of them are among the country's biggest tourist attractions.

Washington, D.C., as the nation's capital, has more monuments and statuary than you could see in a day, but do be sure to visit the Washington Monument (the world's tallest obelisk), the stately Lincoln Memorial, and the incredibly moving Vietnam Veterans Memorial. The city's architecture is also an attraction—the Capitol Building and the White House are two of the most iconic buildings in the country and often serve to represent the whole nation to the world.

Actually, a number of American cities have world-renowned skylines, perhaps none more so than the concrete canyons of Manhattan, part of New York City. The site of the destroyed World Trade Center towers remains a gaping wound in Manhattan's vista, however America's tallest building, the new 1 World Trade Center, now stands adjacent to the site of the former towers. Also, the Empire State Building and the Chrysler Building stand tall, as they have for almost a century. Chicago, where the skyscraper was invented, is home to the country's single tallest building, the (former) Sears Tower, and an awful lot of other really tall buildings. Other skylines worth seeing include San Francisco (with the Golden Gate Bridge), Seattle (including the Space Needle), Miami, and Pittsburgh.

Some human constructions transcend skyline, though, and become iconic symbols in their own right. The Gateway Arch in St. Louis, the Statue of Liberty in Manhattan, the Hollywood Sign in Los Angeles, and even the fountains of the Bellagio casino in Las Vegas all draw visitors to their respective cities. Even the incredible Mount Rushmore, located far from any major city, still attracts two million visitors each year.

Museums and galleries

In the US, there's a museum for practically everything. From toys to priceless artifacts, from entertainment legends to dinosaur bones — nearly every city in the country has a museum worth visiting.

The highest concentrations of these museums are found in the largest cities, of course, but none compare to Washington, D.C., home to the Smithsonian Institution. With almost twenty independent museums, most of them located on the National Mall, the Smithsonian is the foremost curator of American history and achievement. The most popular of the Smithsonian museums are the National Air and Space Museum, the National Museum of American History, and the National Museum of Natural History, but any of the Smithsonian museums would be a great way to spend an afternoon—and they're all 100% free.

New York City also has an outstanding array of world-class museums, including the Guggenheim Museum, the American Museum of Natural History, the Museum of Modern Art (MOMA), the Metropolitan Museum of Art, the Intrepid Sea-Air-Space Museum, and the Ellis Island Immigration Museum.

You could spend weeks exploring the cultural institutions just in D.C. and the Big Apple, but here's a small fraction of the other great museums you'd be missing:

• American Visionary Art Museum — Baltimore, Maryland
• Carnegie Museums of Pittsburgh — Pittsburgh, Pennsylvania
• Children's Museum of Indianapolis — Indianapolis, Indiana
• Exploratorium — San Francisco, California
• Hollywood Walk of Fame — Los Angeles, California
• Monterey Bay Aquarium — Monterey, California
• Museum of Science & Industry — Chicago
• Naismith Memorial Basketball Hall of Fame — Springfield, Massachusetts
• National Aquarium in Baltimore — Baltimore, Maryland
• National Baseball Hall of Fame and Museum — Cooperstown, New York
• Pro Football Hall of Fame — Canton, Ohio
• Rock and Roll Hall of Fame and Museum — Cleveland, Ohio
• San Diego Zoo — San Diego, California
• Strong National Museum of Play — Rochester, New York

Itineraries

Here is a handful of itineraries spanning regions across the United States:

• Appalachian Trail — a foot trail along the spine of the Appalachian Mountains from Georgia to Maine

• Braddock Expedition — traces the French-Indian War route of British General Edward Braddock (and a younger George Washington) from Alexandria, Virginia through Cumberland, Maryland to the Monongahela River near Pittsburgh.

• The Jazz Track — a nation-wide tour of the most important clubs in jazz history and in jazz performance today

• Lewis and Clark Trail — retrace the northwest route of the great American explorers along the Missouri River

• Route 66 — tour the iconic historic highway running from Chicago to Los Angeles

• Santa Fe Trail — a historic southwest settler route from Missouri to Santa Fe

• Touring Shaker country — takes you to one current and eight former Shaker religious communities in the Mid-Atlantic, New England and Midwest regions of the United States.

• U.S. Highway 1 — traveling along the east coast from Maine to Florida

Do

Music — Mid-size to large cities often draw big ticket concerts, especially in large outdoor amphitheaters. Small towns sometimes host concerts in parks with local or older bands. Other options include music festivals such has San Diego's Street Scene or South by Southwest in Austin. Classical music concerts are held year round and performed by semi-professional and professional symphonies. Boston, for instance, occasionally puts on free concerts in the Public Park. Many cities and regions have unique sounds. Nashville is known as Music City because of the large number of country artists that live in the city. It's home to the Grand Ole Opry, one of the most famous music venues in the country. Country music is popular nationwide but is particularly concentrated in the South and rural West. Seattle is the home of grunge rock. Many of the most popular bands are based out of Los Angeles due to the large entertainment presence and concentration of record companies.

Marching Band — In addition to traditional music concerts, a quintessential American experience is the marching band festival. One can find these events almost every weekend between September and Thanksgiving throughout the country and again from March to June in California. Check local event listings and papers to find specifics. Also notable is the Bands of America Grand National Championship held every autumn in Indianapolis. Those looking to see the best of the best should acquire tickets to the "finals" performance, where the twelve best bands of the festival compete for the championship. This event is now held at the Lucas Oil Stadium. Both "street" or parade marching bands as well as "field" or show bands are found at almost every high school and university in America.

Professional sports — The United States has a professional league for virtually every sport, including pillow fighting. However, perhaps because at the national level the only major world team sport that the USA regularly wins at is basketball, many of the most popular leagues are:

MLB — Major League Baseball is very popular and the sport of baseball is often referred to as "America's pastime" (being one of the most widely played in the country). The league has 30 teams (29 in the U.S. and 1 in Canada). Season lasts from April to September with playoff games held in October. With 30 teams playing 162 games per team per season and the cheapest seats usually $10-20, this is possibly the best sporting event for international travelers to watch.

NBA — The National Basketball Association is the world's premier men's basketball league and has 30 teams (29 in the U.S. and one in Canada). Season runs November to April, with playoffs in May-June.

NFL — The National Football League, with 32 teams, is the leading promoter of American football in the world, a sport which has virtually nothing in common with the sports that most other countries call football (Americans know those sports as soccer and rugby). The day of the championship game, called the Super Bowl, is an unofficial national holiday. Season lasts from September to December, with playoffs in January ending with the Super Bowl in February. TV advertisements leading to and on the day of the Super Bowl tend to be comical and creative.

NHL — The premier league for ice hockey in the world, featuring 30 teams (23 in the U.S. and 7 in Canada). A slight majority of players are Canadians, but the league has players from many other parts of the world, mainly the United States, the Nordic countries (primarily Sweden and Finland), Russia, the Czech Republic, and Slovakia. Originally in Northern markets, recent expansions have each major region covered with a NHL team. The season runs from October to April, followed by playoffs that culminate in the Stanley Cup Finals in June.

INDYCAR — Beginning as the original form of American motorsport in 1911 with the first Indianapolis 500. INDYCAR has since come to be the premier open-wheel racing series in North America. The competition in INDYCAR is known to be closer, faster, and far more dangerous than that of NASCAR. Unlike NASCAR which almost races exclusively on "oval" tracks, INDYCAR competes on a wide variety of tracks ranging from city streets, road courses, to ovals like the world-famous Indianapolis Motor Speedway in Speedway, Indiana which plays host to the most famous and prestigious race in the world, the Indianapolis 500, where speeds can reach up to a thrilling 240 miles per hour! INDYCAR holds races all across the United States, as well as Brazil and Canada, from March to October.

NASCAR — Viewed by many as a "regional sport" confined to the more rural areas of the South, the National Association for Stock Car Auto Racing (NASCAR) has seemingly broken away from those misconceptions over recent years to become a major spectator sport across the country. While a majority of the tracks still reside in the Mid-Atlantic and South, NASCAR holds races all across the country, beginning with their marquee event, the Daytona 500, in mid-February and ending in late November.

MLS — Major League Soccer, currently with 19 teams (16 in the U.S. and three in Canada), is the latest attempt to kick start American interest in soccer. While it may not be as popular with the media, MLS is still widely viewed and enjoyed. Foreign travelers can find particularly vibrant and familiar fan experiences in several cities, notably Washington, Chicago, Houston, Kansas City, and especially Portland and Seattle.

College sports — One rare feature of the United States sports landscape, as compared to that of other nations, is the extent to which sports are associated with educational institutions. In many regions of the country, local college or university teams, especially in football and men's basketball, enjoy followings that rival or surpass those of major professional teams. The main governing body for U.S. college sports is the National Collegiate Athletic Association (NCAA), which has over 1,000 member schools, including essentially all of the country's best-known colleges and universities. The college football season runs from roughly September 1 through mid-December, with postseason bowl games running into early January. The basketball regular season begins in mid-November and ends in late February or early March, followed by conference tournaments and then national postseason tournaments that run through early April. The NCAA Division I men's basketball tournament, popularly known as "March Madness" (an NCAA trademark), is especially widely followed even by casual sports fans.

High school sports — Many communities take great pride in their local high school teams, and especially in smaller communities, games are a large part of local culture. If your trip is during the school year (generally late August to late May), a high school game can be a great (and cheap) opportunity to get a major dose of the local culture. The most widely followed sports at this level are generally football and boys' basketball, with ice hockey also having a major presence in certain regions, mainly New England and the upper Midwest. Other sports, such as baseball, girls' basketball, volleyball (almost exclusively a girls' sport in most parts of the U.S.), and wrestling have significant pockets of popularity. In some states, a particular high school sport enjoys a special cultural place. Examples include football in Texas, basketball in Indiana, hockey in Minnesota, and wrestling in Iowa.

Festivals and Fairs — A few days prompt nation-wide celebrations. They include Memorial Day, Independence Day (a.k.a. Fourth of July), and Labor Day. Other major holidays like Thanksgiving Day are marked by private festivities. Many towns and/or counties throw fairs, to commemorate the establishment of a town or the county with rides, games, and other attractions.

Memorial Day — commemorates the ultimate sacrifice made by America's war dead. It is not to be confused with Veterans Day (11th November) which commemorates the service of America's military veterans, both living and deceased. It is the also the unofficial start of summer — expect heavy traffic in popular destinations, especially National Parks and amusement parks.

Independence Day — Celebrates America's independence from Britain. The day is usually marked by parades, festivals, concerts, outdoor cooking and grilling and firework displays. Almost every town puts on some sort of festivity to celebrate the day. Large cities often have multiple events. Washington, D.C. celebrates the day on the Mall with a parade and a fireworks display against the Washington Monument.

Labor Day — The US celebrates Labor Day on the first Monday of September, rather than May 1st. Labor Day marks the end of the summer social season. Some places, such as Cincinnati, throw parties to celebrate the day.

National Parks. There are numerous national parks throughout the United States, especially the vast interior, which offer plenty of opportunities to enjoy your favorite outdoor activities, including Recreational shooting, ATV riding, hiking, bird watching, prospecting, and horseback riding. In more urban areas, some national parks are centered around historic landmarks.

National Trails System is a group of twenty-one 'National Scenic Trails' and 'National Historic Trails' as well as over 1,000 shorter 'National Recreation Trails' for a total length of over 50,000 miles. While all are open to hiking, most are also open to mountain biking, horseback riding, and camping and some are even open for ATVs and cars.

Money

Official currency is the United States dollar ($), divided into 100 cents (¢). Conversion rates vary daily and are available online. The dollar is colloquially known as the buck (a reference to when buck skins were used as a median of exchange in areas far from the coastal mints) so 5 bucks means $5. Foreign currencies are almost never accepted, although some major hotel chains may accept travelers' checks in other currencies. Canadian currency is sometimes accepted at larger stores within 100 miles of the border, but discounted for the exchange rate. (This is more of an issue nowadays with a weak Canadian dollar.) Watch for stores that really want Canadian shoppers and will accept at par. Often, a few Canadian coins (especially pennies) won't be noticed, and do show up in circulation with American coins as they are the same size (but different metal contents and weight). Now that the Mexican peso has stabilized, it is somewhat accepted in a limited number of locations at border towns (El Paso, San Diego, Laredo, etc), but you're better off exchanging your pesos in Mexico, and using US dollars instead, to ensure the best exchange rate.

Common American bills are for $1, $5, $10, $20, while the $2, $50 and $100 bills are less common. All bills are the same size. All $1, $2, and the older $5, $10, $20, $50 and $100 bills are greenish on one side and printed with black and green ink in the other. Newer versions of the $5 (purple), $10 (orange), $20 (green & orange), $50 (pink) and $100 (blue) bills incorporate different gradations of color in the paper and additional colors of ink. As designs are updated every 5-10 years to make it more difficult to counterfeit, you will currently find up to three different designs of some bills in circulation. Almost all vending machines accept $1 bills and a few accept $5 bills; acceptance of larger bills ($50 and $100) by small restaurants and stores is less common. No

US banknotes have been demonetized in the last 80 years. You may even find some vending machines accepting debit/credit cards.

The standard coins are the penny (1¢, copper color), the chunky nickel (5¢, silver color), the tiny dime (10¢, silver color) and the quarter or quarter dollar (25¢, silver color). None of these coins display the numeral of their value, so it is important to recognize the names of each. The size doesn't necessarily correspond to their relative value: the dime is the smallest coin, followed by the penny, nickel, and quarter. Half dollar (50¢, silver) and dollar ($1, silver or gold colored) coins exist but are uncommon in general circulation. Coins haven't been devalued or demonetized, but some may be worth more because of the real silver content (40 - 90% silver) or due to demand in the coin collectors' market. 'Quarters' (25¢) and 'dimes' (10¢) dated before 1965 are 90% real silver and can appear more white in color. 'Half dollars' (50¢) dated before 1971 are also made of real silver at 40% dated 1965 through 1970 and at 90% dated 1964 and earlier. Most have been removed from circulation due to their higher intrinsic value (due to higher silver prices) above legal tender face value and less common but they can still be found in circulation from time to time. Coin-operated machines usually only accept nickels, dimes, and quarters and they may not accept the real silver coins dated before 1965 due to their different weight from the current debased coins (copper core in a nickel clad). Coins dated in the 1940s or earlier, some with a different or similar design or appearance than the current coins are still found in circulation and may be worth more as a collector's item.

Currency exchange and banking

Currency exchange centers are rare outside the downtowns of major coastal and border cities, and international airports, however, many banks can also provide currency exchange services. Note that exchange rates are mediocre at airports and downright terrible at currency exchange centers in the suburbs. It is easiest to exchange major currencies like the euro, the UK pound, the Japanese yen, the Mexican peso, and the Canadian dollar. Visitors in possession of other currencies will find less places willing to accept them, or if at all, at less optimal rates. Major foreign exchange services at airports are provided by either Travelex or ICE Plc (International Currency Exchange)

The Big Four U.S. retail banks are Chase, Bank of America, Wells Fargo, and Citibank, all of which have branches and ATMs in most major cities in the Lower 48 states. Because interstate bank branching was legalized only in 1994, many parts of the U.S. (like Hawaii, Alaska, and the territories) are poorly served by the big retail banks and are dominated by local banks. A few international banks have made inroads into the U.S. like HSBC, BBVA, and

Rabobank, but because the country is so big, they are still relative newcomers and interstate banking laws are so restrictive, their branch networks are relatively limited.

Most automated teller machines (ATMs) can handle foreign bank cards or credit cards bearing Visa/Plus or MasterCard/Cirrus logos; note, however, that many ATMs charge fees of about $3 for use with cards issued by other banks (often waived for cards issued outside of the U.S., but banks in one's home country may charge their own fees). Smaller ATMs found in restaurants etc. often charge higher fees (up to $5). Some ATMs (such as those at Sheetz gas stations and government buildings such as courthouses) have no fee. Another option is withdrawing cash (usually up to $40 over the cost of your goods) when making a debit-card purchase at a large discount store such as Walmart or Target, or at many supermarkets. Stores almost never charge a fee for this service, though the bank that issued your card may.

Unless your debit / credit card is U.S. issued, expect to incur foreign transaction fees from your bank.

Most bank ATMs support at least one language (usually Spanish) in addition to English. ATMs operated by the Big Four banks tend to support many more languages, especially in urban areas.

If you are from a country or territory with the US dollar as an official currency, you will not need to worry about understanding prices and currency transferring. Also if you are from Bermuda, Panama, or Bahamas, the official currency(ies) of the mentioned countries and territories have fixed exchange rates to the US Dollar. Meaning what price is said in the U.S. will be understood with your country's/territory's official currency. Example; $125 US Dollars will equal $125 Bermudian dollars, but you will still have to exchange currencies.

Credit and debit cards

Major credit cards Visa and MasterCard were both launched in the U.S., so it makes sense that today, Visa and MasterCard (and their debit card counterparts/affiliates) are widely used and accepted throughout all 50 states and all inhabited territories. Nearly all large retailers will accept credit cards for transactions of all sizes, even as small as one or two dollars. However, some small businesses and independently-owned stores specify a minimum amount of money (usually $2-5, but can legally charge up to $10 minimum) for credit card use, as such transactions cost them around 30 to 50 cents (this practice is also common at bars when opening a tab). Almost all sit-down restaurants, hotels, and shops will accept credit and debit cards; those that do not post a sign saying "CASH ONLY." Other cards such as American Express and Discover are also accepted by most retailers, but not as widely. Many retailers have a window sticker or counter sign showing the logos of the four big U.S. credit cards: Visa, MasterCard, AmEx, and Discover. However, major retailers might accept only cash or debit cards for payment of prepaid/gift cards/transportation passes.

Historically, logos for foreign cards like JCB and China UnionPay were very hard to find outside of high-end luxury boutiques, although both JCB and China UnionPay have longstanding alliances with Discover and can be used anywhere that takes Discover cards. In 2012, many U.S. stores, including Walmart, added JCB and China UnionPay logos to attract Asian tourists.

When making large purchases, it is typical for U.S. retailers to ask to see some form of photo identification. Shops may also ask for photo identification for foreign issued cards. In certain circumstances, credit/debit cards are the only means to perform a transaction. Hence if you do not have one, you can purchase a prepaid card or gift card with Visa/Mastercard or Amex logo for yourself in a good number of stores but you may need to provide identification before the card is activated.

Transaction authorization is made by signing a paper sales slip or a computer pad, although many retailers will waive the signature requirement for small purchases. The US has not yet implemented the EMV "chip-and-PIN" credit card authorization system used overseas, due to the high cost of upgrading point-of-sale systems and an ongoing dispute among retailers, banks, and credit card firms over who should bear that expense. Between August 2011 and June 2012, the four big credit card networks initially announced target dates in spring 2013 for EMV implementation among their US retailers. The vast majority of retailers failed to meet that deadline. The latest targets for EMV implementation are in 2015 for most retailers, and 2017 for gas stations, although it is still unclear whether those deadlines can be met.

Gas station pumps, selected public transportation vending machines, and some other types of automated vending machines often have credit/debit card readers. Many gas station pumps and some automated vending machines that accept credit cards ask for the ZIP code (i.e., postal code) of the U.S. billing address for the card, which effectively prevents them from accepting foreign cards (they are unable to detect a foreign card and switch to PIN authentication). However, inputting the digits only of a UK Post Code of the UK billing address, or the digits only of the postal code of the Canadian billing address (in both cases, ignore spaces and letters), and adding on as many zeros as necessary to make five digits works often enough to be worth trying and does no harm. Since July

2013, this trick is guaranteed to work for Canadians who use cards with the MasterCard logo at gas stations that require a ZIP code prompt. At gas stations you can use a foreign issued card by paying the station attendant inside.

In many big tourist cities, watch out for merchants trying to convert your USD purchase to your home currency when using your foreign debit / credit card. This is known as dynamic currency conversion and the exchange rate, at the point of sale, is NEVER in your favor; regardless of what you are told by the merchant. Always opt to be charged in USD. You can also avoid this by buying a prepaid debit card as long as you ensure there is sufficient funds in the card.

Gift cards

Each major commercial establishment (e.g. store, restaurant, online service) with a statewide, regional, nationwide or online presence makes its own gift card available to consumers for use at any of its establishments nationwide or its online store. In spite of the word "gift" in gift card, you can actually purchase and use these cards for yourself; however, they are most commonly given to others as gifts. This is a more polite way to give someone money as a gift, and is a standard gift for someone whom you don't know very well. A gift card for a certain establishment can be purchased at any of the establishment's branches. Supermarkets and pharmacies also have a variety of gift cards from different stores, restaurants and other services. Once these are purchased by you or given to you by friends, you can use a particular store or restaurant's gift card at any of its branches nationwide or online store for any amount. In case funds in the gift card are insufficient, you can use other payment methods to pay for the balance (like cash, credit card, a 2nd gift card particular to the establishment). VISA, MasterCard and American Express gift cards work very similarly to their credit/debit card counterparts. The gift card also has instructions on how to check your remaining balance online. Take note that the gift cards are unlikely to be accepted in the establishment's branches outside the U.S. though when you return home you can still use any remaining amount in the gift card in the establishment's online store.

Sales tax

There is no nationwide sales tax (such as VAT or GST), the only exception being motor fuels like gasoline and diesel. As a result, state and/or local taxes (see below) on major purchases cannot be refunded by customs agents upon leaving the United States.

However, most states have a sales tax, ranging from 2.9% to nearly 10% of the retail price; 4-6% is typical. Sales tax is almost never included in posted prices (except for gasoline/diesel, and in most states, alcoholic beverages consumed on-premises), but instead will be calculated and added to the total when you pay. Groceries and a variety of other "necessities" are usually exempt, but almost any other retail transaction – including restaurant meals – will have sales tax added to the total. The price displayed is rarely the final price you pay.

Delaware, New Hampshire and Oregon have no sales tax. Alaska has no statewide sales tax, but allows local governments to collect sales taxes. Montana also has no state-wide sales tax, but a few local governments (mostly in tourism-dominated towns) are allowed to collect sales taxes. Minnesota, Pennsylvania and New Jersey do not collect sales tax on clothes. In Massachusetts, clothing is exempt from any sales tax if the item costs no more than $175 (and sales tax is collected only on the amount over $175); in New York, clothing is exempt from state sales tax statewide and local sales tax in some locations (most notably New York City) if the item costs less than $110. At least two states, Louisiana and Texas, will refund sales tax on purchases made by international travelers taken out of the state.

Regional price variations, indirect hotel and business taxes, etc, will usually have more impact on a traveler's wallet than the savings of seeking out a low-sales-tax or no-sales-tax destination. Many cities also impose sales taxes, and certain cities have tax zones near airports and business districts that are designed to exploit travelers. Thus, sales taxes can vary up to 2% in a matter of a few miles.

However, even accounting for the burden of sales taxes, US retail prices still tend to be much lower than in many other countries. With one exception, the US has not implemented any form of value-added tax, where each segment in the supply chain is required to charge tax on the value it adds towards the final product. Rather, US sales taxes are charged only by the retailer at the time of the sale of the final product to the consumer. This is one reason for why Americans find everything to be so expensive when they visit other countries. The sole exception is the state of Hawaii, which charges a general excise tax that is worse than a value-added tax; it is levied on the entire price of products at every segment of the supply chain, rather than just the value added.

If you are coming to the U.S. from a higher-taxed jurisdiction in search of bargains on luxury goods, note that it is much more difficult to find most of the internationally renowned brands of luxury goods in the no-sales-tax states, as such brands have traditionally positioned their boutique stores in the largest and wealthiest states: California, Texas, New York, Illinois and Florida (all of which have sales taxes). Even if you can find a particular luxury brand in a no-sales-tax state, it will likely be only one of multiple brands carried by a local luxury retailer, meaning their inventory will not be able to match the depth of a boutique dedicated solely to that brand.

Places for shopping

Shopping malls and shopping centers. America is the birthplace of the modern enclosed "shopping mall" as well as the open-air "shopping center". Most large high-end malls are operated by nationwide mall operators like Westfield, Simon, or General Growth Properties. In addition, American suburbs have miles and miles of small strip malls, or long rows of small shops with shared parking lots, usually built along a high-capacity road. Large cities still maintain central shopping districts that can be navigated on public transport, but pedestrian-friendly shopping streets are uncommon and usually small.

Outlet centers. The U.S. pioneered the factory outlet store, and in turn, the outlet center, a shopping mall consisting primarily of such stores. Outlet centers are found along major Interstate highways outside of most American cities. Simon Premium Outlets is the largest chain of outlet centers in the U.S.

Major retailers. American retailers tend to have some of the longest business hours in the world, with chains like Walmart often featuring stores open 24/7 (24 hours a day, 7 days a week). Department stores and other large retailers are usually open from 10 AM to 9 PM most days, and during the winter holiday season, may stay open as long as 8 AM to 11 PM. The U.S. does not regulate the timing of sales promotions as in other countries. U.S. retailers often announce sales during all major holidays, and also in between for any reason or no reason at all. American retail stores are gigantic compared to retail stores in other countries, and are a shoppers' dream come true.

Travelers should be aware that bargaining is generally not practiced at established stores, though it is welcome at other sales venues (see below). While asking for a price reduction due to an item defect is generally acceptable, retail sales personnel often do not have the authority to change prices and may see attempting to haggle as rude or or even threatening. If you want to ask for a discount, be polite and accept whatever answer you are given. If you don't, you may be asked to leave.

Garage sales. On weekends, it is not uncommon to find families selling no longer needed household items in their driveway, garage, or yard. If you see a driveway full of stuff on a Saturday, it's likely a garage sale. Check it out; one person's trash may just be your treasure. Bargaining is expected and encouraged.

Flea markets. Flea markets (called "swap meets" in Western states) have dozens if not hundreds of vendors selling all kinds of usually inexpensive merchandise. Some flea markets are highly specialized and aimed at collectors of a particular sort; others just sell all types of items. Again, bargaining is expected.

Auctions. Americans did not invent the auction but may well have perfected it. The fast paced, sing-song cadence of a country auctioneer, selling anything from farm animals to estate furniture, is a special experience, even if you have no intention of buying. In big cities, head to the auction chambers of Christie's or Sotheby's, and watch paintings, antiques and works of art sold in a matter of minutes at prices that go into the millions.

Major U.S. retail chains

Department stores

According to Deloitte, the largest fashion goods retailer in both the U.S. and the entire world is Macy's, Inc., which operates just over 770 Macy's midrange department stores in 45 states, Puerto Rico, and Guam, plus 37 upscale Bloomingdale's stores and 13 Bloomingdale's Outlet stores. In other words, nearly every mall you visit will have a Macy's.

Unfortunately, not all of them are all worth visiting. Most Macy's stores, especially in smaller cities and middle-class suburbs, tend to heavily feature midrange brands. Most brands featured in those stores are private brands (that is, the brand concept was created by and is exclusive to Macy's itself, and most of them are not associated with a famous fashion designer). Over time, Macy's, like other U.S. department stores, has shifted its product mix in favor of its own private brands over outside designer brands. Obviously, if it owns the brand, it captures more of the profits. Therefore, shopping at most Macy's stores makes sense only if you are actually a fan of Macy's private brands (some of which are quite good and are available overseas in select department stores).

However, in the largest U.S. cities, Macy's operates high-end regional flagship stores which feature many internationally renowned upscale designer brands, and some of those stores have visitor centers catering to international tourists. In general, you should save your time and money for Macy's regional flagship stores or its gigantic original flagship store in New York City.

Nordstrom is another upscale department store that is also found in most states. Other upscale department stores that operate coast-to-coast include Saks Fifth Avenue, Neiman Marcus, and Barney's New York, but they are found only in the wealthiest cities.

Besides Macy's, other midrange nationwide chains include Kohl's, Sears, and JCPenney. The lower end is dominated by Marshalls, TJ Maxx, and Old Navy.

Discount stores, supermarkets, and warehouse clubs

General discount stores like Walmart, Target, and Kmart are ubiquitous, as well as Walmart Supercenters and SuperTargets which are similar to hypermarkets overseas. (Kmart's hypermarket equivalents are called Super Kmarts, but they are extremely rare.) Many discount stores have either a small grocery section or a full supermarket; in fact, Walmart is the country's largest seller of groceries, as well as its largest retail chain.

The two largest supermarket chains are Kroger and Safeway (the latter is in the process of being bought by Albertsons), but both operate under legacy regional nameplates in many states. For example, in the nation's second largest city, Los Angeles, Kroger operates Ralphs and Food4Less, while Safeway operates Vons and Pavilions, and neither operates any stores under their own names. And neither chain operates in the nation's largest city, New York City, where the supermarket business is severely fragmented among a huge number of regional chains. The dominant warehouse club chain in the U.S. is Costco, whose biggest competitor is Sam's Club (operated by Walmart).

Other chains

In several areas of the retail sector, ruthless consolidation has resulted in only one surviving nationwide chain, each of which competes with numerous regional chains and local stores. Examples include bookstores (Barnes & Noble), toys (Toys "R" Us), housewares (Bed Bath & Beyond), convenience stores (7-Eleven) and electronics (Best Buy). Both of the last two compete against several almost national chains that technically operate "coast-to-coast" but are notably absent from certain regions. For example, Circle K does not operate in the Mid-Atlantic states and New York City metro and Fry's Electronics is absent from most of the East Coast except Atlanta.

Some areas of retail have two nationwide chains. The two big sporting goods chains are Sports Authority and Dick's Sporting Goods.

Other areas of retail have stabilized around three big nationwide chains. For example, the three big office stationery chains are Office Depot, OfficeMax, and Staples (although Office Depot and OfficeMax have merged and are now one company). The three big pharmacy chains are CVS, Walgreens, and Rite Aid—although virtually all Walmart, Target, and Kmart stores also have pharmacies, as do many supermarkets.

Keep in mind that even if a discount store or supermarket is open 24/7, its pharmacy will almost never keep that schedule—it will usually have a morning-to-evening schedule and close overnight. This is only an issue if you need to fill a prescription or purchase a decongestant containing pseudoephedrine (in the latter case, pharmacists are required to record sales because it can be used to illegally make the highly addictive drug methamphetamine). Almost all other items sold in the pharmacy section can be paid for at any checkout location.

U.S. pharmacies traditionally use the mortar-and-pestle as their symbol, not the green cross used by some European pharmacists (which in the U.S. is the symbol of medical marijuana). However, many U.S. pharmacies are now marked simply by the word "pharmacy" as part of their logo. U.S. pharmacies are much larger than their counterparts overseas because in the 1950s, they began selling soft drinks, packaged foods, and general merchandise to compete against the small discount stores ("dime stores") that were then widespread, and eventually displaced them altogether. Thus, upon entering the U.S. and reaching your hotel, if you don't see any supermarkets close by, try a pharmacy if you need to stock up on soft drinks and snacks.

One interesting aspect of most U.S. malls is the lack of dedicated bookstores, as most U.S. consumers now order books online and use brick-and-mortar retailers only for impulse purchases. Barnes & Noble may still be found as an anchor tenant at some enclosed malls, but is more frequently found in outdoor power centers or strip malls.

Costs

Unless you live in Australia, Canada, Western Europe, or Japan, the United States is generally expensive, but there are ways to limit the damage. Many foreign visitors come to the United States for shopping (especially electronics, designer apparel, and accessories). While retail prices in the United States for luxury goods are lower than in many countries (as a result of low or nonexistent sales tax), and selection and quality are generally much better (due to the superior bargaining power of the gigantic U.S. retail chains), keep in mind that you could be charged taxes/tariffs on goods purchased abroad. That said, it's easy to go through the "green lane" at many airports and avoid paying any tax.

Additionally, electronics may not be compatible with standards when you return, such as DVD region. That problem is easily avoided by using a "region-free" DVD/Blu-Ray player or by viewing the movies on a computer, where region codes are easy to evade. Your U.S.-bought item may not be eligible for warranty service in your home country.

If you have generous friends from the U.S. who will give gift cards to you for some reason, the cards can sometimes help you defray some costs.

A barebones budget for camping, hostels, and cooking your food could be $30-50/day, and you can double that if you stay at motels and eat at cheap cafes. Add on a rental car and hotel accommodation and you'll be looking at $150/day and up.

There are regional variations too: large cities like New York and Los Angeles are expensive, while prices are usually lower in the suburbs and countryside.

If you intend to visit any of the National Parks Service sites, such as the Grand Canyon or Yellowstone National Park, it is worth considering the purchase of a National Parks and Federal Recreational Lands Pass. This costs $80 and gives access to almost all of the federally administered parks and recreation areas for one year. Considering the price of admission to many parks is at least $20 each, if you visit more than a few of them, the pass will be the cheaper solution. You can trade in receipts from individual entries for 14 days at the entrance to the parks to upgrade to an annual pass, if you find yourself cruising around and ending up visiting more parks than expected.

Many hotels and motels offer discounts for members of certain organizations which anyone can join, such as AAA (formerly the American Automobile Association, now generally referred to as "Triple-A"). If you're a member, or are a member of a club affiliated with AAA (such as the Canadian Automobile Association, The Automobile Association in the UK, or ADAC in Germany), it's worth asking at check-in. In addition, many hotels may offer senior discounts. The criteria for most is 62 (some set at 65) or older. Rates can be the same, greater, or less than AAA. Be prepared to show ID at check-in for age verification.

Tipping

Tipping in America is widely used and expected. While Americans themselves often debate correct levels and exactly who deserves to be tipped, generally accepted standard rates are:

Hairdressers, other personal services: 10-15%

Bartenders: $1 per drink if inexpensive or 15-20% of total

Bellhops: $1-2 per bag ($3-5 minimum regardless)

Hotel doorman: $1 per bag (if they assist), $1 for calling a cab

Shuttle bus drivers: $2-5 (optional)

Private car & limousine drivers: 15-20%

Parking valet: $1-3 for retrieving your car

Housekeeping in hotels: $1-2 per day for long stays or $5 minimum for very short stays (optional)

Food delivery (pizza, etc.): $2-5, 15-20% for larger orders

Tour guides / activity guides $5-$10 if he or she was particularly funny or informative.

Taxis: Tips of 10-20% are expected in both yellow cabs as well as livery cabs. A simple way of computing the tip is to add 10% of the fare and round up from there. Thus, if the meter reads $6.20, you pay $7 and if the meter reads $6.50, you pay $8. Always tip more for better service (for example, if the cabbie helps you with your bags or stroller). Leave a small tip if the service is lousy (for example, if the cabbie refuses to turn on the air conditioning on a hot day). For livery cabs, tip 10-20% depending on the quality of the service, but you don't need to tip at all if you hail the cab on the street and negotiate the fare in advance (leave an extra dollar or two anyway!).

Full-service restaurants: 15-20%. Many restaurants include a mandatory service charge for larger groups, in which case you do not need to tip an additional amount - however, tipping on top of the service charge is always welcomed by waiters especially if two waiters work on one large group and they are splitting the service charge between them. But tipping on top of the service charge is only optional and could be done if the service was particularly spectacular.
It is important to keep in mind that the legal minimum wage for restaurant wait staff and other tip-earners is quite low (just $2.13/hour before taxes), with the expectation that tips bring them up to a more "normal" wage. Thus, in restaurants (and certain other professions) a tip is not just a way to say "thank you" for service, but an essential part of a server's wages.

Remember that while it is expected for you to tip normally for adequate service, you are never obliged to tip if your service was truly awful. If you receive exceptionally poor or rude service and the manager does not correct the problem when you bring it to their attention (and do bring the matter to their attention first), a deliberately small tip (one or two coins) will express your displeasure more clearly than leaving no tip at all. If you do decide not to leave a tip, don't be surprised if the restaurant's manager follows you out of the restaurant to ask you about the reasons for your dissatisfaction. Not leaving a tip is exceptionally rare, and something that will definitely be noticed.

If paying your bill by cash, leave a cash tip on the table when you leave (there is no need to hand it over personally or wait until it's collected), or if paying by credit card you can add it directly to the charge slip when you sign it. Look carefully, as the slip will generally inform you whether a 15% gratuity has already been added.

Tipping is not expected at restaurants where patrons stand at a counter to place their order and receive their food (such as fast-food chains). Some such restaurants may have a "tip jar" by the cash register, which may be used wholly at the customer's discretion in appreciation of good service. Some tipping at a cafeteria or buffet is expected since the wait staff often clears the table for you and provides refills of drinks and such.

The majority of jobs not mentioned here are not customarily tipped, and would likely refuse them. Retail employees, or those in service positions which require high qualifications (such as doctors or dentists) are good examples. Never try to offer any kind of tip to a government employee of any kind, especially police officers; this could be construed as attempted bribery (a felony offense) and might cause serious legal problems.

Comics and cartoons

No.8
SUPERMAN
10¢
JAN.
FEB.
WORLD'S GREATEST ADVENTURE-STRIP CHARACTER!

The United States is known worldwide for its comics and cartoon culture, especially in superheroes and supervillains such as Superman and Joker. The U.S. is also famous for its Comic Cons (Comic Conventions) as they are known for being huge and for the variety of products other than comics. Visitors to the U.S. must be aware that it can be very difficult to find non-English cartoon DVDs and mangas. Although Spanish and French speakers will have less trouble as many DVDs nowadays have French and Spanish languages as optional choices as subtitles. Due to Japanese anime and manga being the second most popular animation products in the U.S. (after American animation and comics), it is possible to find imported anime and manga products in Japanese only. But they are usually found online or in special shops catering only to Japanese products. As with almost everywhere else in the western hemisphere, all DVDs are in formatted in NTSC.

Eat

The variety of restaurants throughout the U.S. is remarkable. In a major city such as New York or Chicago, it may be possible to find a restaurant from nearly every country in the world. One thing that a traveler from Europe or Latin America will notice is that many restaurants do not serve alcohol, or may only serve beer and wine. Some restaurants, especially in larger cities, implement a BYOB (Bring Your Own Booze) policy, in other words, you are invited to bring your own alcoholic beverages. Another is the sheer number and variety of fast food and chain restaurants. Most open early in the morning and stay open late at night; many are open 24 hours a day. A third remarkable fact is the size of the portions generally served by US restaurants. Although the trend has moderated in recent years, portions have grown surprisingly large over the past two or three decades.

Types of restaurants

Fast food restaurants such as McDonald's, Burger King, KFC, and Taco Bell are ubiquitous. But the variety of this type of restaurant in the US is astounding: pizza, Chinese and Mexican food, fish, chicken, barbecued meat, and ice cream only begin to touch on it. Alcoholic beverages are not served in these restaurants; "soda" (often called "pop" in the Midwest through Western New York and Western Pennsylvania, or generically "coke" in the South) or other soft drinks are standard. Don't be surprised when you order a soda, are handed a paper cup and expected to fill it yourself from the machine (refills are often free).

Americans tend to love their soft drinks ice cold so you can expect to see some fellow patrons filling their cups two-thirds with ice and then adding what would seem to be a tiny amount of the actual beverage, but this varies from person to person.

The quality of the food varies, but in general it will be cheap, reliable, and fairly tasty (in a mass-market sort of way - connoisseurs and "foodies" generally avoid these places like the plague), but the menu will be somewhat limited, and aside from a couple token healthy options, generally high in fat, carbs, and salt. The restaurants are usually clean and bright, and the service is limited but friendly. Tipping is not expected but you must clear your table after your meal.

Take-out food is very common in larger cities, for food that may take a little longer to prepare than a fast-food place can accommodate. Place an order by phone (or, at an increasing number of establishments, on the Web) and then go to the restaurant to pick it up and take it away. Many places will also deliver; in fact, in some cities, it will be easier to have pizza or Chinese food delivered than to find a sit-down restaurant. Pizza delivery is especially ubiquitous in the US; almost any town of 5,000 or more people will have at least one establishment offering delivery. The main national pizza chains are Pizza Hut, Domino's, Papa John's, and Little Caesars. Most Pizza Huts are dine-in restaurants that also offer carry-out and delivery. Domino's and Papa John's are delivery and carry-out only. Most Little Caesars locations are carry-out only, though some now offer delivery as well. Especially in larger cities, local pizza places compete successfully against the big national chains, and many of them offer delivery.

Fast-Casual is a fairly recent new genre of restaurants that grew in popularity during the 2000's. They are places that are usually around $5-7 for a meal and involve a little bit of waiting as food is prepared fresh (although much less waiting than sit-down restaurants). They tend to be a bit healthier than most typical fast food chains and offer distinct menus. Notable fast-casuals include: Chipotle, Moe's Southwest Grill, Noodles and Company, Panera Bread, Five Guys (a hamburger chain), and Freddies Burgers.

Chain sit-down restaurants are a step up in quality and price from fast food, although those with discerning palates will probably still be disappointed. They may specialize in a particular cuisine such as seafood or a particular nationality, though some serve a large variety of foods. Some are well-known for the breakfast meal alone, such as the International House of Pancakes (IHOP) which serves breakfast all day in addition to other meals. A few of the larger chain restaurants include Red Lobster, Olive Garden, Applebee's and T.G.I. Friday's, to name a few. These restaurants generally serve alcoholic beverages, though not always.

Very large cities in America are like large cities anywhere, and one may select from inexpensive neighborhood eateries to extravagantly expensive full-service restaurants with extensive wine lists and prices to match. In most medium sized cities and suburbs, you will also find a wide variety of restaurants of all classes. In "up-scale" restaurants, rules for men to wear jackets and ties, while once de rigueur, are becoming more relaxed, but you should check first if there is any doubt. This usually only happens at the most expensive of restaurants.

The diner is a typically American, popular kind of restaurant. They are usually individually run, 24-hour establishments found along the major roadways, but also in large cities and suburban areas. They offer a huge variety of large-portion meals that often include soup or salad, bread, beverage and dessert. They are usually very popular among the locals for breakfast, in the morning or after the bars. Diner chains include Denny's, Norm's, and (in the South) Waffle House, but there are many non-chain diners. Local, non-chain diners are particularly common along the east coast in New York, New Jersey, and Eastern Pennsylvania.

No compendium of American restaurants would be complete without mentioning the truck stop. You will only encounter these places if you are taking an intercity auto or bus trip. They are located on interstate highways and they cater to truckers, usually having a separate area for diesel fuel, areas for parking "big rigs", and shower facilities for truckers who sleep in their cabs. These fabled restaurants serve what passes on the road for "plain home cooking": hot roast beef sandwiches, meatloaf, fried chicken, and of course the ubiquitous burger and fries – expect large portion sizes! In recent years, the concept of the chain establishment has been adopted by truck stops as well, and two of the most ubiquitous of these, Flying J Travel Plazas and Petro Stopping Centers, have 24-hour restaurants at most of their installations, including "all you can eat" buffets. A general gauge of how good the food is at a given truck-stop is to note how many truckers have stopped there to eat.

The most recent newcomer to the American dining scene is the food truck. Food trucks are just what they sound like – trucks, buses or vans that have been converted into mobile restaurants. The quality of the food served ranges to greasy, poor-quality stuff served at construction sites to high-end operations serving gourmet, restaurant quality food (at surprisingly affordable prices) run by renowned chefs. Food trucks are common in large cities (especially on the West Coast), tend to set up shop where large groups of hungry people typically congregate (e.g. office parks and central business districts during lunch hours, and bars/clubs during evening hours. Most trucks are open for business during afternoon and evening hours Monday through Thursday, afternoon, evening and late night hours on Fridays, and late night hours on Saturdays. These trucks frequently use social media such as Twitter to announce to their followers where they'll be setting up on any given day.

Some bars double as restaurants open late at night but may be off-limits to those under 21 or unable to show photo ID, and this may include the dining area.

American restaurants serve soft drinks with a liberal supply of ice to keep them cold (and fill the glass). Asking for no ice in your drink is acceptable, and the drink will still probably be fairly cool. If you ask for water, it will usually be chilled and served with ice, unless you request otherwise. Water will not be carbonated as may be typical in parts of Europe. If desired, "sparkling water" is the term for carbonated water. In many restaurants, soft drinks and tea will be refilled for you at no extra charge, but you should ask if this is not explicitly stated.

Types of service

Many restaurants aren't open for breakfast. Those that do (mostly fast-food and diners), serve eggs, toast, pancakes, cereals, coffee, etc. Most restaurants stop serving breakfast between 10 and 11 AM, but some, especially diners, will serve breakfast all day. As an alternative to a restaurant breakfast, one can grab breakfast food such as doughnuts, muffins, fruits, coffee, and packaged drinks at almost any gas station or convenience store. Coffee shops (of which Starbucks is the most well-known) are popular for breakfast; although they offer pastries and other items, most people frequent them for a morning dose of caffeine. Some chains, like Dunkin' Donuts or Einstein Brothers Bagels, are sometimes liked more for their coffee than their actual food.

Continental Breakfast is a term primarily used by hotels and motels to describe a cold breakfast offering of cereal, breads, muffins, fruit, etc. Milk, fruit juices, hot coffee and tea are the typical beverages. There is usually a toaster for your bread. This is a quick, cheap (usually free) way of getting morning food.

Lunch can be a good way to get food from a restaurant whose dinners are out of your price range.

Dinner, the main meal. Depending on culture, region, and personal preference, is usually enjoyed between 5 and 9pm. Many restaurants serve portions well in excess of what can normally be eaten in one sitting, and will be willing to box up your leftover food (typically referred to as a "to go box"). Do not feel the need to finish what you have been served. Making reservations in advance is a good idea if the restaurant is popular, "up-scale", or you are dining in a large group.

Buffets are generally a cheap way to get a large amount of food. For a single, flat, rate, you can have as many servings of whatever foods are set out. However, since food can be sitting out in the heat for hours, the quality can suffer. Generally, buffets serve American or Chinese-American cuisine.

Many restaurants serve Sunday brunch, served morning through early afternoon, with both breakfast and lunch items. There is often a buffet. Like most other meals, quality and price can vary by restaurant.

Types of food

While many types of food are unchanged throughout the United States, there are a few distinct regional varieties of food. The most notable is in the South, where traditional local fare includes grits (ground maize porridge), collard greens (a boiled vegetable, often flavored with ham and a dash of vinegar), sweet iced tea, barbecue (not unique to this region, but best and most common here), catfish (served deep-fried with a breadcrumb coating), cornbread, okra, and gumbo (a stew of seafood or sausage, rice, okra, and sometimes tomatoes).

Barbecue, BBQ, or barbeque is a delicious American specialty. At its best, it's beef brisket, ribs, or pork shoulder slowly wood smoked for hours. Ribs are served as a whole- or half-rack or cut into individual ribs, brisket is usually sliced thin, and the pork shoulder can be shredded ("pulled pork") or chopped ("chopped pork"). Sauce of varying spiciness may be served on the dish, or provided on the side. Various parts of the U.S. have unique styles of barbecue. Generally, the best barbecue is found in the South, with the most distinct styles coming from Kansas City, Texas, Tennessee, and North Carolina. However, barbecue of some variety is generally available throughout the country. Barbecue restaurants differ from many other restaurants in that the best food is often found at very casual establishments. A typical barbecue restaurant may have plastic dinnerware, picnic tables, and serve sandwiches on cheap white bread. Barbecue found on the menu at a fancy chain or non-specialty restaurant is likely to be less authentic. Ribs and chicken are always eaten with your fingers; pork and brisket are either eaten with a fork or put into a sandwich. Note that the further one gets from the South, the more likely that "barbecue" refers to food cooked on a grill with no smoking, such as hamburgers or hot dogs.

With a rich tradition of immigration, America has a wide variety of ethnic foods; everything from Ethiopian cuisine to Laotian food is available in major cities with large immigrant populations.

Chinese food is widely available and adjusted to American tastes - by default, a "Chinese" restaurant will serve a menu only vaguely related to authentic Chinese food, usually meat in sugary sauce with rice and noodles, often in an all-you-can-eat buffet setting. Authentic Chinese food can be found in restaurants in Chinatowns in addition to communities with large Chinese populations. Japanese sushi, Vietnamese, and Thai food have also been adapted for the American market in recent years. Fusion cuisine combines Asian ingredients and techniques with more traditional American presentation. Indian food outlets are available in most major U.S. cities and towns.

Mexican/Hispanic/Tex-Mex food is very popular, but again in a localized version. Combining in various ways beans, rice, cheese, and spiced beef or chicken with round flatbread loaves called tortillas, dishes are usually topped with spicy tomato salsa, sour cream, and an avocado-based dip called guacamole. Small authentic Mexican taquerias can be found easily in the Southwest, and increasingly in cities throughout the country.

Italian food is perhaps the only cuisine that rivals Mexican for widespread popularity. All manners of pasta can be found here, and American-styled pizzas (typically a thick crust topped with tomato sauce and cheese, in addition to other meats and vegetables) are a popular choice for social events and casual dining. Italian restaurants can be found almost everywhere, and even non-specialty restaurants and grocery stores can provide you with basic pasta meals.

Middle Eastern and Greek foods are also becoming popular in the United States. The gyro (known as "doner kebab" or "schawarma" in Europe) is a popular Greek sandwich of sliced processed lamb on a pita bread topped with lettuce, tomatoes and a yogurt-cucumber sauce. Hummus (a ground chickpea dip/spread) and baklava pastries are frequently found in supermarkets, along with an increasingly widespread and high-quality array of "pita" products.

Vegetarian food is easy to come by in big urban areas. As vegetarians are becoming more common in the U.S., so are the restaurants that cater to them. Most big cities and college towns will have vegetarian restaurants serving exclusively or primarily vegetarian dishes. In smaller towns you may need to check the menu at several restaurants before finding a vegetarian main course, or else make up a meal out of side dishes. Wait staff can be helpful answering questions about meat content, but be very clear about your personal definition of vegetarian, as dishes with fish, chicken, egg, or even small quantities of beef or pork flavoring may be considered vegetarian. This is especially common with vegetable side dishes in the South. Meat-free breakfast foods such as pancakes or eggs are readily available at diners.

People on low-fat or low-calorie diets should be fairly well-served in the U.S., as there has been a continuing trend in calorie consciousness since the 1970s. Even fast-food restaurants have "lite" specials, and can provide charts of calorie and fat counts on request.

For the backpacker or those on very restricted budgets, American supermarkets offer an almost infinite variety of pre-packaged/pre-processed foods that are either ready or almost ready for consumption, e.g. breakfast cereal, ramen noodles, canned soups, etc.

In the largest cities, "corner stores" abound. These small convenience stores carry a variety snacks, drinks, and prepackaged foods. Unlike most convenience stores, their products are sold at relatively low prices (especially by urban standards) and can provide for snacks or even (nutritionally partial) meals for a budget no more than $5 a day.

Seafood is abundant on the coasts, with freshwater and saltwater varieties of fish and shellfish (although finding squid, octopus, and jellyfish will require a bit of effort). The Northeast is famed for its Maine lobsters, and the Southeast has a variety of shrimp and conch. Most of the seafood in Florida is served spicy, as influenced by the Caribbean taste. Seafood dining on the west is equally abundant, and Alaskan salmon is served in high quantity through the Pacific Northwest. The state of Maryland is famous for its Chesapeake Bay blue crabs, which are usually steamed live in a pot with a spicy seasoning. There is a bit of a learning curve to eating Maryland crabs, though any server or local, for that matter, in a crabhouse will gladly give you a lesson. It is not recommended to wear a plastic bib or napkin when eating Maryland crabs or Maine lobster. You will be instantly pegged as a tourist.

Etiquette

It is usually inappropriate to join a table already occupied by other diners, even if it has unused seats; Americans prefer and expect this degree of privacy when they eat. Exceptions are cafeteria-style eateries with long tables, and at crowded informal eateries and cafes you may have success asking a stranger if you can share the table they're sitting at. Striking up a conversation in this situation may or may not be welcome, however.

Table manners, while varying greatly, are typically European influenced. Slurping or making other noises while eating are considered rude, as is loud conversation (including phone calls). It is fairly common to wait until everybody at your table has been served before eating. You should lay cloth napkins across your lap; you can do the same with paper napkins, or keep them on the table. Offense isn't taken if you don't finish your meal, and most restaurants will package the remainder to take with you, or provide a box for you to do this yourself (sometimes euphemistically called a "doggy bag", implying that the leftovers are for your pet). If you want to do this, ask the server to get the remainder "to go"; this term will be almost universally understood, and will not cause any embarrassment. Some restaurants offer an "all-you-can-eat" buffet or other service; taking home portions from such a meal is either not allowed, or carries an additional fee. If you are eating with a group, it is very rude to leave before everyone else is ready to go, even if you came separately. Cleaning your plate is a sign that you enjoyed your meal, and doesn't imply that the host didn't serve enough or should bring more.

Many fast food items (sandwiches, burgers, pizza, tacos, etc) are designed to be eaten by hand (so-called "finger food"); a few foods are almost always eaten by hand (french fries, barbecue, chicken on the bone) even at moderately nice restaurants. If unsure, eating finger food with a fork and knife probably won't offend anyone; eating fork-and-knife food by hand might, as it's considered "uncivilized" and rude.

When invited to a meal in a private home it is considered polite for a guest to ask if they can bring anything for the meal, such a dessert, a side dish, or for an outdoor barbecue, something useful like ice or plastic cups or plates. The host will usually refuse except among very close friends, but it is nonetheless considered good manners to bring along a small gift for the host. A bottle of wine, box of candies or fresh cut flowers are most common. Gifts of cash, prepared ready-to-serve foods, or very personal items (e.g. toiletries) are not appropriate.

An exception is the potluck meal, where each guest (or group/family) must bring a food dish to share with everyone; these shared dishes make up the entire meal. Usually dishes are grouped (e.g., salads, main dishes or casseroles, side dishes, desserts); you should ask the host if they want you to bring something in particular. Ideal dishes for a potluck should be served from a large pot, dish, or bowl, and would be spooned or forked on to diners' plates—hence the emphasis on salads, casseroles, and spoonable side dishes.

Smoking

Smoking policy is set at the state and local levels, so it varies widely from place to place. A majority of states and a number of cities ban smoking in restaurants and bars by law, and many other restaurants and bars do the same by their own policy. Some states (like New York, Illinois, Wisconsin, and California) have banned any smoking indoors, while some still allow designated smoking areas. Check local information, and ask before lighting up; if a sign says "No Smoking," it means it. Breaking the ban may get you ejected, fined, or even arrested - and lots of dirty looks. Native American reservations are sovereign (independent) land and indoor smoking may be allowed on tribal lands even if you're in a state with an indoor smoking ban. In recent decades, smoking has acquired something of a social stigma (more so than in Europe)—even where smoking is permitted, be sure to ask your dining companions if they mind. With the increasing popularity of eCigarette devices, it is important to note that some establishments ask that you do not use them indoors. Although these devices simply produce an odorless, or even pleasant smelling, vapor, there is a somewhat common fear that they are unsafe and that others, especially in bars, may mistakenly assume that smoking is allowed indoors.

Drink

Drinking customs in America are as varied as the backgrounds of its many people. In some rural areas, alcohol is mostly served in restaurants rather than dedicated drinking establishments, but in urban settings you will find numerous bars and nightclubs where food is either nonexistent or rudimentary. In very large cities, of course, drinking places run the gamut from tough local "shot and a beer" bars to upscale "martini bars".

American tradition splits alcoholic drinks into hard liquor and others. Americans drink a wide array of hard liquors, partially divided by region, but for non-distilled spirits almost exclusively drink beer and wine. Other fermented fruit and grain beverages are known, and sold, but not consumed in great quantities; most fruit drinks are soft (meaning 'non-alcoholic', not 'low alcohol volume'). 'Cider' without further qualifiers is a spiced apple juice, and 'hard cider' is a relatively little-consumed alcoholic beverage in spite of the U.S. having been one of its most enthusiastic consumers a mere two centuries ago. Be prepared to specify that you mean a liquor or cocktail in shops not specifically dedicated to alcohol.

Beer is in many ways the 'default' alcoholic beverage in the U.S., but gone are the days when it was priced cheaply and bought without high expectations for quality. In the last 25 years, America has seen a boom in craft brews, and cities like Baltimore, Philadelphia and Boston are becoming renowned among beer lovers. The various idioms for alcohol consumption frequently and sometimes presumptively refer to beer. While most American beer drinkers prefer light lagers – until the 1990s this was the only kind commonly sold – a wide variety of beers are now available all over the U.S. It is not too unusual to find a bar serving 100 or more different kinds of beer, both bottled and "draft" (served fresh in a cup), though most will have perhaps a dozen or three, with a half dozen "on tap" (available on "draft"). Microbreweries – some of which have grown to be moderately large and/or purchased by one of the major breweries – make every kind of beer in much smaller quantities with traditional methods. Most microbrews are distributed regionally; bartenders will know the local brands. Nowadays all but the most basic taverns usually have one or more local beers on tap, and these are generally more full of character than the big national brands, which have a reputation for being generic. Some brew pubs make their own beer in-house, and generally only serve the house brand. These beers are also typically considered superior to the big national brands.

Wine in the U.S. is also a contrast between low-quality commercial fare versus extremely high-quality product. Unlike in Europe, American wines are labeled primarily by the grape (merlot, cabernet sauvignon, Riesling, etc.). The simple categories 'red', 'white', and 'rosé' or 'pink' are also used, but disdained as sole qualifiers by oenophiles. All but the cheapest wines are usually also labeled by region, which can be a state ("California"), an area of a state ("Central Coast"), a county or other small region ("Willamette Valley"), or a specific vineyard ("Dry Creek Vineyard"). (As a general rule, the narrower the region, the higher quality the wine is likely to be.)

Cheap cask wines are usually sold in a box supporting a plastic bag; bottled wines are almost universally priced as semi-luxury items, with the exception of 'fortified wines', which are the stereotypical American answer for low-price-per-milliliter-alcohol 'rotgut'.

All 50 U.S. states now support winemaking, with varying levels of success and respect. California wines are some of the best in the world, and are available on most wine lists in the country. The most prestigious American wine region is California's Napa Valley, although the state also has a number of other wine-producing areas, which may provide better value for your money because they are less famous. Wines from Oregon's Willamette Valley and the state of Washington have been improving greatly in recent years, and can be bargains since they are not yet as well-known as California wines. Michigan, Colorado's

Wine Country, and New York State's Finger Lakes region have recently been producing German-style whites which have won international competitions. In recent years, the Llano Estacado region of Texas has become regionally renowned for its wines. The Northern Virginia area, specifically Fauquier, Loudoun, and Prince William counties are also becoming well known for both their flavor, and organized wine tasting tours, supplemented by the scenery seen on the drives between locations.

Sparkling wines are available by the bottle in up-scale restaurants, but are rarely served by the glass as they often are in western Europe. The best California sparkling wines have come out ahead of some famous brand French champagnes in recent expert blind tastings. They are comparatively difficult to find in 'supermarkets' and some non-alcoholic sparkling grape juices are marketed under that name.

The wines served in most bars in America are unremarkable, but wine bars are becoming more common in urban areas. Only the most expensive restaurants have extensive wine lists, and even in more modest restaurants wine tends to be expensive, even if the wine is mediocre. Many Americans, especially in the more affluent and cosmopolitan areas of the country, consider themselves knowledgeable about wine, and if you come from a wine producing country, your country's wines may be a good topic of conversation.

Hard alcohol is usually drunk with mixers, but also served "on the rocks" (with ice) or "straight up" (un-mixed, with no ice) on request. Their increasing popularity has caused a long-term trend toward drinking light-colored and more "mixable" liquors, especially vodka, and away from the more traditional darker liquors such as whiskey and bourbon that many older drinkers favor. However, this is not an exclusive trend and many Americans still enjoy whiskey and bourbon.

It was formerly wholly inappropriate to drink hard liquor before 5PM (the end of the conventional workday), even on weekends. A relic of this custom is "happy hour", a period lasting anywhere from 30 minutes to three hours, usually between 5PM and 8PM, during which a significant discount is offered on selected drinks. Happy hour and closing time are the only presumptive customs in American bars, although 'ladies night', during which women receive a discount or some other financial incentive, is increasingly common.

Although laws regulating alcohol sales, consumption, and possession vary somewhat by state and county, the drinking age is 21 throughout the U.S. except in Puerto Rico and the U.S. Virgin Islands (where it is 18). Enforcement of this varies, but if you're under 30 you should definitely be prepared to show photo ID when buying alcohol in a store or entering a bar (which often refuse admittance to "minors" under 21). In some states, people who are under 21 are not even allowed to be present in bars or liquor stores. A foreign passport or other credible ID will probably be accepted, but many waiters have never seen one, and it may not even be legally valid for buying alcohol in some places. As a driver's license is the most ubiquitous form of ID in the U.S. and have a magnetic strip for verification purposes, some supermarkets have begun requiring them to purchase alcohol. In such cases, it is the cash register not the cashier which prevents such purchases. It's worth noting that most American ID's have the date of birth laid out as month/day/year, while frequently other countries ID's use year/month/day or day/month/year which may cause further confusion. Using false identification to misrepresent your age is a criminal offense in all 50 states, and while most alcohol vendors will simply refuse to sell or take a blatantly fake ID away, a few also call the police which may result in prosecution.

Most states (currently 45 of them) and Washington D.C. have found and use loupes in the federal law to allow underage drinking, example; in some states like Delaware and Mississippi, underage drinking is legal on private, non-alcohol premises (including private properties not open to the public). As long as he/she is accompanied by the physical presence of a parent or legal guardian who is over the age of 21 and has the approval to consume alcohol, but this varies. In states like Hawaii and Tennessee, Underage consumption of alcohol is allowed for religious purposes. Some states require that the alcohol must be provided by an official religious representative and/or limit the type of alcohol allowed. In states like Texas and Wisconsin, underage consumption of alcohol is allowed on alcohol-selling premises, such as a restaurant or bar, as long as the legal guardian gives the minor the alcohol and is in the presence of the legal guardian. This again varies. In states like Colorado and Nevada, underage consumption of alcohol is allowed for medical purposes. Again, this varies. Alabama, Arkansas, Idaho, New Hampshire, and West Virginia have no exceptions to underage alcohol consumption laws.

Selling alcohol is typically prohibited after a certain hour, usually 2 AM. In some states, most stores can only sell beer and wine; hard liquor is sold at dedicated liquor stores. In Indiana, sales of any type of alcoholic beverage is banned statewide on Sunday, However, bars are still open and serve alcoholic beverages. Several "dry counties" – mostly in southern states – ban some or all types of alcohol in public establishments; private clubs (with nominal membership fees) are often set up to get around this. Sunday sales are restricted in some areas. Some Indian reservations (especially the Navajo Nation) doesn't allow any alcohol on their territory.

Most towns ban drinking in public (other than in bars and restaurants of course), with varying degrees of enforcement. Even in towns which allow public drinking, a visible bottle (rather than one in a small bag, which is so commonly used for it as to be synonymous with public drinking) is either illegal or justifies police attention. All communities have some sort of ban on "drunk and disorderly" behavior, some quite stringent, and as a rule intoxication is an aggravating rather than exculpating factor in all but the most and least severe offenses. Drunk driving comes under fairly harsh scrutiny, with a blood-alcohol level of 0.08% considered "Under the Influence" and many states considering 0.05% "Impaired" - in Washington D.C. it's illegal to drive with any amount of alcohol in your system. If you're under 21, however, most states define a DUI from 0.00-0.02%. Drunk driving checkpoints are fairly common during major "party" events, and although privacy advocates have carved out exceptions, if a police officer asks a driver to submit to a blood-alcohol test or perform a test of sobriety, you generally may not refuse (and in certain states such as New York it is a crime in itself). DUI ("driving under the influence"), OUI ("operating under the influence") and DWI ("driving while intoxicated") are typically punished quite harshly, and as a foreign national it will typically mean the end of your time in the United States - even permanent residents have had their Green Cards revoked and were subsequently deported for DUI. In many jurisdictions catching and enforcing DUIs is the main job of patrolling police; it is watched for zealously and treated severely. It is also usually against the law to have an open container of alcohol anywhere in the car other than in the trunk. Some states have "open bottle" laws which can levy huge fines for an open container in a vehicle, sometimes several hundred dollars per container.

If you're going out to drink with others; always assign at least one person as the designated driver of an automobile. Likewise, you can also arrange a taxi to take you back to your residence. Either way, it is way better than getting a ride in the back of a police car with a DUI on your record.

Nightlife

Nightclubs in America run the usual gamut of various music scenes, from discos with top-40 dance tunes to obscure clubs serving tiny slices of obscure musical genres. Country music dance clubs, or honky tonks, are laid fairly thick in the South and West, especially in rural areas and away from the coasts, but one or two can be found in almost any city. Also, gay/lesbian nightclubs exist in nearly every medium- to large-sized city. Many nightclubs in America have a large area or "dance floor" where people often congregate and dance to the music played by the DJ, although in some areas of the deep south, people also dance to music played by live bands as well. A lot of nightclubs also have multi colored ceiling mounted music lights to brighten up the dance atmosphere. Mostly, a lot of couples and groups go to nightclubs, though singles also go there as well. However, if you go as a single person to a nightclub, remember that, in the United States of America, it is etiquette for the ladies to ask the guys to dance with them.

Until 1977, the only U.S. state with legalized gambling was Nevada. The state has allowed games of chance since the 1930s, creating such resort cities as Las Vegas and Reno in the process. Dubbed "Sin City," Las Vegas in particular has evolved into an end-destination adult playground, offering many other after-hours activities such as amusement parks, night clubs, strip clubs, shows, bars and four star restaurants. Gambling has since spread outside of Nevada to a plethora of U.S. cities like Atlantic City, New Jersey and Biloxi, Mississippi, as well as to riverboats, offshore cruises and Indian reservations throughout the continental United States. Some states have tolerated card rooms for many years, which have since rebranded themselves as "casinos" (notwithstanding their lack of slot machines) to compete for business against true casinos in New Jersey, Nevada, and Indian reservations.

State lotteries and "scratch games" are another, popular form of legalized gambling. However, online gaming and wagering on sports across state lines both remain illegal throughout the U.S.

Sleep

Daily rates for hotel rooms vary widely across the United States. Based on the average daily hotel room rate as of 2012, New York City and Honolulu were the most expensive cities for a hotel stay in the U.S.

Virtually all hotels at check-in will ask for the name of the guest who made the reservation, then demand from that person some kind of photo identification (a passport or driver's license is normally sufficient) and a credit card to cover incidental charges. If you do not have a valid credit card, some hotels will demand a cash deposit instead. Upon check-in, a hotel front desk clerk will almost always issue you a keycard with a magnetic stripe for access to your room, although an increasing number have switched to RFID keycards, which are tapped instead of swiped.

By far the most common form of lodging in rural United States and along many Interstates is the motel. Providing inexpensive rooms to automotive travelers, most motels are clean and reasonable with a limited array of amenities: telephone, TV, bed, bathroom. Motel 6 (+1 800 466-8356) is a national chain with reasonable rates ($30-$70, depending on the city). Super 8 Motels (+1 800 800-8000) provides reasonable accommodations throughout the country as well. Reservations are typically unnecessary, which is convenient since you don't have to arbitrarily interrupt a long road trip; you can simply drive until you're tired then find a room. However, some are used by adults looking to book a night for sex or illicit activities and many are located in undesirable areas.

Business hotels are increasingly available across the country. Generally, they are more expensive than motels, but not as expensive as full-scale hotels, with prices around $70 to $170. While the hotels may appear to be the size of a motel, they may offer amenities typically associated with larger hotels. Examples include Marriott International's Courtyard by Marriott and Fairfield Inn; Hilton's Hampton Inn and Hilton Garden Inn; Holiday Inn's Holiday Inn Express; Starwood's Aloft and Four Points by Sheraton, and Hyatt Place.

Another option are extended-stay hotels directed at business travelers or families on long-term stays (that are often relocating due to corporate decisions). These hotels often feature full kitchens in most rooms, afternoon social events (generally by a pool), and serve continental breakfast. Such "suite" hotels are roughly equivalent to the serviced apartments seen in other countries, though the term "serviced apartments" is not generally used in American English. Examples include Marriott’s ExecuStay, Residence Inn, TownePlace

Suites and SpringHill Suites; Extended StayAmerica; Homestead Studio Suites; Homewood Suites by Hilton; and Summerfield Suites by Hyatt.

Hotels are available in most cities and usually offer more services and amenities than motels. Rooms usually run about $80-$300 per night, but very large, glamorous, and expensive hotels can be found in most major cities, offering luxury suites larger than some houses. Check-out and check-in times almost always fall in the range of 11am-noon and 2pm-4pm respectively. Examples of major hotel chains include Marriott, Renaissance by Marriott, Hilton, Hyatt, DoubleTree by Hilton, Sheraton, Radisson, and Wyndham. Examples of upscale hotels include St. Regis, Fairmont, Waldorf Astoria, Crowne Plaza, InterContinental and Ritz Carlton.

Note that many US cities now have "edge cities" in their suburbs which feature high-quality upscale hotels aimed at affluent business travelers. These hotels often feature all the amenities of their downtown/CBD cousins (and more), but at less exorbitant prices.

In many rural areas, especially on the coasts and in New England, bed and breakfast (B&B) lodging can be found. Usually in converted houses or buildings with less than a dozen units, B&Bs feature a more home-like lodging experience, with complimentary breakfast served (of varying quality and complexity). Bed and breakfasts range from about $50 to $200 per night, with some places being much steeper. They can be a nice break from the impersonal chain hotels and motels. Unlike Europe, most American bed and breakfasts are unmarked; one must make a reservation beforehand and receive directions there.

The two best-known hotel guides covering the US are the AAA (formerly American Automobile Association; typically pronounced "Triple-A") TourBooks, available to members and affiliated auto clubs worldwide at local AAA offices; and the Mobil Travel Guide, available at bookstores. There are several websites booking hotels online; be aware that many of these sites add a small commission to the room rate, so it may be cheaper to book directly through the hotel. On the other hand, some hotels charge more for "drop-in" business than reserved rooms or rooms acquired through agents and brokers, so it's worth checking both.

Camping can also be a very affordable lodging option, especially with good weather. The downside of camping is that most campgrounds are outside urban regions, so it's not much of an option for trips to big cities. There is a huge network of National Parks (+1 800 365-2267), with most states and many counties having their own park systems, too. Most state and national campgrounds are of excellent quality, with beautiful natural environments. Expect to pay $7-$20 per car on entry. Kampgrounds of America (KOA) has a chain of commercial campground franchises across the country, of significantly less charm than their public-sector equivalents, but with hookups for recreational vehicles and amenities such as laundromats. Countless independently owned private campgrounds vary in character.

Some unusual lodging options are available in specific areas or by prior arrangement. For example, you might enjoy staying on a houseboat in Lake Tahoe or the Erie Canal. Or stay in a treehouse in Oregon. More conventional lodging can be found at college or university dormitories, a few of which rent out rooms to travelers during the summertime. Finally, in many tourist areas, as well as big cities, one can rent a furnished house by the day.

Learn

Short courses may be undertaken on a tourist visa. Community colleges typically offer college-credit courses on an open-admissions basis; anyone with a high school degree or its equivalent and the required tuition payment can generally enroll. In large cities, open universities may offer short non-credit courses on all sorts of practical topics, from ballroom dance to buying real estate. They are a good place to learn a new skill and meet people.

Studying full-time in the United States is an excellent opportunity for young adults seeking an advanced education, a chance to see a foreign country, and a better understanding of the U.S. and its people. It can be done independently by applying directly to a college for admission, or through the "study abroad" or "foreign exchange" department of a college in your own country, usually for a single term or one year. (Either approach requires, at minimum, an F or J student visa.) The latter is usually easiest; the two institutions will handle much of the arrangements, and you don't have to make a commitment to four years living in a strange country. Be forewarned, however: many state universities and private colleges are located in small towns, hundreds of miles from any big urban centers. They go out of their way to recruit lucrative international students unfamiliar with U.S. geography. Don't expect to spend your weekends in New York or Los Angeles if your college is in North Dakota unless it is part of the academic activities in your school/course. Furthermore, U.S. higher education institutions are distributed along a wide spectrum in terms of prestige and quality. Outside of an elite group of about 20 to 40 internationally renowned universities, most U.S. colleges and universities aren't that well-known outside of their home state, let alone their home city.

The common requirements to study at a higher education level will include your admissions essay (also known as the statement of purpose or personal statement), transcript of records, recommendation/reference letters, language tests (TOEFL is most widely accepted but it can be waived if your previous school primarily used English as a medium of instruction), standardized achievement tests (SAT for undergraduate, GMAT for graduate business schools, GRE for most other graduate programs), degree certificates. As the TOEFL, SAT, GMAT or GRE are administered by the New Jersey-based ETS, you can sit the exam in your home country well beforehand and arrange for your scores to be directly sent to the school you are applying to. You may need to present these documents including your acceptance letter when applying for a student visa.

The types of schools vary dramatically. (In conversation, Americans tend to use the terms "school" and "college" inclusively: any college or university might be referred to as "school", and a university might be called "college".) State university systems are partially subsidized by state governments, and may have many campuses spread around the state, with hundreds of thousands of students. Private colleges are generally smaller (hundreds or a few thousand students), with a larger percentage of their students living on campus; some are affiliated with churches and may be more religious in character. Other kinds of colleges focus on teaching specific job skills, education for working adults, and providing inexpensive college-level education to local residents. Although nearly all colleges are open to students regardless of race, gender, religion, etc. many were originally established for a particular group (e.g. African-Americans, women, members of a particular religion) and may still attract primarily students from that group. Several private colleges remain female-only, there are a few male-only private colleges, and private religious colleges may expect students to practice the school's faith.

Colleges are funded by "tuition" charged to the student, which is often quite expensive, very commonly reaching into the tens of thousands of dollars per year. The most selective colleges (and hence, often the most desirable) run up to $40,000-50,000 per year, including both tuition and "room & board" in that price. Most US citizens and eligible non-citizens receive substantial financial assistance from the federal government in the form of grants and low-interest loans, which are not available to most non-residents. Often financial aid for foreign students is provided by their home country. They may be eligible for privately-funded "scholarships" intended to provide educational opportunities for various kinds of students. Some U.S. banks offer loans to foreign students, which usually require a citizen to guarantee that they'll be repaid. Contact the Financial Aid Office of any college you are interested in attending for more information about the sources of aid available.

Almost all US colleges and universities operate web sites (in the .edu domain) with information for prospective students and other visitors.

Work

Work in America is best arranged long before you enter the United States. Young people who are full time students of certain nationalities can apply for a J1 "Exchange Visitor" visa which permits paid work as au pairs or summer work for up to 4 months in virtually any type of job. The United States Department of State has full information on applying for this type of visa including the precise categories that qualify.

The H-1B visa allows a limited number of skilled and certain unskilled employees to temporarily work in the United States. It usually requires a bachelor's degree and is based on a petition filed by an American employer. The job you wish to apply for should be related to your degree. The most common careers of hard-to-get H-1B visa holders are nurses, math teachers, and computer science professionals. The H1-B cap was filled the day applications started this year, although proposed immigration changes would increase the cap. On the other hand, there is the more permanent employment-based immigrant visa which has similar requirements to the H-1B visa. An employment-based green card is significantly harder to obtain than an H1B, because the employer needs to first go through a tedious labor certification process, and assuming USCIS approves the petition, lengthy backlogs may occur (depending on nationality).

Paid work is generally not allowed on a B1/B2 visitor visa. Working unlawfully in the United States runs the very real risk of arrest, deportation, and ineligibility to re-enter the country for at least some time. Illegal immigrants also run the risk of working in dangerous conditions without much relief from the law. Note that "paid work" includes receiving any sort of compensation or thing of value in exchange for your labor including "volunteering" in exchange for lodging.

If you are seeking to adjust visa status or to enter the U.S. on a working visa you should first check the official government websites of the US Department of State, which issues visas abroad, and the US Citizenship and Immigration Services which administers immigration programs within the United States. Unfortunately, con artists both in the US and overseas often prey on people's desire to travel or work here. Keep in mind that while visa applications do not usually require an attorney or other intermediary, be wary of and verify any "advice" offered by third parties, especially non-lawyers. If in doubt about properly applying for such visas, it is best to get a licensed immigration attorney.

Keep in mind that anyone entering under the Visa Waiver Program cannot adjust their status for any reason.

Minimum Wage

Federal Minimum Wage is currently at $7.25 an hour. However, most states, the Federal District of Columbia, and all territories have their own set minimum wage. These are almost all higher than this federal minimum and wage floors can also be set even at county or municipal level (city, town or village). For example; minimum wage in the State of California is currently $9.00 an hour, but the City of San Francisco is currently $10.74 an hour, the highest in the U.S., and Seattle is scheduled to eclipse the country by 2022, gradually increasing to $15.00 an hour. While in the Commonwealth of the Northern Mariana Islands (NMI), the lowest in the nation because federal labor laws don't apply to the N.M.I. Minimum wage for tips is $2.13 an hour, again, this varies by state, territory, and municipality. Georgia and Wyoming have a minimum wage for at home workers is $5.15 an hour and some states such as Oklahoma allows a $2 minimum wage for certain workers under small businesses with less than 10 employees and $150,0000 or less in profits. But most are lower than federal minimum wage and others are at the same rate as the minimum wage set by the State, Federal District, or municipality. Note: Minimum wage doesn't often include health insurance coverage. And be aware of the property of which you are working on. As it could be a Federal enclave, and a state's minimum wage law will not apply to the Federal enclave. Also, note that overtime pay which is extra applies to most workers although that also has many exemptions so do your research.

Staying safe

Corruption

Bribery and other corrupt practices are illegal and most Americans will at best pass on your offer and at worst report it to the police and be offended.

Crime

American movies and television shows often give foreigners the inaccurate impression that the US is ravaged by an extremely high level of violent crime. While there are some locations in the United States with high crime rates, most violent crime is heavily concentrated in certain inner city neighborhoods (most of which are specifically identified in the relevant city-specific articles in this travel guide), or poor outlying areas. Few visitors to the US experience any sort of crime.

Much crime is gang- or drug-related in inner city regions or poor areas located along the US-Mexican border. It mostly occurs in areas that are of little interest to visitors, however it can and does also occur in high tourist areas of certain cities. You can all but ensure that you won't experience crime by taking common-sense precautions and staying alert to your surroundings. Locations frequented by tourists and visitors (National Mall in Washington DC, and Manhattan in NYC) often have a police presence and are quite safe for all but the most minor petty crimes (e.g. pick pocketing).

Like other regions of the world, many American urban areas have populations of homeless people, some of whom are drug-addicted and/or mentally ill. In certain cities, aggressive panhandling is a concern. If you feel you are being harassed, say NO firmly and walk away and/or call the police.

Note that security has increased along the United States–Mexico border due to increased illegal immigration and drug-related crime. Only cross the country's borders at official ports of entry.

Police

If stopped by the police while driving, the driver is expected to stay in the car and wait for the police officer to come to the driver or passenger window. It is expected for the driver to roll-down the window the officer is at. When stopped you should stay calm, be polite and cooperative, and avoid making sudden movements. If you need to reach for your purse or wallet to present your identification, state what you are doing and wait for permission to do so. Often police will ask you to keep your hands out of your pockets while speaking to them. This is in no way meant to be offensive, but is for their peace of mind and your safety. American police are always armed on duty, and will respond with force if they believe you present an immediate threat. Furthermore, do not in any way make physical contact or run away from a police officer under any circumstances. Physical contact with a cop can lead to you getting arrested for battery. Do not act aggressively or angrily, as that can and will make a police officer suspicious. Determine if you're being detained or if you're free to go; the police will need evidence to detain you, so do choose your words sparingly.

Any form of communication between yourself and them can and will be written down. If you are being detained, demand that you will not answer further questions without a lawyer. Don’t answer any questions, no matter how seemingly innocuous or trivial, and demand a lawyer immediately or an official from your consulate/embassy.

If you are stopped by a patrol car, turn on your interior car lights and keep your hands on the wheel so they remain visible. Do not exit the vehicle unless told to do so. If you follow the officer's instructions, you will probably not be arrested (unless you have actually committed a crime or resemble someone who recently committed one in the immediate vicinity). Instead, patrol stops typically result in a written citation for a driving offense, or sometimes a simple verbal warning if the offense was minor, as long as you remain appropriately cooperative. If they demand that they search your vehicle, you have a right to refuse it. You could be arrested for doing something you didn't do, such as when a friend may have left something illegal in the car, if you consent to a search. Be firm and polite when it comes to that situation.

If a police officer stops by at your residence and demands to search it, determine if they have a warrant from a state or federal authority to search your residence. It is against the law for a police officer to search your place without a warrant. If further assistance is needed, please call your lawyer or consulate/embassy official.

Do not offer bribes to a police officer in any way or under any circumstances. While bribery may be expected in other countries, the stark opposite is true in the US; bribery is actually a crime for which one can and will be arrested and detained. Foreigners are seldom given the benefit of the doubt, even if they are from a country where bribery is common. Even a vague gesture that could be interpreted as an attempt at bribery will offend the officer. If you need to pay a fine, the officer can direct you to the appropriate police station, courthouse, or government office. Most minor traffic infractions can be paid by mail. Don't even think about paying a fine directly to the officer who cited you, since that will probably be interpreted as a bribe. An exception to this rule is found in Montana, where fines can be paid to the officer by cash, check, or even a credit or debit card.

Texting and driving

Distracted driving is a major problem in the United States, but despite the high dangers, Texting and driving is not considered illegal under federal law. But each state, territory, and Washington D.C. has laws on distracted driving. According to the Governors Highway Safety Administration, no state, territory, nor Washington D.C. except Illinois bans all uses of cellphone while driving. So, when driving or crossing the street, it's best to be aware of distracted driving.

911 Emergency services

During any emergency, dialing 911 (pronounced "nine-one-one") on any telephone will connect you to a dispatcher for the emergency services in the area (police, fire, ambulance, etc). Calls to 911 are free from pay phones and any mobile phone capable of connecting to any local carrier. Give the facts. The dispatchers will send help. Unless you are calling from a mobile phone, the 911 operator can almost certainly trace your line instantly and pinpoint the exact structure you are calling from.

With mobile phones it is more difficult; in some states, you may be connected to the regional office for the state police or highway patrol, which will then have to transfer you to the appropriate local agency once they talk to you and determine what you need. In recent years, many mobile phones have incorporated GPS devices that will display the user's precise geographical location to the 911 operator (known as Enhanced 911 or E-911), so that the operator can direct units to that location even if the caller is incapacitated.

If you are staying in one area, it may be helpful to have the phone numbers for the local emergency services so as to get through directly to the local dispatch. Moreover, in most locations, 911 calls are recorded and are open, public records, while the conversation with the local emergency dispatchers cannot be accessed by the public. Remember that if you dial emergency dispatchers directly instead of through 911, the operator may not be able to trace your location.

Note also that if you have a GSM mobile phone (the standard technology in most of the world, especially in Europe), you can also dial 112, which is the standard emergency number for GSM networks worldwide. All US GSM carriers (AT&T, T-Mobile, and smaller regional operators) automatically redirect 112 calls to 911.

As with most countries, misuse of the emergency services number will result in, at the very least, a call back from authorities; if particularly egregious, you will be heavily fined or even arrested.

Border patrol

You may encounter the United States Border Patrol if you're transiting through or visiting cities geographically close to Canada (such as Detroit) or Mexico (San Diego) as well as in Southern coastal areas (Florida Keys). Border Patrol has the authority to verify immigration status and enforce immigration laws in places designated as "border zones" — generally within 40 miles of Canada and 75-100 miles of Mexico (although the law allows for 100 miles from any border, including international bodies of water like the seas and Great Lakes; this includes the entirety of some states and the majority of population centers). Border patrol is visible near Canada, though less so than on the southern border, (with guards primarily checking domestic long distance buses, Amtrak trains and their associated terminals, and rarely air travelers on arrival or departure). On the border with Mexico and in Southern coastal areas, systematic vehicle checkpoints or being pulled over by Border Patrol for a document check is much more common.

Foreign nationals are legally required to have passport, visa, and I-94(W) entry record (or Green Card) in their possession at all times. Consequences for not having them during a document check may be severe; you may be delayed or detained until your status can be verified. Long-term visa holders and permanent residents have been fined, or in extreme cases had their visas canceled for being found without their documents. If your documents are in order, you generally won't be questioned. Even US citizens are increasingly being advised to carry proof of citizenship, or at the very least identification of some kind, in areas under Border Patrol jurisdiction.

Border Patrol does not have much of a presence outside the border zones; its inland counterpart, Immigration and Customs Enforcement, generally doesn't target tourists unless it suspects them of trying to work during their tourist visits. In most states, police and other local authorities cannot question you about your immigration status or ask to see passports or visas unless you're arrested and charged with a crime, and then only for the purpose of connecting you with a representative from your country's embassy or diplomatic mission.

Natural disasters

The U.S. is a huge country with varied geography, and parts of it are occasionally affected by natural disasters: hurricanes in June through November in the Gulf and Atlantic coastal states, including Florida, extreme heat throughout the country, blizzards and extreme cold in the far north, large and violent tornadoes mostly in the Great Plains, the Mid-West, and the South, floods in areas all over the United States, wildfires in the late summer and early fall in the west, dust storms in any arid areas, and tsunamis, earthquakes, and volcanic eruptions in the west, as well as large thunderstorms throughout the country. See the regions in question for more details.

Because tornadoes are so common between the Rocky Mountains and the Appalachian Mountains, this area has earned itself the colloquial name Tornado Alley. The west of the country sits along the pacific ring of fire, and as a result, is an area very prone to tectonic and geothermal disasters.

Gay and lesbian

Homosexuality is legal between consenting adults in all states as of 2003, and same-sex marriage was legalized in all states in 2015. Some states and cities have anti-discrimination codes, including public accommodations in hotels, restaurants and transportation. Some Americans take a live-and-let-live approach to sexuality, but there are significant exceptions. It can be a problem to be open about one's sexual orientation and you may receive unwanted attention, remarks, threats, violent attacks, and be refused service, a big amount of this occurs in Texas, Wyoming, the Midwest and the South. Attitudes toward homosexuality vary widely, even in regions with a reputation for tolerance or intolerance. Tolerance is most common in major cities throughout the country especially around the Pacific Coast, some parts of the Northeast and Hawaii. Gay-friendly destinations include New York's Chelsea, Cape Cod, Rochester in Western New York State, Chicago's Boystown, Seattle's Capitol Hill, San Francisco's Castro Street, Washington's Dupont Circle, Miami Beach's South Beach, Atlanta's Midtown and Los Angeles' West Hollywood. Even outside of gay neighborhoods, many major cities are gay-friendly, especially in the West Coast and some areas of the Notheast. Massachusetts is an especially tolerant state as a whole. An increasing number of resort areas are known as gay-friendly, including Fire Island, Key West, Asheville, Provincetown, Ogunquit, Rehoboth Beach, Saugatuck, and parts of Asbury Park. In a few smaller cities, there are neighborhoods where gay people tend to congregate, many have resource centers for LGBTQ people. Some gay-friendly businesses like to advertise themselves as such with a rainbow flag or a small pink triangle or three-vertical-striped sticker in the window. Men planning to engage in any sex, should be aware the heightened risk of HIV and other infections in the United States. A gay American man is 44 times more likely to contract HIV than a heterosexual one, and 46 times more likely to contract syphilis. This risk grows greatly among men likely to engage in one-night stands and other higher-risk behavior. In a nation where 0.5% of the population are infected with HIV, unprotected sex is a very real risk. Precautions, including safer sex, are strongly advised during your stay. Most cities have affordable or free testing and treatment centers for STIs at least for gay men, though hours may be limited and waits may be long. Lesbians and trans face the same risk. The life-long repercussions of HIV or other STIs aren't covered by healthcare providers and seeking health care elsewhere can be very pricey.

Illicit drugs

Street drugs, including but not limited to cocaine, heroin, and methamphetamines, are illegal under federal law throughout the US.

Marijuana use is more widely accepted than other drugs. Although a few states have passed laws legalizing the medical use of marijuana, this will not protect any foreign citizen caught in possession. Outside of drug-using circles, most Americans frown upon illicit drug use regardless of quantity. This is especially true in more conservative jurisdictions (Such as Utah). And travelers would be wise to avoid using such substances in the United States, even in the jurisdictions that allow it. Penalties can be very severe, and can include mandatory minimum jail terms for possession of personal quantities in some states. Also, ANY drug possession near a school, however slight the quantity, will land you a heavy jail term. Attempting to bring any quantity into the US possess a serious risk of being arrested for "trafficking".

Legal marijuana

Notable exceptions to the precautions above are the states of Alaska, California, Colorado, Maine, Massachusetts, Nevada, Oregon and Washington, the District of Columbia (Washington, D.C.) and several recognized Indian Reservations, which have all recently legalized recreational use of marijuana. According to these new local laws, you can possess up to 1 ounce (8 ounces in Oregon, 2.5 ounces in the city of Portland, Maine and 2 ounces in Washington D.C.) of marijuana from a licensed seller and use it personally if you are over 21 years old. Indian Reservations have recently been allowed by the Federal government to regulate cannabis on their recognized reservation, so laws within the reservation vary widely, and can be different from state laws. Example; while cannabis is legal in the state of Washington, the Yakima Nation (an Indian reservation in Washington State) declares cannabis illegal on their land. So, by default, both federal and laws of the Indian Reservation apply. However, use on public streets or inside public buildings is illegal, so if you do use it, use it in private.

The federal government of the United States still considers marijuana illegal, so the use is still illegal in territory under direct federal government jurisdiction within states where marijuana use has legalized such as the Lewis-McChord Military Reservation in Washington state. Likewise, mailing of marijuana from Washington state to Colorado through the US Postal Service or bringing in some 'BC Bud' from British Columbia to Washington state is still illegal. The future of these laws is uncertain, but for now, they stand (with the exceptions in recognized Indian Reservations and federal territory).

Marijuana possession and use is still illegal everywhere else, so do NOT under any circumstances bring marijuana into any U.S. jurisdiction where it is illegal, nor across adjacent international borders. This includes any Indian Reservation that deems it illegal on their land as you will risk facing criminal charges if you are caught with it. Depending on which country of your residence or you're traveling to after leaving the U.S., you may face criminal charges in your home country (or a third country) if found in possession of cannabis (or even in very small amounts) on arrival from the U.S. or having it in your urine or through other means of testing for drug use from a person's body, even if it was completely consumed in the U.S. prior to departure. The US reports crimes to other countries even ones who enforce the death penalty for drug offences so keep that in mind.

Do not bring cannabis or any other federally illegal drug onto any Federal enclave, as federal drug laws are heavily enforced.

Racism

Most travelers to the US will not encounter overt racism. However, free speech is protected in the United States, so, as such, racist speech is still legal to a large extent (racial discrimination and hate crimes are illegal). You may come across familiar hate signs when traveling across the US. There is an extremely small chance of running into someone who is a member of a supremacist group such as, the Ku Klux Klan, New Black Panther Party, La Raza, "Neo Nazi" or various other hate groups. Symbols like swastikas and other Nazi imagery are legal in the US, and may be found in tattoo art among members. However, they usually cover these up in public to avoid drawing hostility from others. For the most part, racist hate groups tend to prefer to be reclusive due to the mainstream unpopularity of their views. Most such groups choose to inhabit remote, rural, isolated areas (some of which may be crudely constructed compounds) that are difficult for outsiders to come upon incidentally. Occasionally, they may appear in public just to exercise their "free speech rights", even if they don't intend to commit any violent or obviously illegal acts. If you come across any racist, just walk away from them. It isn't worth starting a fight with them and if they are in public they could become violent.

Islam

"Islamophobia" or the "fear of Islam" does exist in the United States, and has seen an uptick since the early 2000's. There is an internal US debate on whether to accept Syrian refugee's due to the crisis in the Middle East with ISIS and other radical groups. Despite this, Muslims are generally not discriminated against on a personal level. However, there may be isolated cases in rural and urban settings alike.

Curfew

Some cities don't allow minors below a certain age to wander alone after a certain hour at night, unless accompanied by a legal guardian. Similar rules may apply to driving.

Animals

It is illegal to hunt, kill, or keep any of a bald eagle's feathers. Keeping its feathers will result in a $100,000 fine for each feather you possess. As well as a year in prison, repeated offenses will change your sentence. However, Indian reservations are somewhat excluded from the possession of bald eagle feathers. But you must have a certification of tribal membership and the appropriate registration license to possess one. If not, federal law applies. The U.S. has one of the highest populations of venomous snakes (32), and a high number of potentially dangerous animals compared to many other countries. Please exhibit caution in any wilder areas of the country (even suburban areas.). Animal fighting and abuse in general is illegal.

Prostitution

Prostitution is not prohibited by Federal law. States, Territories, and the Federal District are allowed to make their own laws. Even so, prostitution remains illegal in all areas except at licensed brothels in rural Nevada counties. Prostitution remains illegal in Las Vegas and Reno, Nevada, and street-walking prostitutes are always illegal. Elsewhere in the US, tolerance and enforcement of prostitution laws vary considerably, but be aware that police routinely engage in "sting" operations in which an officer may pose as a prostitute to catch and arrest persons offering to pay for sex. This is not considered entrapment by US laws since the arrested person was consciously intending to commit an illegal act.

Firearms

Like it or not, firearms are an entrenched feature of the American culture. Legal ownership of firearms is supported by the Second Amendment of the United States Constitution, most (but not all) of the fifty states have similar wording in their state constitutions. Because of this, the U.S. has become a major destination for "Gun tourism", and currently the largest destination.

Many Americans (but certainly not all) own a firearm, and firearm ownership is legal in all jurisdictions with varying degrees of restriction by State, Territory, and Federal District. Legally carried firearms can range from hunting rifles and shotguns to revolvers and semi-automatic handguns.

Non-immigrant aliens that are in the country for fewer than 180 days cannot possess a firearm or ammunition, unless they came here specifically for hunting or sporting purposes, or they have a valid hunting license from the state they are visiting. Passport + Visa + State Issued Hunting License = firearm possession / use. Entry in a recognized shooting competition can substitute for the hunting license. Anything else is strictly illegal.

The vast majority of Americans are non-violent except in self-defense; they are responsible with their firearms and use/carry them appropriately and within the limits of the law. All States have laws regarding self-defense which allow a person to use force, up to and including deadly force, in defense of themselves or others when in reasonable fear of seriously bodily injury or death. This right to self-defense extends to protection of one's home, and, in some states, to other types of personal property.

Your chances of a firearm-related injury in the U.S.A. are very low, but please keep the following in mind:

• Concealed carry: All fifty states and Washington DC have "concealed carry" laws which enable people with the appropriate license to possess a concealed (and loaded) handgun on their person.

• Open carry: Many states also allow people to "open carry" a handgun. Seeing a person with an openly carried handgun or a (poorly) concealed handgun is only a cause for concern if the person's behavior is otherwise non-law abiding. The vast majority of Americans who carry firearms (either concealed or openly) do so within the limits of the law. While so called 'open carry' may seem highly unusual to individuals from nations (or other American states) without a gun culture, the general attitude among those who open carry is that criminals do not carry openly.

• When approaching a stranger's house or apartment, especially at night, make special effort to stand within the view of the door's peephole or in the light, so you can clearly be seen from the inside.

Hunting is a popular sport in rural America. In general, while hiking, travel on marked trails - this will not put you in any danger, but if venturing off the beaten path, it is a good idea to inquire if any hunting is currently afoot and where. If there is hunting in the area, wear bright colors (particularly "Blaze Orange") to differentiate yourself from terrain and prey. If you have a dog with you, you should also put a blaze orange vest on it as well. If you wish to hunt you will need to obtain a hunting license (usually available at outdoors stores among other places) and should review local regulations.

Property owners may defend their homes with firearms during a burglary or home invasion. If in rural areas, it is common courtesy not to cross land posted as private property.

Shooting is a popular recreational activity in America that many tourists wish to participate in. Many shooting ranges are more than happy to accommodate tourists and will have a variety of firearms available to rent and shoot at the range. However, due to the laws restricting non-immigrant aliens from possessing firearms, you will most likely need to be accompanied by a US citizen who satisfies the local requirements for firearm possession.

If you come from a country where firearm ownership is discouraged or prohibited, there is a possibility that your American host will offer to take you shooting. On a shooting trip, your host will most likely explain basic firearm safety and quiz you on it before allowing you to handle their guns. They may also watch you closely and point out any accidental safety violations. This is all done out of gun safety concerns, and should never be interpreted as impertinent or disrespectful.

Other conflicts

It is never worth getting into a street fight or a bar fight if such a thing can be avoided. Many states in the USA now allow licensed concealed carry holders to carry their pistols into establishments (such as bars) that serve alcohol on the premises, so long as the individual with the pistol refrains from consuming any alcohol. If you get drunk and wind up attacking somebody or threatening somebody with a pool stick, a chair, a glass bottle, a knife, or any sort of weapon, you open yourself to the possibility of somebody using a pistol against you in self-defense, aside from the fact that you open yourself to being arrested and charged with numerous felonies (which could carry years in prison). Always know your limits and drink responsibly. Do not drink to the point where you become prone to violent or reckless behavior. If you are at a reputable and clean establishment in a decent/safe neighborhood you will generally find that bar fights are extremely uncommon while in other bars that are known to get "rough" there may be bouncers (unarmed security who will forcibly eject you if you become disruptive/menacing) and in some bars (particularly those in bad neighborhoods) there may be armed security or the bar-tender/owner may be carrying a weapon. Use common-sense, if a misunderstanding occurs, politely but firmly apologize, back away from the situation, and avoid escalation. If somebody asks you to "step outside" or "go out back" or "let's take this into the parking lot" decline, tell him that you do not want any trouble, and if he persists in challenging you, speak with the bar-tender or a bouncer, or phone the police if he persists or tries to follow you, but do not go outside with him.

Staying healthy

Personal hygiene

The average American takes a bath or shower at least once per day, and expects others to do the same. Excessive body odor is frowned upon, as is excessive use of perfumes and colognes.

American men either shave their faces daily, or if they grow beards and/or mustaches, keep them neatly trimmed. American women shave their legs if walking around in shorts or high-cut skirts that expose bare skin. Most also shave their underarms and some shave their arms.

Bad breath (halitosis) is also frowned upon. Americans are taught from a young age to brush and floss their teeth twice daily.

Disease

Being a highly industrialized nation, the United States is largely free from most serious communicable diseases found in many developing nations; however, the HIV rate is higher than in Canada and Western Europe, with about a 0.5% infection rate in the overall population. This is due to Americans being more likely to have multiple partners at younger ages (down to 12 years of age,) than residents of Canada or Western Europe.

Two diseases that, while rare, are worth becoming educated about are rabies and Lyme disease. Rabies is more prevalent in eastern regions of the country and may be contracted from animal bites; if you are bitten by any mammal see a doctor quickly—do not wait for symptoms. Lyme disease is spread via the deer tick, which are prevalent in the woodlands and open fields of many rural areas. When venturing into the outdoors, it is a good idea to apply an insect repellent onto exposed skin surfaces that is effective against deer ticks.

Other diseases that are endemic within the United States, but are of far less concern, include Hantaviral Pulmonary Syndrome (found in western regions), Dengue fever (in areas from the southern Mid-West down to the Gulf and Hawaii,) Chikungunya (almost all regions,) Bubonic Plague (Pacific Northwest,) Rocky Mountain Spotted Fever (mostly in the Rocky Mountain region), West Nile Virus (all regions) and Eastern/Western Equine Encephalitis (particularly in the mid-west region).

All of the above listed diseases are extraordinarily rare and the medical system of the United States is very much capable of handling any of these when necessary.

For the latest in traveler's health information pertaining to the United States, including advisories and recommendations, visit the Centers for Disease Control and Prevention Destination United States website.

Health care

Health care in America is the most expensive in the world. Millions of working Americans struggle to pay their medical bill, even though the Affordable Care Act (commonly called "Obamacare" by Americans) enacted by President Barack Obama in 2010 helped to alleviate the problem. The same drug sold in the United States can cost up to 5 or 6 times the price of other countries. Americans generally use private health insurance, paid either by their employer or out of their own pocket; some risk paying high hospital bills themselves, or depend on government subsidized health plans. As a traveler, you should have travel insurance or you will potentially face very high costs if you need medical care.

Most metropolitan areas will have a mix of public and private hospitals, and in turn, US private hospitals can be either non-profit or for-profit. Public hospitals located in wealthy suburbs can be as good as private ones, but in poorer inner-city areas, public hospitals are usually overcrowded and run-down and should be avoided by tourists. However, many public hospitals are also the Level I regional trauma centers for their respective metro areas (i.e., they guarantee 24-hour on-site availability of all major types of medical specialists), which means that you will be taken there if critically injured.

In a life-threatening emergency, call 911 to summon an ambulance to take you to the nearest hospital emergency room ("ER"), or in less urgent situations get to the hospital yourself and register at the ER's front desk. Emergency rooms will treat patients without regard to their ability to pay, but you will still be presented with a bill for all care. Do not use ERs for non-emergency walk-in care. Not only can this be 3-4 times more expensive than other options, but you will often wait many hours (or days) before being treated, as the staff will give priority to patients with urgent needs. In most areas, the charge for an emergency room visit starts around $500, in addition to any specific services or medications you may require. Most urban areas have minor emergency centers (also called "urgent care", etc.) for medical situations where a fully equipped emergency room would be excessive, such as superficial lacerations. However, their hours may be limited, and few are open overnight.

Walk-in clinics are another place for travelers to find routine medical care, letting patients see a doctor or nurse-practitioner without an appointment (but often with a bit of a wait). They are typically very up-front about fees, and always accept credit cards. To find one, check the yellow pages under "Clinics", or call a major hospital and ask. Make sure to tell the clerk you will be paying "out of pocket"; if they assume an insurance company will be paying for it, they may order tests that are not medically essential and in some cases bill for services that aren't actually provided.

Dentists are readily available throughout the United States (again, see the yellow pages). Dental offices are accustomed to explaining fees over the phone, and most will accept credit cards. Be prepared to pay for all services up front as this is a common requirement for most dental practices.

Please note the Affordable Care Act (ACA), commonly referred to by Americans as Obamacare (named after the U.S. President Barack Obama who started the idea) is a law that requires everyone to have affordable health insurance to avoid paying a hefty price on their medical bills. It took effect March 1, 2014. It is however, not applicable to U.S. visitors so if you get sick you have to pay full price for medical bills.

Most counties and cities have a government-supported clinic offering free or low-cost testing and treatment for sexually transmitted diseases; call the Health Department for the county you are in for more details. Many county clinics offer primary health care services as well, however these services are geared towards low-income residents and not foreign travelers.

Restrooms/Toilets

The full-time restroom attendants often seen in certain European countries are extremely rare in the US. Some facilities may be pristine, such as in upscale shopping malls, fine restaurants, or commercial office buildings. Others will be shockingly unkempt, such as at many gas stations and bars. Public universities and big box retail stores will have a medium level of cleanliness. Nearly all public buildings are required to have restrooms accessible to the disabled. Many restrooms increasingly offer baby changing stations in both the men's and women's restrooms (especially in shopping centers and restaurants). A few places offer a separate, third "family" restroom which is single-occupancy but spacious. For little children who need to be monitored or assisted, it's generally acceptable for them to use the restroom of the parent they're with (little girls can go with dad to the men's room, and vice versa). The other way around (dad going to the ladies' room) is usually not okay.

North Carolina and a few other states have a law that transgender people use the bathrooms that matches their biological sex. However, law enforcement has not yet figured out how to effectively enforce it. You may face jail time if discovered to be transgender in the restroom of the gender that you identify as, but this is not a concern if you pass. In fact, it is safer for a passing trans woman to use the women's restroom; if you are a trans woman, using the men's restroom may lead to sexual assault, and severe physical beating if discovered to be transgender.

Water

Tap water is generally chlorinated and may also include fluorine. Nevertheless, some Americans use filter pitchers (common brands for both include Brita and Pur). Although tap water is not dangerous, some Americans prefer to filter (and sometimes boil) tap water before drinking. It has more to do with taste than actual safety.

Ice in restaurants is typically made with ice machines. Water is always served for free in restaurants.

Truly isolated rural areas or sources in condemned buildings may be suspect water sources-use your best judgement-but this is exceptionally rare.

While tap water in most urban and suburban areas is safe to drink, many Americans are more comfortable drinking either filtered or bottled water. This should not be seen as a sign that the water is unsafe, rather that some prefer to always have portable bottled water on hand. You can carry a reusable water bottle (heavy plastic or metal) and refill with water from public drinking fountains, some of which are even now filtered for taste, or have a vertical spout to make dispensing water directly into a bottle easier.

These considerations, of course, bar natural disasters or other disturbances to the water supply system. Again, use your best judgement. After an earthquake or a tornado or the like you can check with the local authority, and they will have maps zoned out where unsafe water may be found. Many cities water municipal properties with 'greywater' (reclaimed or otherwise not-processed) water, and there will be signs stating that the water is unsafe to drink from the sprayers. This should not be a huge problem, as parks tend to have drinking water fountains if you find yourself in a desperate situation.

In hot states such as Arizona and New Mexico, all businesses must provide tap water upon request.

Cope

News

News media in the U.S. is almost entirely privately-owned and profit-driven, and so conforms itself to its consumers and advertisers. The result is a wide range of information and opinion, some of it focused entirely on political ideology or special interests, with others attempting to be broad and impartial to appeal to a wide audience. As a very general rule (there are always exceptions) radio news has right-wing opinions, while print and cable news has a left-wing inclination. Other publications or channels will offer a range of right, center, and left opinions, but this is relatively uncommon.

Newspapers

The five most important newspapers are as follows:

• Los Angeles Times - the second-largest metropolitan newspaper in circulation in the United States in 2008 and the fourth most widely distributed newspaper in the country. Center-left stance on news pages, left-wing stance on editorial pages.

• The New York Times - the largest local metropolitan newspaper in the United States and third-largest newspaper overall, behind The Wall Street Journal and USA Today. It is the national newspaper of record and is generally considered to be the most prestigious newspaper in the United States. It also takes a center-left stance on news pages and a left-wing stance on editorial pages.

• The Wall Street Journal - primarily covers American economic and international business topics, and financial news and issues. Its name derives from Wall Street, located in New York City, which is the heart of the financial district; it has been printed continuously since its inception on July 8, 1889, by Charles Dow, Edward Jones, and Charles Bergstresser. The newspaper has won the Pulitzer Prize thirty-four times. Mixed political stance—center-right on editorial pages, center-left on news pages.

• USA Today - known for synthesizing news down to easy-to-read-and-comprehend stories. In the main edition seen in the US and some Canadian cities, each edition consists of four sections: News (the oft-labeled "front page" section), Money, Sports, and Life. On Fridays, two Life sections are included: the regular Life for entertainment (subtitled Weekend; section E), which features television, a DVD column, film reviews and trends, and a travel supplement called Destinations & Diversions (section D). Centrist stance. Often found at many hotels (for which they either charge a "newspaper fee" or bundle it into a larger "resort fee").

• The Washington Post - well-known for its coverage of national politics, especially major scandals like the Watergate scandal. Center-left stance.

Most good newsstands (especially at major airports) always carry the NYT, the WSJ, and USA Today, as well as one or more local newspapers. In addition, they may also carry either the LA Times or the Washington Post (depending on whether they sit west or east of the Mississippi River). Local newspapers can generally be found at sidewalk vending machines in the cities they cover, together with USA Today. Starbucks Coffee shops and other coffee houses often also carry newspapers. However, many bookstores (such as Barnes & Noble) no longer carry newspapers since most Americans now read news online.

Cable news channels

Cable News Network (CNN) - broadcasts, primarily, from studios in Atlanta. Delivers the latest breaking news and information on the latest top stories, weather, business, entertainment, politics, and more. It has been labeled as having a center to left stance.

Fox News Channel - broadcasts from studios in New York City. Presents a variety of programming with up to 17 hours of live programming per day. Audio simulcasts of the channel are aired on XM Satellite Radio and Sirius Satellite Radio. Right-wing stance.

MSNBC - broadcasts, primarily, from studios in New York City. Features news, information, and political opinion programming. Left-wing stance.

Dress

Today, dress in the US tends to be fairly casual. For everyday clothes, jeans and T-shirts are generally acceptable, as are shorts when the weather is suitable. Sneakers (athletic shoes) are common; flip-flops, tank tops, and sandals are also popular in warm weather.

At the workplace, business casual (slacks, understated collared shirts without a tie, and non-athletic shoes) is now the default at many companies; more traditional industries (e.g. finance, legal, and insurance) still require suits and ties, while others (e.g. computer software) are even more casual, allowing jeans and even shorts.

When dressing up for nice restaurants or upscale entertainment, a pair of nice slacks, a collared shirt, and dress shoes will work almost everywhere. Ties for men are rarely necessary, but jackets are occasionally required for very upscale restaurants in big cities.

At the beach or pool, men prefer loose bathing trunks or board shorts, and women wear bikinis or one-piece swimsuits. Nude bathing is illegal under Federal law except at certain private beaches or resorts; women going topless is also illegal under Federal law. Many establishments, such as water parks, will enforce rules on improper swimwear; for example, insufficient covering of the intimate parts or offensive language. Staff members may ask you to either change into swimwear more appropriate or be escorted out of the park (typically without a refund).

Generally, Americans accept religious attire such as hijab, yarmulke, and burqa without comment. However, do be aware that in places of heightened security such as banks, municipal buildings, and so on, wearing clothing which covers the face may be regarded as suspicious behavior and is generally unadvised.

Respect

The number one rule of respect among Americans is that it must be earned by your actions and integrity. Being honest, polite, and open-minded will win you much more respect than your age, wealth, or level of education.

Some Americans will show great courtesy to elders, women, priests, military veterans, teachers, and so on, but this is purely a matter of personal preference, and behaving as though you expect superior treatment will guarantee the opposite.

When Americans refer specifically to "lower class," "middle class" or "upper class" people, they are referring strictly to economic status, not social status. Disrespecting someone because they have less money than you is widely regarded as terrible behavior.

Some Americans find foreign culture and language fascinating and you will likely be bombarded with questions about your home. Questions such as these are nearly always meant in a friendly and inquisitive manner.

Americans value their right to free expression, and may encourage visitors to voice their feelings and opinions, but some topics are best treated with care and respect:

Many Americans are openly critical of their government and its policies, but disparaging remarks about the U.S. military or foreign policy are rarely welcome from outsiders. In addition, many Americans will take offense to questions about American stereotypes (obesity, firearms, etc) and even if meant in a joking way, it will still be seen as very disrespectful; the US is a very large country with all types of people. Most Americans will change the subject or excuse themselves from the conversation if they think you are being inappropriate. If this happens, do not pursue the offending topic further. Upon becoming better acquainted with someone, political discussion and criticism may become more acceptable. Pride in the American military is very strong, and at many sporting events and institutions, military members often receive recognition. Americans are free to respectfully disagree with military policy, but questioning the honor, integrity or behavior of American soldiers themselves is usually unacceptable. As an outsider you should do neither unless you know the person very well.

Given the variety of religions practiced throughout the States, you should expect to be surrounded by many who disagree with your beliefs, though most are tolerant of such differences. While you're unlikely to offend an American by politely asking about their religion or offering to explain your own, aggressive proselytizing or disparaging remarks of other faiths will not earn you any respect.

Leftists are generally found in the states where the Democratic Party is predominant, but can also be found in even the most conservative towns. Generally, though, one should not mention these views unless their host does so first, or has already displayed their allegiance to such views via a T-shirt, bumper sticker, etc.

Nazism and other Fascist ideologies are viewed negatively. Holocaust denial is not tolerated in the United States. Americans strongly support the Jewish people as they were victims of a mass genocide during the Second World War and also support having a strong alliance with Israel more than any other Western nation.

Jokes at the expense of a specific race, ethnic group, etc. are generally not tolerated. Such jokes are often considered a sign of bigotry and most Americans will not find them humorous, even if they are not a member of the offended group. For example, making fun of black people in an exclusively white setting will still offend most Americans. In return, you can expect Americans to not mock your race and country of origin.

Understand that Americans value directness and self-confidence, particularly in public/professional life. To make a good impression, you will want to greet someone you've never met before with direct eye contact, a firm handshake and a smile. If you come from a country such as Japan, where directness is usually considered uncomfortable, rude and/or disrespectful, these aspects of interaction may take some getting used to, but can go long way in determining how positively or negatively you're perceived.

Unless it is extremely crowded, leave about an arm's length of personal space between yourself and others. On public transportation, it is considered invasive to sit directly next to a stranger if there are open seats available elsewhere. With the exception of handshakes, Americans do not like to be touched by members outside of their family and will respond aggressively if poked, pushed, or grabbed by a stranger. Unlike many cultures, Americans do not perform cheek kissing as a way of greeting strangers, and if they do cheek kissing at all, it is only with family members.

As a result of the country's extensive history of racial discrimination, coupled with the country's push toward racial equality, Americans are exceptionally sensitive about issues of race. If you must reference race, Black or African-

American, Asian, Latino or Hispanic, Native American or American Indian, and White or Caucasian are acceptable terms.

Note also that when Americans use the term "Asian" by itself to refer to people, they are often specifically referring to East Asians (including Southeast Asians), and not to people from South Asia. In most parts of the US, East Asian communities are larger and more established than South Asian communities. (Note that this usage is exactly opposite that of British English, in which "Asian" by itself refers exclusively to South Asians, and East Asians are usually called "Oriental" which is considered offensive in America.)

Smoking indoors is heavily frowned upon and is illegal in most public buildings. If you're in a private home and want to smoke, politely excuse yourself and go outside.

Adults should never approach or speak directly to children they don't know. American children are taught to be wary of strangers. If you have something you'd like to say to a child, address the adult he or she is with.

Videotaping in any indoor public-use place is highly frowned upon in the United States of America and can rather easily result in expulsion from the premises, even without warning. Places that prohibit or restrict videotaping by visitors include shopping malls, stores, restaurants, museums, arcades, movie theaters, nightclubs, bars, taverns, and stadiums. Additionally, cameras (both still and motion picture) are generally prohibited at strip clubs and clothing-optional facilities. Videotaping is usually permitted at most amusement parks, but is highly restricted and oftentimes prohibited on rides, especially at chain parks like Six Flags and Cedar Fair. Different stadiums, and even different events at the same stadium can have different photo policies. It is always best to ask about the photo and video policy to determine acceptability.

Public display of affection, including hugging, gets various types of reactions depending on the region it occurs in. Generally, in the northern tier states (especially within northern states such as Alaska, Montana, and such), public displays of affection more demonstrative than hugging are seen as tacky and inconsiderate. Also, many schools and work places prohibit public display of affection. Public display of affection is generally more permitted and open in the southern states area. It even occurs, especially in deep southern states (Texas, Florida, South Carolina, Mississippi, and such) that waitresses do occasionally hug their customers.

There are Native American reservations scattered throughout the country, particularly in the Upper Midwest and the Southwest. Many of these

reservations are home to sites that are sacred to the tribe, and certain places may be off-limits to outsiders. If you enter a reservation's territory, please be sure to respect the land. They also have unique legal status allowing them to regulate themselves. Laws and customs may be different in these regions.
The Bald Eagle is the national animal, and is beloved by many Americans and is a sacred animal in many Indian reservations. Respect national wildlife.

The United States has been through several waves of feminism since the mid 20th century and has been influenced by feminism more than any other country in the world. Many countries, of course, have a custom of reverence towards older women or women of higher status but males should be careful in how they address or interact with any American adult females, younger or older, regardless of their apparent status. The issue of sexual harassment and sexual assault is a very serious matter in the United States for both man and women, as sexual assault and harassment are a problem for both genders.

Avoid slang terms that you might hear Americans use for women ("babe", "broad", "chick") and to be safe, avoid any equivalents in your language. It is just best to simply address an American woman by her given name. A majority of American women consider men who use such terms as disrespectful. Catcalls and whistles, which may be traditionally considered harmless in your native country, are considered to be a form of sexual harassment and you will find yourself in court.

Be aware of your surroundings when discussing LGBT rights. It is a very sensitive issue on both sides of the aisle, so saying the wrong thing could cause great offense or argument.

In regard to pets, many Americans value their pet as a family member. It would not be a good idea to make a rude comment about somebody's dog or cat. Such remarks will often be greeted with hostility.

Contact

By phone

U.S. telephone numbers are governed by the North American Numbering Plan (NANP) and are invariably written in one of these formats:

XXX-YYY-ZZZZ
(XXX) YYY-ZZZZ
YYY-ZZZZ

The numbers YYY-ZZZZ make up the local part of the telephone number (specifically, the telephone exchange number and line number). You must dial all seven digits even if the YYY portion is the same as the line you are calling from. The numbers XXX denote the area code. Densely populated areas often have several area codes (e.g. the six area codes within the borders of New York City), while some sparsely-populated states will have one or two codes for the entire state (e.g. Montana).

Ordinarily, if the number you are dialing is within the same area code as the one for the line you are dialing from, dial YYY-ZZZZ; otherwise, dial 1-XXX-YYY-ZZZZ. However, many metropolitan areas, and even some entire states (such as Maryland and West Virginia) have implemented 10-digit dialing, where all local calls must be dialed as XXX-YYY-ZZZZ. (In such areas, you must still dial "1" to distinguish long-distance calls.) Mobile phones are much simpler and can be dialed with all 10 digits regardless of whether the call is local or long distance.

You may occasionally see phone numbers for business which spell out words, such as "1-800-FLOWERS". Almost all phones have letters written on each number ("2" is "ABC", "3" is "DEF", etc.) which you use to dial the number; for example, "FLOWERS" becomes "356-9377". This is a legacy of the old alphabet letter codes which were previously used for telephone exchanges. In the case of mobile phones, most feature phones (i.e., not smartphones) have the letters printed along with the numbers. As for smartphones, most touchscreen phones have virtual phone keypads that display the corresponding letters along with the numbers. Smartphones without touchscreens, such as some older BlackBerry devices, often allow you to enter letters as part of a phone number. In either case, entering "1-800-FLOWERS" and pressing the send button should connect you to that business.

Long-distance calls are calls to lines outside the "local calling area" of the line from which you are dialing. The long-distance prefix (in some countries called the "trunk" prefix) in the U.S. is "1", so a long-distance call should be dialed 1-XXX-YYY-ZZZZ. As with local calls, dialing incorrectly will result in an automated message informing you how to properly dial the number. Mobile phones typically do not require you to dial "1" for long-distance.

Canada and certain Caribbean islands also participate in the NANP. This means they can be dialed using "1" as if they were in the U.S., although the call will be billed at international rates. As a general rule, calls to Canada are more expensive than U.S. domestic calls, but cheaper than calls to other countries. Calls to other locations require using the international access code ("011") followed by the country code of the destination number. For example, a call from the United States to the British Museum in London would be dialed as 011-44-20-7323-8000.

At some locations with internal phone systems (e.g. businesses and hotels), you will need to dial an access code (usually "9" or "8") to reach an outside line before dialing the number as usual.

Numbers with the area code 800, 888, 877, 866, or 855 are toll free within the U.S., meaning that the cost of the call is paid by the recipient. Outside the country, dial 880, 881, 882, and 883 respectively, but these aren't toll free. The area code 900 is used for services with additional charges applied to the call (e.g. "adult entertainment"). This is also true of "local" seven-digit phone numbers starting with 976.

Most visitor areas and some restaurants and bars have directories with two listings of telephone numbers (often split into two books): the white pages, for an alphabetical listing; and the yellow pages, an advertising-filled listing of business and service establishments by category (e.g. "Taxicabs"). Directory information can also be obtained by dialing 411 (for local numbers) or 1-area code-555-1212 (for other areas). If 411 doesn't work locally, try 555-1212 or 1-555-1212. Directory information is normally an extra cost call. As an alternative, directory information is available for free via 1-800-Free411, which is ad-supported. Information directories are also available online at each regional telephone company's web site (most often AT&T, Verizon, or CenturyLink; also Frontier in West Virginia and FairPoint in northern New England), as well as www.free411.com. Although each claims to have all the local phone numbers of the others, using the site of the region you are searching for yields the best results (i.e. AT&T for most of California, Verizon for the Northeast, etc.) Many residential land-line phones and all mobile phones are unlisted.

Historically, pay phones were ubiquitous on sidewalks all over the United States, and commonplace in other places such as gas stations. After 2000, cell phone usage soared and pay phone usage collapsed, so the regional landline telecom monopolies exited the pay phone business. The small companies that took over the legacy pay phones have ripped out most of them and increased prices on the ones that remain. Today, prices are typically 50 cents for the first three minutes, and a quarter for each additional minute. You will probably have to enter a store or restaurant to find one, though some are against the outer wall of such businesses, usually in front, or near bus stops. Most pay phones are coin operated (quarters, dimes and nickels) and do not accept paper bills. An online directory of pay phones can be found at Pay Phone Directory. Dialing 9-1-1 to report an emergency is still a free call on pay phones, it's just a matter of locating one to use.

Long-distance telephone calling cards are available at most convenience stores. Most calling cards have specific destinations in mind (domestic calls, calls to particular countries), so make sure you get the right card. Some cards may be refilled by phoning a number and giving your Visa/MasterCard number, but often operators refuse foreign cards for this purpose. Moreover, calls may cost more if a payphone or toll-free number is used or if a mobile number is dialed or if more calls are made (rather than few but longer calls).

Another option is using a virtual number service. That way you can avoid paying for roaming.

Mobile phones

American mobile phone services (known as cell phones regardless of the technology used) are not very compatible with those offered abroad. While GSM has been gaining in popularity, the US uses the unusual 1900 and 850MHz frequencies; check with your operator or mobile phone dealer to see if your phone is a tri-band or quad-band model that will work here. Roaming fees for foreign mobiles are high and text messages may not always work due to compatibility issues between networks.

Depending on the length of your trip and the amount of calling you plan on doing, it may be less expensive to obtain an American mobile phone. If you are arriving and departing from the same city, consider that most larger airports will have a boutique that rents mobile phones (rates start around $3/day). Alternatively, prepaid phones and top-up cards can be purchased at mobile phone boutiques and at many discount, electronics, office supply and convenience stores. A very basic mobile handset and credit for an hour or two's worth of calls can be had for under $40, though be aware that international calling will, if it is in fact available, use up those credits much more quickly than a domestic call. It is possible to purchase a prepaid SIM card for an unlocked mobile, although these are not nearly as common in the United States as in other countries so you will probably have to purchase it from a GSM provider's boutique. The four major national carriers are AT&T, Verizon, Sprint, and T-Mobile, which operate boutiques in most, if not all, metropolitan areas and offer pre-paid service. Historically, the AT&T and T-Mobile networks have used GSM, while Verizon and Sprint have used the different CDMA standard (whose phones did not use SIM cards). Today, all four carriers are quickly migrating to the newer LTE standard (which uses SIM cards), and some Verizon and Sprint phones (mostly smartphones) support LTE, CDMA, and GSM. Other providers of mobile phone service include TracFone, Boost Mobile, Virgin Mobile, and various regional operators. To work out whether a regional operator might work better (as their deals are more flexible over their local areas of service) OpenSignal provide independent US coverage maps

Unlike in many countries, there is no surcharge for dialing a mobile phone (calls to mobile phones are charged the same as calls to land lines outside your geographic area), but on the other hand mobile phone users are charged for incoming and outgoing calls and SMS (you won't be able to contact someone who does not have sufficient balance to receive phone calls). Numbers that are toll-free from land lines however are not free when dialed from a mobile phone. Packages as low as $25/month are available to allow you to make hundreds of minutes' worth of calls. Take note that a failed attempt at making a call (or a "missed call") will be deducted from your balance since you are charged from the moment you dial.

If you are going to be in the United States for a long time, you may wish to consider a long-term service contract. A service contract will give you the best rates on calls, SMS and data, and will also usually include a free or discounted handset. On the other hand, they are almost always two-year agreements with stiff penalties for early cancellation (anywhere from $150 to $350, depending on carrier and phone model), so consider the length of your stay and your needs before signing one. T-Mobile has recently become the major exception to this rule—in March 2013, it eliminated service contracts for new customers. New T-Mobile customers have the choice of paying for their phone up front, or buying the phone at a discounted price and paying the balance, interest-free, over a 20-month period. Users who choose the second option may prepay part or all of the remaining cost of their phone without penalty; canceling service has no penalty apart from re-payment of any remaining cost of the phone. In the case of T-Mobile, the length of your stay will still be a factor—if you do not pay the entire retail cost of your phone up front, the remaining balance at the time you leave may be more than another carrier's cancellation fee.

Conversely, if you are only going to be in the US for a short period (e.g. a week or less), some carriers (most notably T-Mobile) offer a plan that allows unlimited calling, texting, and data for $2-3 per day. This will not include international calling, however.

By mail

The United States Postal Service (USPS) operates a gigantic network of post offices and mailboxes throughout the country. The bright blue metal mailboxes of the USPS are a ubiquitous sight in rural and urban settings, indoors and outdoors, in every U.S. state and territory. They are normally serviced once, twice or even thrice a day, Monday through Saturday. Pickup times are always listed on a label on the box. In suburban areas, it is common to see mailboxes located on a drive-through lane outside of a post office.

Each post office has different hours, but most are open 9:00 am to 5:00 pm, Monday through Saturday. In high crime areas, post offices are completely closed to the public when not open. In low crime areas, the lobby is divided into two areas. The retail counter area is closed after hours, but the rest of the lobby can be open 24/7 (or may only be open longer hours like 6 a.m. to 10 p.m.) and normally includes access to Post Office Boxes as well as at least one Self-Service Kiosk (SSK). The SSK is an easy-to-use self-service touchscreen kiosk that accepts credit cards. It can weigh packages and print out a variety of different types of postage and labels.

Addressing

In general, the addressee's section of the piece of mail should appear as follows:

(name of recipient)
(street address, which contains the house number and street name)
(apartment, suite or room number if any)
(city or town), (two-digit state abbreviation) (ZIP code)

For example:
John & Jane Doe
555 Main St
Apt #1
Houston, TX 77002-0001

To send items to any destination within the U.S. by post, the most important item in the addressee's section of the mail piece is the ZIP code (postal code).

The importance of the ZIP code arises from the Postal Service's highly automated process for handling mail. USPS personnel dump all newly received mail pieces into a scanning machine that runs optical character recognition on the destination address and then sprays or prints an Intelligent Mail Barcode corresponding to the ZIP+4 code. The Intelligent Mail Barcode is then scanned by high-speed automatic sorting machines at each step in the system, in order to route the mail piece into the bag or tray of the letter carrier whose route includes that ZIP+4 code. Thus, if the ZIP+4 code and Intelligent Mail Barcode are incorrect, the error will not be detected until the mail piece gets to the wrong letter carrier. The USPS requires a particular combination of house number and street name to be unique within the same city, but does not require a street name to be unique across an entire metropolitan area. Since there are often many cities in a single metropolitan area that have streets with the same name, writing the correct ZIP code is essential to prompt delivery of your mail piece.

When you do not know of or are unsure of the correct ZIP code, visit USPS.com, the website of the USPS. It enables users to look up ZIP codes by city and by street address. Entering a full street address may return a ZIP code (first 5 digits) and ZIP+4 (next 4 digits) to a total of 9 digits. The ZIP (first 5 digits) usually encompasses a greater area such as a section of a city, an entire town or across an expansive (rural) area encompassing several small towns. University campuses, large hospitals, governmental agencies, military bases, sections of the U.S. military or a single large building may have their own unique ZIP code and any mail sent to that particular ZIP code goes to that institution's internal mail room for onward delivery. Depending upon the complexity of a particular place, the unique ZIP+4 code (next for 4 digits) may correspond to anything from a segment along a letter carrier's route to the entire route (which may cover an entire small town); a group of apartments, offices or storefronts in a single address; an office within a specific building (which is often the case in big cities); or a department, office, mail stop or a building on an university campus or some large entity with its own unique zip code.

The "+4" portion of the ZIP code is optional. For nearly all addresses, as long as the written address in its entirety corresponds to an actual and unique address, the OCR machine will be able to link it to that address, quickly identify the correct "+4" portion, and print the correct Intelligent Mail Barcode. But the ZIP code (the first 5 digits) is always necessary.

Pricing

First class (airmail) postcards and letters (if not oversized, or over one ounce/28.5 grams) are $1.15 internationally including to Canada and Mexico. It is no longer necessary to mark "AIR MAIL" on items going overseas as everything is now sent abroad on airplane by default. All addresses with a USPS ZIP code are considered "domestic", including Alaska, Hawaii, Puerto Rico, U.S. Virgin Islands, Guam, American Samoa, Federated States of Micronesia, Marshall Islands, Palau, U.S. military bases abroad (identified with an 'APO' or 'FPO' address), U.S. Navy ships at sea (usually 'FPO' addresses) and U.S. diplomatic missions abroad ('DPO' addresses). Domestic postcards are sent for $0.34 while a letter in an envelope weighing within 1 oz. is mailed for $0.49. If you put a solid object like a coin or a key in an envelope, you'll pay a surcharge.

"Forever" stamps are always valid for the first ounce for all first-class domestic mail items, with no surcharge after a price increase. (For all other kinds of price increases and historically for first-class domestic mail price increases, the USPS sells one and two-cent stamps which must be added to cover the difference between the face value of stamps sold before an increase and the current rate.) However, Forever stamps are not valid for international use.

If for whatever reason you have stamps that don't add up to the correct exact amount, you can try overpaying by adding one more stamp. The USPS stamp canceling machines are intelligent enough to recognize that fact and allow the mail piece through.

Due to sagging demand, the USPS has taken away the vending machines through which one could formerly purchase a variety of pre-printed stamp booklets in post office lobbies. The SSKs as initially deployed could regularly dispense at least one type of pre-printed stamp booklet year-round, but that feature has been withdrawn as well. The USPS will still make stamp booklets available sometimes through the SSKs, but only on an intermittent and seasonal basis.

Therefore, at this time, the only always-available method for buying postage at a post office when the retail counter is closed is to use the SSK in the lobby to print bar-coded postage labels. However, besides post office retail counters, stamp booklets are also available from many retailers, including pharmacies, supermarkets, and certain banks.

Receiving mail via General Delivery

You can receive mail sent both domestically and from abroad by having it addressed to you as "General Delivery." In other countries, this is often called

Poste Restante. There is no charge for this service. You just go to the main post office, wait in line, and they will give you your mail after showing ID such as a passport.

John Doe
General Delivery
Seattle, Washington 98101-9999
U.S.A.

The last four digits of the ZIP (postal) Code for General Delivery is always '9999'. If the city is large enough to have multiple post offices, only one (usually in the center of downtown) will have the General Delivery service. This means, for example, if you're staying in the Green Lake district of Seattle (a few miles north of downtown), you cannot receive your mail at the Green Lake Post Office, and must travel downtown to get it. On the other hand, if you're completely outside of the city of Seattle, and in a smaller town with only one post office, you can have it sent there.

The two largest private courier services, UPS and FedEx, also have a "Hold for Pickup" option. Both can hold a package at the nearest depot, while FedEx can also hold packages at FedEx Office locations.

By Internet

Most Americans have Internet access, mostly in their homes and offices. Internet cafes, therefore, are not common outside of major metropolitan, tourist and resort areas. However, you almost always have several options for Internet access, except perhaps in the most remote, rural areas.

If you bring your own computer or tablet:

Most public libraries have free Wi-Fi available even without a library card. In some instances, the Wi-Fi remains on 24/7, so even if the library is closed, you may be able to sit outside and access the Internet in the early morning or on Sunday.

Chain hotels usually provide in-room Internet connections, sometimes wireless. Some chains include Wi-Fi with the price of the room and others (especially luxury chains) will demand an additional per-day charge. Local establishments like bed-and-breakfasts and roadside motels are less likely to have Internet access.

Many coffee shops, book stores, and some fast food restaurants provide free wireless Internet access, though you are generally expected to make a purchase first before taking a seat. Among them are major national chains like McDonald's, Burger King, Starbucks, and Barnes & Noble.

Some cities have free Wi-Fi access that spans a central business district (several square miles) or even citywide.

Many colleges and universities offer free Wi-Fi in their libraries and student centers, but non-students may have trouble accessing the network, or even the buildings. However, if you are a university student at a major university around the world that uses the eduroam network, you may be able to access the network of participating universities in the US seamlessly. Ask around.

Airports, even smaller regional ones, usually provide Wi-Fi within passenger terminals, sometimes for a nominal charge.

There are some paid Wi-Fi chains, where you can receive access to numerous hotspots for a small charge, such as Boingo.

If driving, in a pinch you can always park in a chain hotel parking lot or near a commercial strip by coffee shops or libraries, and grab Wi-Fi access from your car. Be sure to check the name of the network—"Joe's Coffeehouse" is likely a public network, "Linksys 10" or "az13t0dug" probably aren't. Using a private network (even if it doesn't have a password) can be risky and in most cases is illegal (again, even if it lacks a password), although enforcement is nearly non-existent.

You can also purchase a mobile broadband modem which can be attached to your laptop via the USB port and subscribe to a prepaid plan. Service providers include Verizon Wireless and Virgin Mobile (which uses the Sprint network). Make sure to check a coverage map before you buy, each company has large areas with bad or no coverage. Also, these plans are subject to data limits which are easy to exceed unknowingly! Avoid watching videos when using a mobile network.

If your tablet (e.g. iPad) has cellular capabilities built in, consider buying a SIM from the nearest AT&T store. You will be able to insert the SIM into your device or ask the store staff to help you with it. You will need a debit/credit card (one from your home country with a Visa/MasterCard logo will be good enough) and you can decide to terminate the service any time before the next cycle without penalty. To maximize your available mobile data, switch cellular data off whenever free/complimentary Wi-Fi is available and use the said Wi-Fi service instead.

If you don't have your own computer:

Internet cafes can still be found in some larger cities (e.g., New York and Los Angeles).

Some locations such as airports and shopping malls have pay-per-use Internet access terminals, where 3-5 minutes of Web time can be purchased for $1.

However, such terminals are becoming quite rare, due to the popularity of smartphones and Wi-Fi. Often a cluster of Internet terminals will share an ageing ISDN or T1 connection, meaning that each user will receive the equivalent of an old dial-up connection.

Nearly all public libraries have PC terminals with broadband Internet access (and usually productivity software such as Microsoft Word) available for free, public use (this is the reason why the US lacks Internet cafes!). You may need a library card to access services and persons living outside the area may need to pay a small fee. Time limits are usually 1-2 hours, although you may be able to ask for an extension.

The best bet for computer rental is a "photocopy shop" such as FedEx Office (+1 800 GOFEDEX/+1 800 463 3339; when prompted by the voice menu, say "FedEx Office" or press "64"), which is a national chain. Most FedEx Office stores are open long hours; at least one in each metro area is open 24 hours. All stores have several Internet-connected computers with Microsoft Office, Adobe Design Suite, and a selection of Web browsers, and at least one computer always has a scanner attached. All FedEx Office branches also have self-service equipment for copying and printing (both in monochrome and color), for sending and receiving faxes, and for printing digital photographs in a variety of sizes. Larger, full-service FedEx Office branches offer professional print shop services. However, keep in mind that you will pay for all this convenience, as FedEx Office charges very high per-minute and/or per-page fees for its various services. Of course, all FedEx Office stores can also ship packages by FedEx.

Most higher-end hotels offer "business centers" with basic Internet access through one or more on-site desktop computers, a fax machine, a laser printer, and a photocopier. At over 80 upscale hotels across the U.S., the business center is a FedEx Office.

Electronics stores that sell computers, such as Best Buy or the Apple Store, sometimes allow customers to access the Internet from the computers on sale on the floor for at least a short while. This is generally a courtesy, and you should not depend on it for regular usage, but it sometimes makes for a convenient option. The Apple Store is particularly generous with their policy, and will not ask you to leave if you come just to access the Internet. However, some websites, such as Facebook, are blocked.

Another, albeit less likely, possibility is a university library. Private universities in larger cities generally restrict library access to enrolled students and faculty. Public university libraries are generally required by law to be open to the public (at least as far as books go), but almost invariably a student login is required to access computer terminals. Public university libraries sometimes have one or two computer terminals set up for casual visitor use, but it's always best to call ahead to be certain first. Furthermore, most universities sit on large campuses.

Alabama

A blend of thought-provoking history, modern cities, and natural beauty make this state "Sweet Home Alabama." Antebellum homes dot Huntsville, where the Saturn rocket was designed, and Montgomery's modern state government buildings stand near the First White House of the Confederacy. Birmingham, a major medical research center, has 99 historic neighborhoods.

Rocky, wooded hills and vast caves, perfect for hiking and spelunking, lay to the north. Expansive lakes and rivers mark the interior and white-sand beaches rim the Gulf Coast. Scenic vistas line well-maintained highways leading to colonial forts, Civil War sites, and charming towns.

Summers are hot and humid, yes, but Alabama's year-round mild climate also means winter temperatures rarely dip below 55°F, perfect weather for exploring 26 courses on the Robert Trent Jones Golf Trail.

Alabama cuisine is a regional buffet. Sample the coast's fresh seafood, the center's barbecue, and the soul food served everywhere. City-based chefs work culinary magic at some of the American South's best restaurants.

History suffuses Alabama, a description which could be true of many states. But there are few places where the perception of said history is so emotionally fraught. The Mississippian Native American culture built great mound cities here, and Mobile is dotted with Franco-Caribbean architecture. But for many, the word Alabama is synonymous with the American Civil Rights movement.

Perhaps such a struggle, and all of the nobility and desperation it entailed, was bound for a state like this, with its Gothic plantations, hardscrabble farmland and fiercely local sense of place. From the smallest hunting town to river-bound cities, Alabama is a place all its own, and its character is hard to forget. Some visitors have a hard time looking beyond the state's past, but the troubling elements of that narrative are tied up in a passion that constantly manifests in Alabama's arts, food and culture.

Sights in Alabama

Birmingham Civil Rights Institute

Price: Adult/senior/child $12/5/3, sun free

Hours: 10am-5pm Tue-Sat, 1-5pm sun

Contact: http://www.bcri.org, 866-328-9696

Location: 520 16th St, N, Birmingham, USA

A maze of moving audio, video and photography exhibits tell the story of racial segregation in America, and the Civil Rights movement, with a focus on activities in and around Birmingham. There's an extensive exhibit on the 16th Street Baptist Church (located across the street), which was bombed in 1963; it's the beginning of the city's Civil Rights Memorial Trail.

Ave Maria Grotto

Price: adult/child $7/4.50

Hours: 9am-5pm

Contact: http://www.avemariagrotto.com

Location: 1600 St. Bernard Dr, Birmingham, USA

Located 50 miles north of Birmingham on the grounds of the only Benedictine monastery in Alabama, the amazing Ave Maria Grotto is more or less the work of one man, Brother Joseph Zoettl, who spent the better part of 35 years hand-sculpting stone and cement miniatures of the world's most prominent religious buildings. The attention to detail and level of skill in the 125 pieces is amazing, regardless of your personal views on religion. From an art perspective, it's even more miraculous yet – after all, this was just Brother Joseph's hobby.

Rosa Parks Museum

Price: adult/child 4-12yr $7.50/5.50

Hours: 9am-5pm Mon-Fri, 9am-3pm Sat

Contact: http://www.troy.edu/rosaparks, 334-241-8615

Location: 251 Montgomery St, Montgomery, USA

This museum, set in front of the bus stop where she took her stand, features a video re-creation of that pivotal moment that launched the 1955 boycott. The experience is very managed - you're given a small opportunity to explore on your own, but otherwise the museum feels something like an interactive movie. For the price of an additional full admission ticket, you can visit the children's wing, a kids-oriented time travel exhibit to the Jim Crow South.

Alaska

Alaska is America's last frontier, with landscapes that stretch out seemingly to infinity. From the lush rain forests of Southeast to the vast, flat tundra in the north, you can stare in awe at the same things that take an Alaskan's breath away: calving glaciers, volcanic valleys, jagged sea cliffs, the northern lights, and more. Here you can kayak to icebergs, fly over the highest peak in North America, stay out all night celebrating the midnight sun, and spot wildlife from eagles to whales. For lovers of nature, few places exhilarate like Alaska.

Bears larger than bison, national parks the size of nations, and glaciers bigger than other US states. The word 'epic' barely does Alaska justice.

Wilderness – land free of strip malls, traffic jams and McDonald's restaurants – is the best attraction Alaska has to offer. Within Alaska is the largest national park in the country (Wrangell-St Elias), the largest national forest (Tongass), and the largest state park (Wood-Tikchik). This is where people play outdoors. During 20-hour days, they climb mountains, canoe wilderness rivers, strap on crampons and trek across glaciers. In July, they watch giant brown bears snagging salmon; in November they head to Haines to see thousands of bald eagles gathered at the Chilkat River. They hoist a backpack and follow the same route that the Klondike stampeders did a century earlier or spend an afternoon in a kayak, bobbing in front of a 5-mile-wide glacier continually calving icebergs into the sea around them. In Alaska these are more than just outdoor adventures. They are natural experiences that can permanently change your way of thinking.

The 49th state is the longest trip in the USA and probably the most expensive. From elsewhere in the country it takes a week on the road, two to three days on a ferry, or a $700 to $900 airline ticket to reach Alaska. Once there, many visitors are overwhelmed by the distances between cities, national parks and attractions. Alaskan prices are the stuff of legends. Still, the Final Frontier is on the bucket list of most adventurous travelers, particularly those enamored of the great outdoors. Those who find the time and money to visit the state rarely regret it.

Alaska is big and so is everything about it. There are mountains and glaciers in other parts of North America, but few on the same scale or as overpowering as those in Alaska. At 20,320ft, Mt McKinley is not only the highest peak in North America, it's also a stunning sight when you catch its alpenglow in Wonder Lake. The Yukon is the third-longest river in the USA, Bering Glacier is larger than Switzerland, and Arctic winters are one long night while Arctic summers are one long day. The brown bears on Kodiak Island have been known to stand 14ft tall; the king salmon in the Kenai River often exceed 70lb; in Palmer they grow cabbages that tip the scales at 127lbs. A 50ft-long humpback whale breaching is not something easily missed, even from a half mile away.

Isolation fosters peculiarities. A trip into the Alaskan wilderness can be as much about the off-beat people as the off-the-beaten-track location. Take tiny Chitina with its handful of subsistence-hunting locals, or the crusty boom-and-bust town of Nome, or the jokey gold-mining punch line that is Chicken. Ever since the US bought Alaska for 2 cents an acre in 1867, the land that styles itself as America's last frontier has attracted contrarians, rat-race escapees, wanderers, dreamers, back-to-the-landers and people imbued with the spirit of the Wild West. In a land of immense natural beauty, the Alaskan people are an oft-forgotten part of the brew.

Alaska's economic, political and social chatter tends to follow hot-button national trends. Like the rest of the US, Alaskans grapple with resource management, environmental responsibility, same-sex marriage, the legalization of marijuana, systemic poverty, recovery from the Great Recession, and a number of related social issues that mirror those in the Lower 48. But being so big, so isolated and so independent, Alaska's discourse often diverges from that of the mainstream at its very roots.

Pure, raw, unforgiving, and humongous in scale, Alaska is a place that arouses basic instincts and ignites what Jack London termed the 'call of the wild'. Yet, unlike London and his gutsy, gold-rush companions, visitors today will have a far easier time penetrating the region's vast, feral wilderness. Indeed, one of the beauties of the 49th state is its accessibility. Nowhere else in North America is it so easy to climb an unclimbed mountain, walk where – quite possibly – no human foot has trodden before, or sally forth into a national park that gets fewer annual visitors than the International Space Station.

People-watching takes second place to wildlife-spotting in a state where brown bears snatch leaping salmon out of angry waterfalls and curious moose pose majestically on national park roadsides. But the real thrill for wilderness purists is to go off in search of fauna in its natural habitat. Fly out into unguarded backcountry and you'll quickly get the sense of swapping your seat on a bush plane for one in the food chain. The landscapes of the far north might be the domain of musk oxen, gray wolves and bears, but, keep your wits about you, and they'll quietly accept you as a guest.

Alaska is, without a doubt, America's grittiest outdoor playground where skilled bush pilots land with pinpoint accuracy on crevasse-riddled glaciers, and backcountry guiding companies take bravehearts on bracing paddles down almost virgin rivers. With scant phone coverage and a dearth of hipster-friendly coffee bars to plug in your iPad, this is a region for 'doing' rather than observing. Whether you go it alone with bear-spray and a backpack, or place yourself in the hands of an experienced 'sourdough' (Alaskan old-timer), the rewards are immeasurable.

Sights in Alaska

Denali, Mountain in Denali National Park

What makes 20,237ft Denali (formerly Mt McKinley) one of the world's great scenic mountains is the sheer independent rise of its bulk. McKinley begins at a base of just 2000ft, which means that on a clear day you will be transfixed by over 18,000 feet of ascending rock, ice and snow. By contrast, Mt Everest, no slouch itself when it comes to memorable vistas, only rises 12,000 feet from its base on the Tibetan Plateau.

Despite its lofty heights, the mountain is not visible from the park entrance or the nearby campgrounds and hotel. Your first glimpse of it comes between Mile

9 and Mile 11 on Park Rd, if you're blessed with a clear day. The rule of thumb stressed by the National Park Service (NPS) rangers is that Mt McKinley is hidden two out of every three days, but that's a random example – it could be clear for a week and then hidden for the next month. While the 'Great One' might not be visible for most of the first 15 miles of Park Rd, this is the best stretch to spot moose because of the proliferation of spruce and especially willow, the animal's favorite food. The open flats before Savage River are good for spotting caribou and sometimes brown bears.

Unalaska & Dutch Harbor

On the road from the ferry terminal to Unalaska and Dutch Harbor, two things catch your eye: concrete pillboxes and crab pots. In a nutshell, that's the story of these twin towns on Unalaska and Amaknak Islands: the pillboxes are a violent WWII reminder of the past, while the crab pots acknowledge the important role of commercial fishing in the towns' future.

Located at the confluence of the Pacific Ocean and the Bering Sea, one of the world's richest fisheries, Dutch Harbor is the only natural deep-water port in the Aleutians. More than 400 vessels call here each year from as many as 14 countries. From this industrialized port of canneries and fish-processing plants, the newly rebuilt Bridge to the Other Side arches over to the residential community of Unalaska.

The area, and Dutch Harbor in particular, shot into the limelight in 2007, when Discovery Channel's The Deadliest Catch (now in its 10th season) emerged as a popular TV reality show. Each week viewers tune in to watch crab boats and their crews battle four-story-high waves, icy temperatures and paralyzing fatigue, to fill their holds with a gold mine of king crab, before heading back to Dutch Harbor.

Ironically, since the dramatic crash of the king-crab fishery in 1982, it has been pollock, an unglamorous bottom fish, that has been the backbone of Unalaska and Dutch Harbor's economy. Pollock accounts for more than 80% of all seafood processed, and is the reason the towns have been the country's number-one commercial fishing port for the past 20 years. In 2006 Dutch Harbor set a record when 911 million lbs. of seafood, at an export value of $165 million, crossed its docks.

During the 1970s Unalaska and Dutch Harbor were Alaska's version of the Wild West, with drinks, money and profanity flowing freely at every bar in town. With the crash of the king crab, the towns became more community-oriented, and with the recent drop of the pollock fishery, residents are now trying to survive another downturn in the boom-and-bust cycle of fishing.

Unfortunately, short-time visitors returning on the ferry don't have an opportunity to soak in the color and unique character of these towns. To stay longer, you need to splurge on an expensive airline ticket. Those who do discover that a few days in Unalaska and Dutch Harbor can be a refreshing cure from an overdose of RVs, cruise ships and tour buses.

Kodiak Island

Kodiak is the island of plenty. Consider its famous brown bears, the largest ursine creatures in the world. Thanks to an unblemished ecosystem and an unlimited diet of rich salmon that spawn in its lakes and rivers, adult male bears can weigh up to 1400lb. Part of the wider Kodiak archipelago and the second largest island in the US after Hawaii's Big Island, Kodiak acts as a kind of ecological half-way house between the forested Alaskan panhandle and the treeless Aleutian Islands. Its velvety green mountains and sheltered ice-free bays were the site of the earliest Russian settlement in Alaska and are still home to one of the US's most important fishing fleets.

Largely off the big cruise-ship circuit, the island's main attraction – beyond the obvious lure of its bears – is its quiet Alaskan authenticity. Only a small northeastern section of Kodiak is populated. The rest is roadless wilderness protected in the Kodiak National Wildlife Refuge.

Elsewhere, Kodiak harbors one of the largest coastguard stations in the US, hides smatterings of abandoned WWII defenses and retains some genuine Russian colonial heritage. On a (rare) sunny day it's a sublime place to be.

Anchorage Museum

Price: adult/child $15/7

Hours: summer 9am-6pm

Contact: http://www.anchoragemuseum.org

Location: 625 C Street, Anchorage, USA

What was once simply Alaska's best museum is now a world-class facility thanks to the 2010, $106 million expansion of Anchorage's cultural jewel. The West Wing, a four-story, shimmering, mirrored facade, added 80,000 sq. ft. to what was already the largest museum in the state. Its flagship exhibit is the Smithsonian Arctic Studies Center with more than 600 Alaska Native objects – art, tools, masks and household implements – which was previously housed in Washington DC.

It's the largest Alaska Native collection in the state and it's surrounded by large video screens showing contemporary Native life. Nearby is the Listening Space where you can listen to storytellers and natural sounds from Arctic Alaska.

The museum also contains the Imaginarium Discovery Center, a hands-on science center for children that was previously housed in a separate downtown location. On the 1st floor of the original East Wing you will still find the Art of the North Gallery, with entire rooms of Alaskan masters Eustace Ziegler and Sydney Laurence. On the 2nd floor, the Alaska History Gallery is filled with life-size dioramas that trace 10,000 years of human settlement, from early subsistence villages to modern oil dependency.

There are also galleries devoted to traveling art exhibits, a planetarium and the KidSpace Gallery designed for young children (and their parents) to explore the worlds of art, history and science through hands-on play. Clearly, this is a place where you can spend an entire afternoon.

Aleutian WWII National Historic Area

Location: Unalaska & Dutch Harbor, USA

In 1996 Congress created this 134-acre national historic area to commemorate the bloody events of WWII that took place on the Aleutian Islands.

To learn about the 'Forgotten War,' begin at the Aleutian WWII Visitor Center, near the airport, in the original air-control tower built in 1942. Downstairs, exhibits relive the Aleutian campaign, including the bombing of Dutch Harbor by the Japanese. Upstairs is the re-created air-control tower, and in a theater you can watch documentaries about the war.

Most of the park preserves Fort Schwatka, on Mt Ballyhoo, the highest coastal battery ever constructed in the US. Looming nearly 1000ft above the storm-tossed waters of the Bering Sea, the Army fort encompassed more than 100 concrete observation posts, command stations and other structures built to withstand earthquakes and 100mph winds. The gun mounts here are still among the best preserved in the country, and include tunnels and bunkers that allowed gunners to cart ammunition from one side of the mountain to the other.

The 1634ft mountain of military artifacts is behind the airport and can be reached on foot or by vehicle via Ulakta Rd, picked up half a mile north of the ferry terminal, along Ballyhoo Rd. If on foot, the gravel road is an hour's climb to the top, but the views of Unalaska Island on the way up, and on top, are excellent. Pick up the free Fort Schwatka Self-Guided Tour brochure at the visitor center.

Alaska Native Heritage Center

Price: adult/child $25/17

Hours: 9am-5pm

Contact: http://www.alaskanative.net, 330-8000

Location: 8800 Heritage Center Dr, Anchorage, USA

To experience Alaska Native culture firsthand, you can travel to the Bush or come to this 26-acre center and see how humans survived – and thrived – before central heating. This is much more than just a museum: it represents a knowledge bank of language, art and culture that will survive no matter how many sitcoms are crackling through the Alaskan stratosphere. It's a labor of love, and of incalculable value.

The main building houses meandering exhibits on traditional arts and sciences – including kayaks and rain gear that rival outdoors department store REI's best offerings. It also features various performances, among them the staccato Alaghanak song, lost for 50 years: the center collected bits and pieces of the traditional song from different tribal elders and reconstructed it. Outside, examples of typical structures from the Aleut, Yupik, Tlingit and other tribes are arranged around a picturesque lake. Docents explain the ancient architects' cunning technology: check out wooden panels that shrink in the dry summers (allowing light and air inside) but expand to seal out the cold during the wet winter. Dog cart rides and private and audio tours are all available for an extra charge.

Arizona

From the vastness of the Grand Canyon to Sedona's red rocks and the living Sonoran Desert, Arizona's landscapes are awe-inspiring. The state's spectacular canyons, blooming deserts, raging rivers, petrified forests, and scenic mountains enthrall lovers of the outdoors in pursuit of hiking, rafting, golf, or picturesque spots to watch the sunset. But there is more to Arizona than beautiful vistas. World-renowned spas in Phoenix provide plenty of pampering, while Native American cultures thrive throughout the state.

Arizona is made for road trips. Yes, the state has its showstoppers – Monument Valley, the Grand Canyon, Cathedral Rock – but it's the drives between these icons and others that really breathe life and context into a trip. For a dose of mom-and-pop friendliness, follow Route 66 into Flagstaff. To understand the sheer will of Arizona's mining barons, take a twisting drive through rugged Jerome. Native American history becomes contemporary as you drive past the inhabitants of a mesa-top Hopi village dating back 1000 years.

Controversies about hot-button issues – immigration, gay rights – have grabbed headlines recently, but these legislative issues are perhaps best left to the politicians, here only temporarily. The majestic beauty of the Grand Canyon, the saguaro-dotted deserts of Tucson, the sunset glow of Camelback Mountain and the red rocks of Sedona… they're here for the duration.

Sights in Arizona

Fort Bowie National Historic Site

Hours: trail sunrise to sunset; visitor center Sat & Sun 8am-4pm May–mid-Oct, varies seasonally

Contact: http://www.nps.gov/fobo, 520-847-2500

Location: Old Fort Bowie Rd, Southern Arizona, USA

Somewhere between the abandoned stagecoach stop and the sun-bleached cemetery, it hits you: this hike is a little spooky. Why? Because the 1.5-mile trail to Fort Bowie is the closest you'll come to time travel in the Southwest. The fort was established in 1862 in response to raids by the Chiricahua Apache, and the interpretive trail through this lonely place passes violent skirmish sites.

As you walk, you can easily imagine Apache warriors watching your every move from hiding places on the rocky hills that flank the trail. To flip the picture, the trail returns to the parking lot along the ridge of one of those very hills, offering the Apache perspective of the activity below. In the 1880s and 1890s, that activity would have been pioneers and soldiers invading your turf.

The fort itself is mostly in ruins, but black-and-white photos beside various buildings illuminate the 19th-century scene. The fort's location was strategic: it's close to the regionally important Apache Spring, which sits beside the trail. Inside the visitor center, check out the heliograph. This mirrored device was placed on a nearby hilltop to send messages to other heliographs along a series of lofty military outposts.

To get here, Follow Hwy 186 south from Willcox and the I-10 for 22 miles to the turnoff. Here, an unpaved but graded road, with mileage signs, runs 8 miles east to the trailhead.

Musical Instrument Museum

Price: adult/child 13-19yr/under 13yr $18/14/10

Hours: 9am-5pm Mon-Sat, 10am-5pm Sun, to 9pm first Fri of the month

Contact: http://www.themim.org, 480-478-6000

Location: 4725 E Mayo Blvd, Greater Phoenix, USA

From Uganda thumb pianos to Hawaiian ukuleles to Indonesian boat lutes, the ears have it at this lively museum that celebrates the world's musical instruments. More than 200 countries and territories are represented within five regional galleries, where music and video performances begin as you stop beside individual displays. You can also bang a drum in the Experiences Gallery and listen to Taylor Swift rock out in the Artist Gallery.

The wireless headsets are a necessity, but simple to use – just don't dash between the Alice Cooper and the Fife & Drums displays in the United States gallery! The museum is 20 miles north of downtown Phoenix, just off Hwy 101.

Heard Museum

Price: adult/child 6-12yr & student/senior $18/7.50/13.50

Hours: 9:30am-5pm Mon-Sat, 11am-5pm Sun

Contact: http://www.heard.org, 602-252-8848

Location: 2301 N Central Ave, Greater Phoenix, USA

This extraordinary museum spotlights the history, life, arts and culture of Native American tribes in the Southwest. Visitors will find art galleries, ethnographic displays, a get-creative kids exhibit and an unrivaled Hopi kachina gallery (many of the pieces were a gift from Barry Goldwater). The Heard emphasizes quality over quantity and is one of the best museums of its kind in America.

The moving Boarding School Experience gallery examines the controversial federal policy of removing Native American children from their families and sending them to remote boarding schools in order to 'Americanize' them. Keep a lookout for unexpected treasures – like the Harry Potter bowl tucked amongst more traditional pottery. Guided tours run at noon, 2pm and 3pm at no extra charge. Overall, allow two to three hours to explore. Also check out the busy events schedule, the well-stocked bookstore and the superb gift shop.

Parking is free. Valley Metro light-rail stops beside the downtown museum at Encanto/Central Ave.

Arizona-Sonora Desert Museum

Price: adult/child 13-17yr $19.50/15.50

Hours: 8:30am-5pm Oct-Feb, 7:30am-5pm Mar-Sep, to 10pm Sat Jun-Aug

Contact: http://www.desertmuseum.org, 520-883-2702

Location: 2021 N Kinney Rd, Tucson, USA

Home to cacti, coyotes and palm-sized hummingbirds, this ode to the Sonoran desert is one part zoo, one part botanical garden and one part museum – a trifecta that'll entertain young and old for easily half a day. Desert denizens, from precocious coatis to playful prairie dogs, inhabit natural enclosures. The grounds are thick with desert plants, and docents give demonstrations.

There are two walk-through aviaries, a mineral exhibit inside a cave, a half-mile desert trail and an underground exhibit with windows into ponds where beavers and otters frolic. Strollers and wheelchairs are available, and there's a gift shop, art gallery, restaurant and cafe. A tip: wear a hat and walking shoes, and remember that the big cats are most active in the morning. The museum is off Hwy 86, about 12 miles west of Tucson, near the western section of Saguaro National Park.

Museum of Northern Arizona

Price: adult/senior/child 10-17y $10/9/6

Hours: 10am-5pm Mon-Sat, noon-5pm Sun

Contact: http://www.musnaz.org, 928-774-5213

Location: 3101 N Fort Valley Rd, Flagstaff, USA

An attractive Craftsman-style stone building amid a pine grove, this small but excellent museum spotlights local Native American archaeology, history and culture, as well as geology, biology and the arts. It's on the way to the Grand Canyon, and makes a wonderful introduction to human and natural history of the region.

From May through August, the museum hosts recommended Thirsty Thursdays ($5, 5pm to 9pm), with storytelling, dancing and hands-on events in the museum courtyard. One night Lowell Observatory may come with their lunar telescope, and another the Arboretum puts on a raptor show. There's a cash bar, and guests have full access to the museum. Check the website for a calendar of events, workshops and field classes.

Arkansas

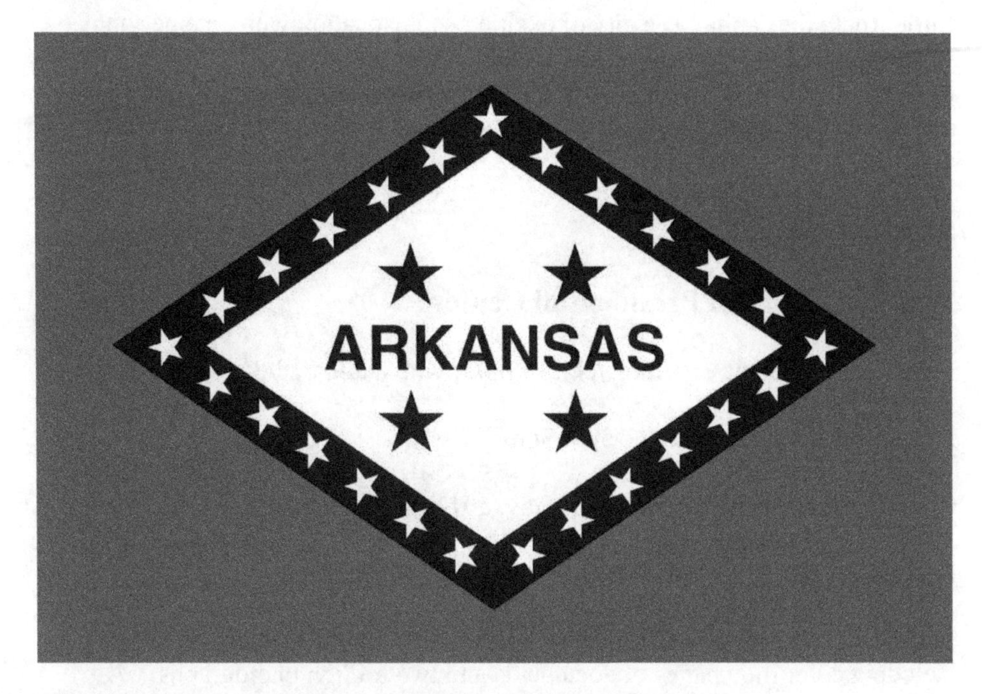

Forming the mountainous joint between the Midwest and the Deep South, Arkansas (ar-kan-saw) is an often-overlooked treasure of swift rushing rivers, dark leafy hollows, crenellated granite outcrops and the rugged spine of the Ozark and the Ouachita (wash-ee-tah) mountains. The entire state is blessed with exceptionally well-presented state parks and tiny, empty roads crisscrossing dense forests that let out onto breathtaking vistas and gentle pastures dotted with grazing horses. Mountain towns juke between Christian fundamentalism, hippie communes and biker bars, yet all of these divergent cultures share a love of their home state's stunning natural beauty.

Arkansas, "The Natural State," rolls out a welcome mat of lush terrain. The Ozark and Ouachita mountain ranges cradle northern and western regions, draping 10 scenic byways in a tapestry of brilliant fall color. To the east, Delta farmland is as rich as her musical heritage. Further south, tall pines populate the Timberlands. Overall, more 600,000 acres of lakes and 9,700 miles of streams and rivers make the state a prime playground for outdoor enthusiasts who enjoy fishing, float trips and water sports, hunting, and camping. A network of trails provides routes for mountain bikes, motorcycles, horses, hikers, and all-terrain vehicles. Seven national park sites plus 2.5 million acres of national forests and 52 state parks preserve and interpret Arkansas's diverse heritage, traditions, and natural resources.

Little Rock, the capital, is a city of exciting sophistication with an emerging culinary landscape. And a burgeoning arts culture in Bentonville — anchored by the renowned Crystal Bridges Museum of American Art — is the most recent capstone to the thriving, small, arts towns of Hot Springs and Eureka Springs.

Sights in Arkansas

William J Clinton Presidential Center

Price: adult/students & seniors/child $7/5/3, with audio $10/8/6

Hours: 9am-5pm Mon-Sat, 1-5pm Sun

Contact: http://www.clintonlibrary.gov, 501-748-0419

Location: 1200 President Clinton Ave, Little Rock, USA

This library houses the largest archival collection in presidential history, including 80 million pages of documents and two million photographs (although there's not a lot related to a certain intern scandal.). The entire experience feels like a time travel journey to the 1990s. Peruse the full-scale replica of the Oval Office, the exhibits on all stages of Clinton's life, or gifts from visiting dignitaries. The complex is built to environmentally friendly 'green' standards.

Riverfront Park

Contact: 501-371-6848

Location: LaHarpe Boulevard, Little Rock, USA

Just northwest of downtown, Riverfront Park rolls pleasantly along the Arkansas River and both pedestrians and cyclists take advantage of this fantastic city park. It's a truly fine integration of a landscape feature (the river) into an urban setting. You can't miss the Big Dam Bridge, a pedestrian-cyclist-only span that connects 17 miles of multiuse trails which form a complete loop thanks to the renovation of the Clinton Presidential Park Bridge.

NPS Visitor Center

Hours: 9am-5pm

Contact: http://www.nps.gov/hosp, 501-620-6715

Location: 369 Central Ave, Hot Springs, USA

On Bathhouse Row, set up in the 1915 Fordyce bathhouse, the NPS visitor center and museum has exhibits about the park's history, first as a Native

American free-trade zone, and later as a turn-of-the-20th-century European spa. Most fascinating are the amenities and standards set forth by an early-20th-century spa; the stained-glass work and Greek statues are opulent, but we could pass on the bare white walls, grout and electro-shock therapy.

California

California's endless wonders, from Yosemite National Park to Disneyland, are both natural and man-made. Soul-satisfying wilderness often lies close to urbane civilization. With the iconic Big Sur coast, dramatic Mojave Desert, and majestic Sierra Nevada mountains, sunny California indulges those in search of great surfing, hiking, and golfing. Other pleasures await, too: superb food in San Francisco, studio tours in Los Angeles, winery visits and spas in Napa and Sonoma. Follow a beach picnic with a city stroll and live the California dream.

From towering redwood forests in foggy Northern California to perfectly sun-kissed surf beaches in Southern California, this Golden State alongside the Pacific is a prize.

Don't be fooled by its perpetually fresh outlook and gung-ho attitude: California is older than it seems. Coastal bluffs and snowy peaks were created over millennia of tectonic upheavals that have threatened to shake California right off the continent. After unchecked 19th-century mining, logging and oil-drilling threatened to undermine the state's natural splendors, California's pioneering environmentalists – including John Muir and the Sierra Club – rescued old-growth trees and spurred the creation of national and state parks that still astound visitors today.

The wonder about hitting California's highways and byways is that things get more dramatic with every winding mile you detour from the big cities – trees get bigger, picturesque towns cuter and beaches more idyllic. Hug scenic oceanfront cliffs on Hwys 1 and 101 from Mexico to Oregon, or take an equally winding jaunt through historic Gold Country along Hwy 49. Follow pastoral back roads between vineyards in California's many wine countries (it's not just Napa), or take a weekend for a loop drive around Lake Tahoe. It's enough for a lifetime of road trips.

From the Gold Rush to the dot-com bubble, California has survived extreme booms and busts, often getting by on its wits. Hollywood still makes most of the world's movies and TV shows, fed by a vibrant performing arts scene on stages across the state. Trends are kick-started here not by moguls in offices, but by motley crowds of surfers, artists and dreamers concocting the out-there ideas behind anything from skateboarding to biotechnology. If you linger in art galleries, cafes and bars, you may actually see the future coming.

Because California produces most of the fresh produce in the US, minor menu decisions here can have nationwide impact. Every time they sit down to eat, Californians take trend-setting stands on mealtime moral dilemmas: certified organic versus spray-free, farm-to-table versus urban-garden-grown, veganism versus grass-fed humanely raised meats. But no matter what you order, it's likely to be local and creative, and it had better be good. For a chaser, California produces over 90% of the nation's wine-making grapes, and has twice as many breweries as any other state.

Sights in California

Golden Gate Bridge

Price: northbound free, southbound $6.25-7.25

Contact: http://www.goldengatebridge.org/visitors, 877-229-8655

Location: Hwy 101, San Francisco, USA

San Franciscans have passionate perspectives on every subject, especially their signature landmark, though everyone agrees that it's a good thing that the navy didn't get its way over the bridge's design – naval officials preferred a hulking concrete span, painted with caution-yellow stripes, over the soaring art-deco design of architects Gertrude and Irving Murrow and engineer Joseph B Strauss, which, luckily, won the day.

As far as best views go, cinema buffs believe Hitchcock had it right: seen from below at Fort Point, the 1937 bridge induces a thrilling case of Vertigo. Fog aficionados prefer the north-end lookout at Marin's Vista Point, to watch gusts billow through bridge cables like dry ice at a Kiss concert.

To see both sides of the Golden Gate debate, hike or bike the 1.7-mile span. MUNI bus 28 runs to the parking lot, and pedestrians and cyclists can cross the bridge on sidewalks. For drivers, bridge tolls are billed electronically to your vehicle's license plate; for details, see www.goldengate.org/tolls.

Muir Woods National Monument

Price: adult/child $10/free

Hours: 8am-8pm mid-Mar–mid-Sep, to 7pm mid-Sep–early Oct, to 6pm Feb–mid-Mar & early Oct-early Nov, to 5pm early Nov-Jan

Contact: http://www.nps.gov/muwo, 415-388-2595

Location: 1 Muir Woods Rd, Muir Woods National Monument, USA

Wander among an ancient stand of the world's tallest trees in 550-acre Muir Woods. The 1-mile Main Trail Loop is a gentle walk alongside Redwood Creek to the 1000-year-old trees at Cathedral Grove; it returns via Bohemian Grove, where the tallest tree in the park stands 254ft high. The Dipsea Trail is a good 2-mile hike up to the top of aptly named Cardiac Hill. Come midweek to avoid crowds; otherwise arrive early morning or late afternoon.

No camping or picnicking is permitted. Because the parking lot is often full, ride the seasonal Muir Woods Shuttle. You can also walk down into Muir Woods by taking trails from the Panoramic Hwy, such as the Bootjack Trail from the Bootjack picnic area, or from Mt Tamalpais' Pantoll Station campground, along the Ben Johnson Trail.

TCL Chinese Theatre

Price: Tours & movie tickets adult/senior/child from $16/15/14

Contact: http://www.tclchinesetheatres.com, 323-461-3331

Location: 6925 Hollywood Blvd, Los Angeles, USA

Ever wondered what it's like to be in George Clooney's shoes? Just find his footprints in the forecourt of this world-famous movie palace. The exotic pagoda theater – complete with temple bells and stone heaven dogs from China – has shown movies since 1927 when Cecil B DeMille's The King of Kings first flickered across the screen.

To see the inside, buy a movie ticket or join a half-hour guided tour offered throughout the day (check in at the gift shop). Of course, most Tinseltown tourists are content to find out how big Arnold's feet really are or to search for Betty Grable's legs or Whoopi Goldberg's braids.

Alcatraz

Price: day tours adult/child/family $33/21/100, night tours adult/child $40/24

Hours: call center 8am-7pm, ferries depart Pier 33 half-hourly 8:45am-3:50pm, night tours 5:55pm & 6:30pm

Contact: http://www.nps.gov/alcatraz, 415-981-7625

Location: San Francisco, USA

Alcatraz: for over 150 years, the name has given the innocent chills and the guilty cold sweats. Over the decades, it's been the nation's first military prison, a forbidding maximum-security penitentiary and disputed territory between Native American activists and the FBI. No wonder that first step you take onto 'the Rock' seems to cue ominous music: dunh-dunh-dunnnnh!

It all started innocently enough back in 1775, when Spanish lieutenant Juan Manuel de Ayala sailed the San Carlos past the 22-acre island he called Isla de Alcatraces (Isle of the Pelicans). In 1859 a new post on Alcatraz became the first US West Coast fort, and soon proved handy as a holding pen for Civil War deserters, insubordinates and those who had been court-martialed. Among the prisoners were Native American scouts and 'unfriendlies,' including 19 Hopis who refused to send their children to government boarding schools where speaking Hopi and practicing their religion were punishable by beatings. By 1902 the four cell blocks of wooden cages were rotting, unsanitary and otherwise ill-equipped for the influx of US soldiers convicted of war crimes in the Philippines. The army began building a new concrete military prison in 1909, but upkeep was expensive and the US soon had other things to worry about: WWI, financial ruin and flappers.

When the 18th Amendment to the Constitution declared selling liquor a crime in 1922, rebellious Jazz Agers weren't prepared to give up their tipple – and gangsters kept the booze coming. Authorities were determined to make a public example of criminal ringleaders, and in 1934 the Federal Bureau of Prisons took over Alcatraz as a prominent showcase for its crime-fighting efforts. 'The Rock' averaged only 264 inmates, but its roster read like an America's Most Wanted list. A-list criminals doing time on Alcatraz included Chicago crime boss Al 'Scarface' Capone, dapper kidnapper George 'Machine Gun' Kelly, hot-headed Harlem mafioso and sometime poet 'Bumpy' Johnson, and Morton Sobell, the military contractor found guilty of Soviet espionage along with Julius and Ethel Rosenberg.

Today, first-person accounts of daily life in the Alcatraz lockup are included on the award-winning audio tour provided by Alcatraz Cruises. But take your headphones off for just a moment, and notice the sound of carefree city life traveling across the water: this is the torment that made perilous escapes into rip tides worth the risk. Though Alcatraz was considered escape-proof, in 1962 the Anglin brothers and Frank Morris floated away on a makeshift raft and were never seen again. Security and upkeep proved prohibitively expensive, and finally the island prison was abandoned to the birds in 1963.

Native Americans claimed sovereignty over the island in the '60s, noting that Alcatraz had long been used by the Ohlone as a spiritual retreat, yet federal authorities refused their proposal to turn Alcatraz into a Native American study center. Then on the eve of Thanksgiving 1969, 79 Native American activists swam to the island and took it over. During the next 19 months, some 5600 Native Americans would visit the occupied island. Public support eventually pressured President Richard Nixon to restore Native territory and strengthen self-rule for Native nations in 1970. Each Thanksgiving Day since 1975, an 'Un-Thanksgiving' ceremony has been held at dawn on Alcatraz, with Native leaders and supporters showing their determination to reverse the course of colonial history. After the government regained control of the island, it became a national park, and by 1973 had already become a major draw. Today the cell blocks, 'This Is Indian Land' water-tower graffiti and rare wildlife are all part of the attraction.

Hearst Castle

Price: tours adult/child 5-12yr from $25/12

Hours: from 9am

Contact: http://www.hearstcastle.org, 800-444-4445

Location: 750 Hearst Castle Rd, San Simeon, USA

Hearst Castle is a wondrous, historic, over-the-top homage to material excess, perched high on a hill. The estate sprawls across acres of lushly landscaped gardens, accentuated by shimmering pools and fountains, statues from ancient Greece and Moorish Spain and the ruins of what was in Hearst's day the world's largest private zoo (look for zebras grazing on the hillsides of neighboring Hearst Ranch). To see anything of this historic monument, you have to take a tour (try to book ahead).

The most important thing to know about William Randolph Hearst (1863–1951) is that he did not live like Citizen Kane. Not that Hearst wasn't bombastic, conniving and larger than life, but the moody recluse of Orson Welles' movie? Definitely not. Hearst also didn't call his 165-room estate a castle, preferring its official name, La Cuesta Encantada ('The Enchanted Hill'), or more often calling it simply 'the ranch.'

From the 1920s into the '40s, Hearst and Marion Davies, his longtime mistress (Hearst's wife refused to grant him a divorce), entertained a steady stream of the era's biggest movers and shakers. Invitations were highly coveted, but Hearst had his quirks – he despised drunkenness, and guests were forbidden to speak of death.

California's first licensed woman architect Julia Morgan based the main building, Casa Grande, on the design of a Spanish cathedral, and over the decades she catered to Hearst's every design whim, deftly integrating the spoils of his fabled European shopping sprees including artifacts from antiquity and pieces of medieval monasteries.

Much like Hearst's construction budget, the castle will devour as much of your time and money as you let it. In peak summer months, show up early enough and you might be able to get a same-day tour ticket, but it's always better to make reservations in advance. For holiday and evening tours, book at least two weeks to a month beforehand.

Tours usually depart starting at 9am daily, with the last leaving the visitor center for the 10-minute ride to the hilltop by 4pm (later in summer). There are three main tours: the guided portion of each lasts about an hour, after which you're free to wander the gardens and terraces, photograph the iconic Neptune Pool and soak up views. Best of all are Christmas holiday and springtime evening tours, featuring living-history re-enactors who escort you back in time to the castle's 1930s heyday.

Dress in plenty of layers: gloomy fog at the sea-level visitor center can turn into sunny skies at the castle's hilltop location, and vice versa. At the visitor center, a five-story-high theater shows a 40-minute historical film (free admission included with daytime tour tickets) about the castle and the Hearst family. Other facilities are geared for industrial-sized mobs of visitors. Before you leave, take a moment to visit the often-overlooked museum area at the back of the center.

It's closed on Thanksgiving, Christmas and New Year's Day, closing time varies throughout the year. RTA bus 15 makes a few daily round-trips to Hearst Castle via Cambria and Cayucos from Morro Bay ($2, 55 minutes), where you can transfer to bus 12 to San Luis Obispo.

San Diego Zoo

Price: 1-day admission adult/child from $50/40; 2-visit pass to zoo and/or safari park adult/child $90/70

Hours: 9am-9pm mid-Jun–early Sep, to 5pm or 6pm early Sep–mid-Jun

Contact: http://zoo.sandiego.org, 619-231-1515

Location: 2920 Zoo Dr, San Diego, USA

This justifiably famous zoo is one of SoCal's biggest attractions, showing more than 3000 animals representing more than 650 species in a beautifully landscaped setting, typically in enclosures that replicate their natural habitats. Its sister park is San Diego Zoo Safari Park in northern San Diego County.

Arrive early, as many of the animals are most active in the morning – though many perk up again in the afternoon. Pick up a map at the entrance to the zoo to find your own favorite exhibits.

The guided double-decker bus tour gives a good overview of the zoo with informative commentary: sitting downstairs puts you closer to the animals. Once you've made the loop, your ticket remains good for an express bus service in the park, a big help if you're unable to walk far. The Skyfari cable car goes right across the park and can save you some walking time, though there may be a line to get on it. Either way, you're going to do a lot of walking: carry quarters for the electric foot-massagers located around the park. Inquire about facilities for disabled visitors.

The koalas are so popular that Australians may be surprised to find them a sort of unofficial symbol of San Diego (they're featured in the Conrad Prebys Australian Outback exhibit), and the giant pandas run a close second. The Komodo dragon, an Indonesian lizard that can grow up to 10ft long, looks fearsome and strides menacingly around the reptile house.

Other bioclimatic environments include the 7.5-acre Elephant Odyssey; Tiger River, a re-created Asian rainforest; Gorilla Tropics, an African rainforest; and the Sun Bear Forest, where the Asian bears are famously playful.

Absolutely Apes is devoted to the apes of Indonesia, including orangutans and siamangs climbing in lush forests. The large, impressive Scripps Aviary and Rainforest Aviary have well-placed feeders to allow some close-up viewing. And you can walk right beneath 100 species of winged creatures inside the Owens Aviary. Finally, don't miss Africa Rocks, an 8-acre exhibit for African plants and animals, opening in 2017.

The zoo gardens are renowned and some of the plants are used for the specialized food requirements of particular animals. Pick up a brochure for the self-guided botanical gardens tour.

And, of course, the zoo is made for kids, from animal shows to a children's zoo exhibit (where youngsters can pet small critters). Both children and adults will enjoy the animal nursery, where you can see the zoo's newest arrivals. Babies are born every spring and summer.

To leave the zoo and return the same day, get a hand stamp from the information booth near the entrance. The zoo is located in the northern part of Balboa Park. The (free) parking lot and the zoo fill up on weekends. Bus 7 will get you there from downtown.

Colorado

Spectacular vistas, endless powder runs and mountain towns with echoes of the Old West. Colorado is a place that has forever beckoned people to adventure.

A playground for nature lovers and outdoor enthusiasts, Colorado has majestic landscapes, raging rivers, and winding trails perfect for activities from biking to rafting. The heart of the Rocky Mountains has scores of snow-capped summits towering higher than 14,000 feet and trails from easy to challenging for exploring them—as well as roads offering spectacular drives. Skiers flock to the slopes here for the champagne powder and thrilling downhill runs. Need a break from the outdoors? Urban adventures await in cool cities like Denver, Boulder, and Aspen.

The best known of the Rocky Mountain states, with the highest concentration of peaks above 14,000ft, Colorado owes its public adoration to the mountainous backbone that rises and rolls from the Front Range westward. But there are also mesas, desert canyons and sagebrush hills. Some 300-plus sunny days per year contribute to hiking, biking, river running and rock climbing that's unrivaled anywhere in the US West. Even during the peak summer season, when millions of tourists flood the state, visitors can still find solitude at a remote mountain lake or meadow, or atop a craggy summit. In Rocky Mountain National Park, the state's premier attraction, there are dozens of backcountry hikes and campsites that see few visitors – unless you count that moose or family of foxes that wandered by.

In the hulking shadow of the Rockies, Colorado's urban culture is vibrant and progressive. Industries like high tech, communications and education propel a robust economy. Former cow town Denver boasts iconic sports arenas, a revitalized downtown and plenty of bike routes, breweries and hipster hangouts. Nearby university towns of Boulder and Fort Collins pair stunning natural settings with progressive vibes. Even Aspen is known almost as much for its summer music festival and think-tank intellect as its adventure opportunities. South of the Arkansas River, Colorado was once Mexico, and pockets of Hispanic culture still thrive. Native American culture persists in the Ute Mountain and Southern Ute Indian Reservations in southwest Colorado.

With heavy snowfalls and light powder, the long winters of the Colorado high country are the stuff of legend. Hares and mountain lions leave white tracks, boarders and skiers weave through pine forests and open bowls, and hearth fires roar in mountain lodges. With the longest ski run in the USA (Vail), some of the highest snowfall (Wolf Creek), and legendary ski-parking-lot BBQs (Arapahoe Basin), Colorado may have the best downhill skiing on earth. Remarkable cross-country and backcountry terrain bring a whole other dimension to winter – one where lift lines don't exist. If you're among the hard core, you can make turns from Halloween until early June. Iconic resorts like Aspen, Vail and Telluride attract visitors in droves, and after the last lift, parties kick into gear.

Sights in Colorado

Rocky Mountain National Park

Though Rocky Mountain National Park doesn't rank among the largest national parks in the USA (it's only 265,000 acres), it's rightly among one of the most popular, hosting four million visitors every year.

This is a place of natural spectacle on every scale: from hulking granite formations – many taller than 12,000ft, some over 130 million years old – to the delicate yellow burst of the glacier lily, one of the dozen alpine wildflowers that explode in a short, colorful life at the edge of receding snowfields for a few days every spring.

And though it tops many travelers' itineraries and can get maddeningly crowded, the park has miles of less-beaten paths, and the backcountry is a little-explored nature-lovers' wonderland. It's surrounded by some of the most pristine wild area in the west: Comanche Peak and Neota Wilderness Areas in the Roosevelt National Forest to the north and Indian Peaks Wilderness to the south. The jagged spine of the Continental Divide intersects the park through its middle. Excellent hiking trails crisscross alpine fields, skirt the edge of isolated high-altitude lakes and bring travelers to the wild, untamed heart of the Rockies.

Boulder

Twenty-five square miles surrounded by reality. That's the joke about Boulder that never goes away. The weather is perfect, the surroundings – stone Flatirons, gurgling creek, ponderosa trails and manicured college campus – beg idylling. And the populace – fit do-gooders with the beta on the best fair-trade coffee – seals the stereotype.

Boulder's mad love of the outdoors was officially legislated in 1967, when Boulder became the first US city to tax itself specifically to preserve open space. Thanks to such vision, people (and dogs) enjoy a number of city parks and open space while packs of cyclists whip up and down the Boulder Creek corridor.

In many ways it is Boulder, not Denver, that is the region's tourist hub. The city is about the same distance from Denver International Airport, and the hub puts you 45 minutes closer to the ski resorts west on I-70 and the extraordinary Rocky Mountain National Park.

Aspen

Here's a unique town, unlike any place else in the American West. It's a cocktail of cowboy grit, Euro panache, Hollywood glam, Ivy League brains, fresh powder, live music and lots of money. It's the kind of place where no matter the season you can bring on a head rush in countless ways. Perhaps you dropped into an extreme vertical run, or stomped to the crest of Buckskin Pass in under three hours? It could also come while relaxing at the local music festival, peering down into the bowl of a superpipe or climbing an ice wall. It's possible the horse-drawn sleigh took off too fast for you while you were peering over at yet another $10 million estate, or that cycling to the top of Independence Pass has left you exhausted but smiling. Then again it may have been that way-brainy conversation with a slurring but extraordinarily literate barfly.

Whatever and whomever you've seen, heard or done, there is a common Aspen cure-all. One that has served every Olympic champion, gonzo journalist, world-class musician, thinker, artist or actor that has ever arrived in this athletic, cultural, intellectual, artistic, absurd ski town. Simply take your body to the frothing hot tub under the stars and leave the head behind. But do bring the bottle. After all, Aspen is nothing if not a place of excellence, extravagance and, most of all, indulgence. Just remember, whatever you do, don't stand up too fast.

Dinosaur National Monument

Price: 7-day pass per vehicle $10

Hours: 24hr

Contact: http://www.nps.gov/dino

Location: off Hwy 40, Northern Colorado, USA

Straddling the Utah-Colorado state line, Dinosaur National Monument protects one of North America's largest dinosaur fossil beds, discovered here in 1909. Though both state's sections are beautiful, Utah has the bones. Don't miss the Quarry Exhibit (9am-4pm), which is an enclosed, partially-excavated wall of rock with more than 1600 bones protruding - quite the sight to see.

In summer, hours may be extended a little and you will have to take a shuttle to see the quarry; out of season you may be required to wait until a ranger-led caravan of cars is scheduled to drive up. From below the quarry parking lot, follow the Fossil Discovery Trail (2.2 miles round-trip) to see a few more giant femurs and such sticking out of the rock. The rangers' interpretive hikes are highly recommended. Plus, there's easily-accessible Native American rock art to see on the Utah side.

In Colorado, the Canyon Area is at a higher elevation - with some stunning overlooks - but is closed to snow until late spring. Both sections have numerous hiking trails, interpretive driving tours (brochures for sale), Green or Yampa river access and campgrounds ($8 to $15 per camp site). The Quarry portion of the park is 7 miles north of Jensen, UT, on Hwy 149. The Canyon Area is roughly 30 miles east, outside Dinosaur, CO.

Stations of the Cross

Location: cnr Hwys 142 & 159, San Luis, USA

Following a path up a small hill, local sculptor Huberto Maestas' 15 dramatic life-sized statues of Christ's crucifixion are a powerful testament to the Catholic heritage of communities near the 'Blood of Christ' Mountains. They are stationed along a 1-mile pathway, an excellent chance to stretch the legs.

Beginning with Jesus being condemned to death, the bronze statues continue through the Resurrection. From the crucifixion on the mesa summit during late afternoon sunsets you can observe the reddish light cast on the Sangre de Cristo mountain range, including Culebra Peak (14,069ft), giving the mountains their 'Blood of Christ' name. You can also look out over San Luis and its surrounding fields and pasture. For many years, San Luis residents re-enacted the capture, trial and crucifixion of Christ during Holy Week (Easter) and also made pilgrimages to the Stations of the Cross every Friday during Lent. During the Centennial Jubilee of the Sangre de Cristo Parish in 1986, parish members conceived the Stations of the Cross Shrine to formalize this re-enactment.

Pikes Peak

Price: highway per adult/child $12/5

Hours: 7:30am-8pm Jun-Aug, 7:30am-5pm Sep, 9am-3pm Oct-May

Contact: http://www.springsgov.com, 719-385-7325

Location: Colorado Springs, USA

Pikes Peak (14,110ft) may not be the tallest of Colorado's 54 14ers, but it's certainly the most famous. The Ute originally called it the Mountain of the Sun, an apt description for this majestic peak, which crowns the southern Front Range. Rising 7400ft straight up from the plains, over half a million visitors climb it every year.

Its location as the easternmost 14er has contributed heavily to its place in American myth. Zebulon Pike first made note of it in 1806 (he called it 'Grand Peak' but never made it to the top) when exploring the Louisiana Purchase, and Katherine Bates, a guest lecturer at Colorado College in 1893, wrote the original draft of America the Beautiful after reaching the summit.

Today there are three ways to ascend the peak: The Pikes Peak Hwy (about a five hour round-trip), which was built in 1915 by Spencer Penrose and winds 19 miles to the top from Hwy 24 west of town; the cog railway; and on foot via the Barr Trail.

Connecticut

Known for its commuter cities, New York's neighbor is synonymous with the affluent lanes and mansions of The Stepford Wives and TV's Gilmour Girls. In old-moneyed Greenwich, Litchfield Hills and the Quiet Corner, these representations ring true, although many regard the state as a mere stepping stone to the 'real' New England, of whose tourist boom Connecticut was spared.

The upside is that Connecticut retains a more 'authentic' feel. The downside is a slow decaying of former heavyweights like Hartford and New London, where visitors can ponder the price of progress and get enthused about urban renewal. New Haven, home of Yale University, is one such place rewiring itself as a vibrant cultural hub.

Dense with historical attractions and the kind of bucolic nature that continues to inspire artists as it has for over a century, Connecticut begs for your attention and a well-deserved spot on your New England itinerary.

You can travel from just about any point in Connecticut to any other in less than two hours, yet the land you traverse — fewer than 60 miles top to bottom and 100 miles across—is as varied as a drive across the country.

Connecticut's 253 miles of shoreline blows salty sea air over beach communities like Old Lyme and Stonington, while patchwork hills and peaked mountains fill the state's northwestern corner, and once-upon-a-time mill towns line rivers such as the Housatonic. Connecticut has seemingly endless farmland in the northeast, where cows might just outnumber people, as well as chic New York City bedroom communities such as Greenwich and New Canaan, where boutique shopping bags are the dominant species.

Just as diverse as the landscape are the state's residents, who numbered more than 3½ million at last count. There really is no such thing as the definitive "Connecticut Yankee." Yes, families can trace their roots back to the 1600s, when Connecticut was founded as one of the 13 original colonies, but the state motto is "He who transplanted still sustains." And so the face of the Nutmegger is that of the family from Naples now making pizza in New Haven and the farmer in Norfolk whose land dates back five generations, the grandmother in New Britain who makes the state's best pierogi and the ladies who lunch in Westport, the celebrity nestled in the Litchfield Hills and the Bridgeport entrepreneur working to close the gap between Connecticut's struggling cities and its affluent suburbs.

One quality all Connecticut Yankees have in common, however, is inventiveness; Nutmeggers are historically known for both their intellect and their desire to have a little fun. The nation's first public library opened in New Haven in 1656 and its first state house in Hartford in 1776. Tapping Reeve developed America's first law school in Litchfield in 1784, and West Hartford's Noah Webster published the first dictionary in 1806. On the fun side, Lake Compounce in Bristol was the country's first amusement park; Bethel's P. T. Barnum staged the first three-ring circus; and the hamburger, the lollipop, the Frisbee, and the Erector Set were all invented here.

Not surprisingly, Nutmeggers have a healthy respect for their history. For decades, Mystic Seaport, which traces the state's rich maritime past, has been the premier tourist attraction. Today, however, Foxwoods Casino near Ledyard, run by the Mashantucket Pequots, is North America's largest casino, drawing more than 40,000 visitors per day. Thanks in large part to these lures, not to mention rich cultural destinations, cutting-edge restaurants, shopping outlets, first-rate lodgings, and abundant natural beauty (including 92 state parks and 30 state forests), tourism is one of the state's leading industries. Exploring Connecticut reveals a small state that's big in appeal.

Sights in Connecticut

Yale University

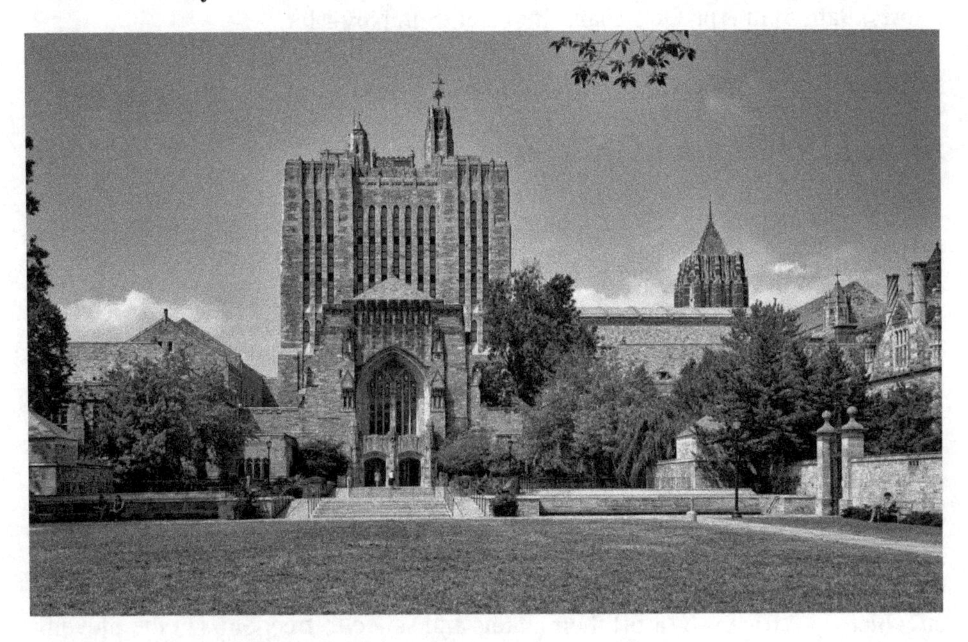

Hours: visitor center 9am-4:30pm Mon-Fri, 11am-4pm Sat & Sun

Contact: http://www.yale.edu/visitor, 203-432-2300

Location: cnr Elm & Temple Sts, New Haven, USA

Each year, thousands of high-school students make pilgrimages to Yale, nursing dreams of attending the country's third-oldest university, which boasts such notable alums as Noah Webster, Eli Whitney, Samuel Morse, and Presidents William H Taft, George HW Bush, Bill Clinton and George W Bush. You don't need to share the students' ambitions in order to take a stroll around the campus, just pick up a map at the Visitor Centre (at the address listed) or join a free, one-hour guided tour.

Although the tour overflows with tidbits about life at Yale, the guides refrain from mentioning the various secret societies and their buildings scattered around the campus, but feel free to ask them!

Mystic Seaport Museum

Price: adult/child $26/17

Hours: 9am-5pm Apr-Oct, 10am-4pm Thu-Sun Nov-Mar

Contact: http://www.mysticseaport.org, 860-572-0711

Location: 75 Greenmanville Ave, Mystic, USA

More than a museum, Mystic Seaport is the re-creation of an entire New England whaling village spread over 17 acres of the former George Greenman & Co Shipyard. To re-create the past, 60 historic buildings, four tall ships and almost 500 smaller vessels are gathered along the Mystic River. Interpreters staff the site and are glad to discuss traditional crafts and trades. Most illuminating are the demonstrations on such topics as ship rescue, oystering and whaleboat launching.

Visitors can board the Charles W Morgan (1841), the last surviving wooden whaling ship in the world; the LA Dunton (1921), a three-masted fishing schooner; or the Joseph Conrad (1882), a square-rigged training ship. The museum's exhibits include a replica of the 77ft schooner Amistad, the slave ship on which 55 Africans cast off their chains and sailed to freedom. (In the Steven Spielberg movie Amistad, the museum was used to stage many of the scenes that actually took place in colonial New London.)

At the Henry B DuPont Preservation Shipyard, you can watch large wooden boats being restored. Be sure not to miss the Wendell Building, which houses a fascinating collection of ships' figureheads and carvings. Close by is a small 'museum' (more like a playroom) for children aged seven years and under. The seaport also includes a small boat shop, jail, general store, chapel, school, pharmacy, sail loft, shipsmith and ship chandlery.

If the call of the sea beckons during your visit, you can visit the Boathouse and captain your own sailboat. Rides are also available on the 20ft Crosby catboat Breck Marshall ($7); and full-day charters to Fishers Island are possible aboard the 33ft Herreshoff auxiliary ketch Araminta ($375 per person, June to October). Week-long teen charters, sailing programs and boat-building workshops are regular summer sell outs, so book well in advance.

Wadsworth Atheneum

Price: adult/child $15/5

Hours: 11am-5pm Wed-Fri, from 10am Sat & Sun

Contact: http://www.thewadsworth.org, 860-278-2670

Location: 600 Main St, Hartford, USA

On September 19, 2015, the nation's oldest public art museum completed a five-year, $33-million renovation, renewing 32 galleries and 15 public spaces. The Wadsworth houses nearly 50,000 pieces of art in a castle-like Gothic Revival building. On display are paintings by members of the Hudson River School, including some by Hartford native Frederic Church; 19th-century impressionist works; 18th-century New England furniture; sculptures by Connecticut artist Alexander Calder; and an outstanding array of surrealist, postwar and contemporary works.

The renovation project also brought the Beaux-Arts Morgan Memorial Building back to its historic splendor, showcasing over 1000 works of European painting, sculpture and decorative arts.

Barely known outside art circles, the Wadsworth was founded by generous Hartford art lover Daniel Wadsworth, scion of one of the oldest settler families in Connecticut. His father made the family fortune in trade, manufacturing, banking and insurance, and Daniel bolstered the family's reputation with his marriage to Faith Trumbull, niece of celebrated artist John Trumbull. The museum was built on the site of the family home and Daniel donated its first Hudson River School paintings. Where Daniel left off, Elizabeth Hart Jarvis Colt, widow of Samuel Colt, picked up. In 1905 she bequeathed the museum more than 1000 items, purchased from the sale of Colt's weapons to the military.

As if the mind-blowing array of the permanent exhibits isn't enough, the Amistad Foundation Gallery has an outstanding collection of African American art and historical objects and the Matrix Gallery features works by contemporary artists.

On the first Thursday of the month the museum stays open until 8pm. Most evenings there are also lectures, which are open to the public and free.

New London

During its golden age in the mid-19th century, New London, then home to some 200 whaling vessels, was one of the largest whaling centers in the US and one of the wealthiest port cities. In 1858 the discovery of crude oil in Pennsylvania sent the value of whale oil plummeting and began a long period of decline for the city, from which it has never fully recovered. Even so, New London retains strong links with its seafaring past (the US Coast Guard Academy and US Naval Submarine Base are here) and its downtown is listed on the National Register of Historic Places.

Despite lacking the sanitized tourism push of nearby Mystic and Stonington, remnants of New London's glorious and opulent times are still evident throughout the city, making it one of Connecticut's most surprising destinations for those interested in history, architecture and urban sociology.

Mark Twain House & Museum

Price: adult/child $19/11

Hours: 9:30am-5:30pm, closed Tue Jan-Mar

Contact: http://www.marktwainhouse.org, 860-247-0998

Location: 351 Farmington Ave, Hartford, USA

For 17 years, encompassing the most productive period of his life, Samuel Langhorne Clemens (1835–1910) and his family lived in this striking orange-and-black brick Victorian house, which then stood in the pastoral area of the city called Nook Farm. Architect Edward Tuckerman Potter lavishly embellished it with turrets, gables and verandahs, and some of the interiors were done by Louis Comfort Tiffany. Admission to the house and museum is by guided tour only. Advance purchase is recommended.

Though Twain maintained that it was difficult to write in the house, it was here that he penned some of his most famous works, including The Adventures of Tom Sawyer, The Adventures of Huckleberry Finn and A Connecticut Yankee in King Arthur's Court. A tour, which focuses largely on the house's beautifully restored interior design, is included in the admission fee.

Delaware

Wee Delaware, the nation's second-smallest state (96 miles long and less than 35 miles across at its widest point) is overshadowed by its neighbors – and often overlooked by visitors to the Capital Region. And that's too bad, because Delaware has a lot more on offer than just tax-free shopping and chicken farms.

Long white sandy beaches, cute colonial villages, a cozy countryside and small-town charm characterize the state that happily calls itself the 'Small Wonder.'

Delaware's founding fathers signed the U.S. Constitution before others, earning Delaware the nickname "the First State." Although rich in colonial political history, today the state is a business leader — 64% of Fortune 500 companies are here. Shoppers love Delaware, too, as the state imposes no sales tax.

Varied landscapes keep Delaware from feeling like America's second-smallest state. Rolling hills and hardwood forests lay north. Vast tidal marshes and dunescapes line the shore. Gleaming corporate center Wilmington is a short train ride to New York, Philadelphia, and Washington, D.C. Find colonial

charm in New Castle, tourist bustle at Rehoboth Beach, and calm at Bombay Hook bird sanctuary in Smyrna.
Industrial giant E. I. du Pont dominated Delaware for generations. Many public institutions bear the du Pont name. Family estates and the company's early headquarters and gunpowder works are showplace museums. Major northern parks and preserves were carved from family holdings.

Most of the state lies on the flat, fertile Delmarva Peninsula. Until the mid-20th century, this region was devoted to agriculture, shipping, fishing, and shipbuilding. Towns display a diverse architectural legacy. Medieval elements appear in Lewes, settled by the Dutch in 1637. Rehoboth Beach's Victorian past emerges in gingerbread-style cottages.

Sights in Delaware

Air Mobility Command Museum

Price: admission free

Hours: 9am-4pm Tue-Sun

Contact: http://www.amcmuseum.org, 302-677-5938

Location: 1301 Heritage Rd, Dover, USA

If you're into aviation, you'll enjoy it; the nearby airfield is filled with restored vintage cargo and freight planes, including C-130s, a Vietnam War-era C-7 and World War 2 era "Flying Boxcar."

Dover Air Force Base (AFB) is a visible symbol of American military muscle and a poignant reminder of the cost of war. This is the location of the Department of Defense's largest mortuary, and traditionally the first stop on native soil for the remains of American service members killed overseas.

First State Heritage Park Welcome Center & Galleries

Hours: 9am-4:30pm Mon-Sat, 1:30-4:30pm Sun

Contact: http://www.destateparks.com/park/first-state-heritage, 302-739-9194

Location: 121 Martin Luther King Blvd N, Dover, USA

Delve into the history of Delaware at the First State Heritage Park, which serves as a welcome center for the city of Dover, the state of Delaware and the adjacent state house. This so-called 'park without boundaries' includes some two dozen historic sites within a few blocks of one another. Start out at the Welcome Center & Galleries, which has exhibitions exploring Delaware's history. You can also pick up more info here on other key sites nearby.

Bombay Hook National Wildlife Refuge

Price: admission per vehicle/pedestrian $4/2

Hours: sunrise-sunset

Contact: http://www.fws.gov/refuge/Bombay_Hook, 302-653-9345

Location: 2591 Whitehall Neck Rd, Delaware, USA

Hundreds of thousands of waterfowl use this protected wetland as a stopping point along their migration routes. A 12-mile wildlife driving trail, running through 16,251 acres of saltwater marsh, cordgrass and tidal mud flats, manages to encapsulate all of the soft beauty of the DelMarVa peninsula in one perfectly preserved ecosystem. There are also short walking trails and observation towers.

Florida

With its accessible and varied pleasures, Florida is a favorite of many. Drawn to the colonial charm of St. Augustine, Miami's pulsing nightlife, the glitz of Palm Beach, or the quiet expanse of the Everglades, almost all visitors find something to love here. From the powdery white beaches of the Panhandle to the vibrant coral reefs of the Florida Keys, the ocean is always calling — for sailing, fishing, diving, swimming, and other water sports. Stray off the path a few miles, and you might glimpse a bit of the Florida of old, including cigar-makers and mermaids.

A hundred worlds – from magic kingdoms and Latin American and Caribbean capitals to mangrove islands, wild wetlands and artist colonies – are all contained within this flat peninsula.

While many know Florida for beaches and theme parks, few understand this is one of the most populous states in the country, a bellwether for the American experiment. And that experiment – and this state – is more diverse than ever. From rural hunters and trappers in her geographically northern, culturally Southern climes, to Jewish transplants sitting side by side with Latin arrivals from every Spanish-speaking nation in the world, it's hard to beat Florida when it comes to experiencing the human tapestry at its most colorful and vibrant.

Tan, tropical Florida is smarter and more culturally savvy then her appearance suggests. This state, particularly South Florida, has a reputation for attracting eccentrics and idiosyncratic types from across the United States, Latin America and Europe. Many of these folks, and their descendants, have gone on to create or provide patronage for the arts, as evidenced by enormous concert spaces in Miami, a glut of museums on the Gulf Coast, and a long, literary tradition – Florida has produced more than her fair share of great American authors.

Sights in Florida

Miami

Miami is so many things, but to most visitors, it’s mainly glamour, condensed into urban form.

They’re right. The archaic definition of ‘glamour’ is a kind of spell that mystifies a victim. Well, they call Miami the Magic City. And it is mystifying. In its beauty, certainly: the clack of a model’s high heels on Lincoln Rd, the teal sweep of Biscayne Bay, flowing cool into the wide South Florida sky; the blood-orange fire of the sunset, setting the downtown skyline aflame.

Then there’s less-conventional beauty: a poetry slam in a converted warehouse, or a Venezuelan singing Metallica en español in a Coral Gables karaoke bar, or the passing shalom/buenas días traded between Orthodox Jews and Cuban exiles.

Miami is so many things. All glamorous, in every sense of the word. You could spend a fun lifetime trying to escape her spell.

Walt Disney World

'Here in Florida, we have something special we never enjoyed at Disneyland…the blessing of size. There's enough land here to hold all the ideas and plans we can possibly imagine'.
-Walt Disney

Minutes before the Magic Kingdom opens, Alice in Wonderland, Cinderella, Donald Duck and others stand where all can see them, sing 'Zippidee Doo Dah' and throw sparkly Mickey Mouse confetti into the crowds. They dash off on an open-windowed train, the gates open, and children, adults, honeymooners, grandparents and everyone in between enter the park, some strolling, others dashing down the impeccably clean Main Street toward Cinderella's Castle. That iconic image is as American as the Grand Canyon, a place as loaded with myth and promises of hope as the Statue of Liberty. If only for these few minutes, this is indeed the Happiest Place on Earth.

Yes, there will be lines with seemingly endless waiting and sure, you'll spend more money than you intended on a Mickey Mouse sweatshirt that you wouldn't have dreamed of buying before you came. That Pirates of the Caribbean ride may not be everything everyone said it'd be, and you may get stuck behind the guy who spreads his shopping bags and empty stroller parallel to the curb so your kids can't sit down to see the parade ('I got here first,' he growls). You'll return to the hotel exhausted and aching, vaguely dissatisfied with the day's meals, carrying your sleeping Belle, her face painted with now-smudging sparkles and her poofy yellow dress stained with ice cream, cotton candy and that green punch so tantalizingly named Tinker Bell and Friends. You swear that next time you'll take a real vacation… Until those last minutes before you fall asleep, when everything you need to do is done and you're finally relaxing in bed, your eyes closed. You see your child's face staring adoringly at Winnie the Pooh as he gives a big ol' bear hug, or your child's arms reaching out to grab the Donald Duck that pops out from the 3-D movie. And it's OK. That beach vacation can wait.

Walt Disney World itself is like a child. One minute, you think you can't take another cafeteria-style restaurant serving fried food and bad coffee or another second in an overstuffed shuttle bus. And the next, it does something right – maybe it's the fireworks, maybe it's a particular turn in a particular ride, maybe it's the corny joke of the guy who drives the horse-drawn carriage down Main Street.

And all is forgiven.

The Everglades

There is no wilderness in America quite like the Everglades. Called the 'River of Grass' by its initial Native American inhabitants, this is not just a wetland, or a swamp, or a lake, or a river, or a prairie, or a grassland – it is all of the above, twisted together into a series of soft horizons, long vistas, sunsets that stretch across your entire field of vision and the creeping grin of a large population of dinosaur-era reptiles.

When you watch anhinga flexing their wings before breaking into a corkscrew dive, or the slow, Jurassic flap of a great blue heron gliding over its domain, or the sun kissing miles of unbroken saw grass as it sets behind humps of skeletal cypress domes, you'll have an idea of what we're speaking of. In a nation where natural beauty is measured by its capacity for drama, the Everglades subtly, contentedly flows on.

Key West

The Keys, like any frontier, have always been defined by two 'E's': edge and eccentric. And when it came to the far frontier, the very edge, the last outpost of America – out here, only the most eccentric would dare venture. And thus, Key West: the most beautifully strange (or is it strangely beautiful?) island in the US. This place is seriously screwy, in a (mostly) good way. There's no middle separating the high and low brow, that's for sure. On one side of the road, literary festivals, Caribbean villas, tropical noir and expensive art galleries. On the other, an S&M fetishist parade, frat boys vomiting on their sorority girlfriends and 'I Love to Fart' T-shirts (seriously).

Where the other Keys are a bit more country-fried, Key West, a historical haven for homosexuals and artists, remains a little more left of center. The locals revel in their funky nonconformity here, probably because weirdness is still integral to the Key West brand. But past these idiosyncrasies is simply a beautiful tropical island, where the moonflowers bloom at night and the classical Caribbean homes are so sad and romantic it's hard not to sigh at them.

Ringling Museum Complex

Price: adult/child 6-17yr $25/5

Hours: 10am-5pm daily, to 8pm Thu

Contact: http://www.ringling.org, 941-359-5700

Location: 5401 Bay Shore Rd, Sarasota, USA

The 66-acre winter estate of railroad, real-estate and circus baron John Ringling and his wife, Mable, is one of the Gulf Coast's premier attractions and incorporates their personal collection of artworks in what is now Florida's state art museum. Nearby, Ringling's Circus Museum documents his theatrical successes, while their lavish Venetian Gothic home, Cà d'Zan, reveals the impresario's extravagant tastes. To get the best out of the complex, don't miss the PBS-produced film on Ringling's life, which is screened in the Asolo Repertory Theatre.

John & Mable Ringling Museum of Art

The Ringlings aspired to become serious art connoisseurs, and they amassed an impressive collection of 14th- to 18th-century European tapestries and paintings. Housed in a grand Mediterranean-style palazzo, the museum covers 21 galleries showcasing many Spanish and baroque works, and includes a world-renowned collection of Rubens canvases including the Triumph of the Eucharist cycle. One wing presents rotating exhibits of contemporary art, and in 2011 the Searing Wing opened Joseph's Coat, a stunning 3000 sq. ft. James Turrell-designed 'Sky Space.'

Cà d'Zan

Ringling's winter home Cà d'Zan (1924–26), or 'House of John,' displays an unmistakable theatrical flair evocative of his two favorite Venetian hotels, the Danieli and the Bauer Grunwald. Ceilings are painted masterpieces, especially Willy Pogany's Dancers of Nations in the ballroom, and even the patio's zigzag marble that fronts Sarasota Bay dazzles. Self-guided tours include the 1st floor's kitchens, tap room and opulent public spaces, while guided tours ($5) add the 2nd floor's stupendous bedrooms and bathrooms.

Circus Museum

This is actually several museums in one, and they are as delightful as the circus itself. One building preserves the hand-carved animal wagons, calliopes and artifacts from Ringling Bros' original traveling show. Other exhibits trace the evolution of the circus from sideshow to Cirque du Soleil. Yet in the center ring, so to speak, is the miniature Howard Bros Circus: a truly epic recreation at 1/12th scale of the entire Ringling Bros and Barnum & Bailey Circus in action. This intricately detailed work occupies its own building, and is mostly the 50-year labor of love of one man, Howard Tibbels.

Wizarding World of Harry Potter – Hogsmeade

Price: theme park admission required

Hours: 9am-6pm, hours vary

Contact: http://www.universalorlando.com, 407-363-8000

Location: Islands of Adventure, USA

Poke around among the cobbled streets and impossibly crooked buildings of Hogsmeade; munch on Cauldron Cakes; and mail a card via Owl Post – all in the shadow of Hogwarts Castle. Two of Orlando's best rides are here – Harry Potter and the Forbidden Journey and Dragon Challenge. Come first thing when the park gates open, before the lines get too long and the crowds become unbearable. Guests staying at Universal Orlando Resort hotels get one hour early admission.

Harry Potter and the Forbidden Journey Wind through the corridors of Hogwarts, past talking portraits, Dumbledore's office and other well-known locations, to one of the best rides in Orlando. You'll feel the cold chill of Dementors, escape a dragon attack, join a quidditch match and soar over the castle with Harry, Hermione and Ron. Though it's not a fast-moving thrill ride, this is scary stuff. Little ones can enjoy the castle but sit out the ride with a parent in the Child Swap waiting room. There's a single rider line as well, but it's tricky to find – ask at the Hogwarts entrance.

Dragon Challenge Gut-churning dueling roller coasters twist and loop, narrowly avoiding each other; inspired by the first task of the Triwizard Tournament in Harry Potter & the Goblet of Fire.

Ollivander's Wand Shop Floor-to-ceiling shelves crammed with dusty wand boxes and a winding staircase set the scene for a 10-minute show that brings to life the iconic scene in which the wand chooses the wizard. Come first thing, as the line quickly extends upwards of an hour.

Flight of the Hippogriff (Express Pass) Family-friendly coaster passes over Hagrid's Hut; listen for Fang's barks and don't forget to bow to Buckbeak!

Honeydukes Sweet Shop Bertie Botts Every Flavor Beans, Chocolate Frogs, Rock Cakes and other Harry Potter–inspired goodies.

Owl Post & Owlery Buy Wizarding World stamps and send a card officially postmarked Hogsmeade.

Filch's Emporium of Confiscated Goods Souvenir Shop featuring the Marauders Map on display.

Three Broomsticks & Hog's Head Tavern Surprisingly good shepherd's pie, pumpkin juice and Hogs Head Brew.

Dervish & Banges Magical supplies and Hogwarts robes for sale.

Salvador Dalí Museum

Price: adult/child 6-12yr $24/10, after 5pm Thu $10

Hours: 10am-5:30pm Mon-Wed & Fri-Sat, to 8pm Thu, noon-5:30pm Sun

Contact: http://www.thedali.org, 727-823-3767

Location: 1 Dali Blvd, St Petersburg, USA

The theatrical exterior of the Salvador Dalí Museum augurs great things: out of a wound in the towering white shoebox oozes the 75ft geodesic atrium Glass Enigma. Even better, what unfolds inside is like a blueprint of what a modern art museum should be, or at least, one devoted to understanding the life, art and impact of a single revolutionary artist. Salvador Dalí is often trivialized as a foppish visual trickster, but he was a passionate, daring intellectual and a true 20th-century visionary. Even those who dismiss his dripping clocks and curlicue mustache are swept away by this museum and grand works such as the Hallucinogenic Toreador.

The Dalí Museum's 20,000 sq. ft. of gallery space is designed specifically to display all 96 oil paintings in the collection, along with 'key works from every moment and in every medium': drawings, prints, sculptures, photos, manuscripts, even movies. Everything is arranged chronologically and explained in context. You get photographer Philippe Halsman's famous portraits (such as Dalí Atomicus), and the sublimely absurd and still shocking 1929 film Un Chien Andalou. The museum is so sharp it includes a 'contemplation area' with nothing but white walls and a window. The garden is also a great breather; it's small but, like everything, shot through with cleverness. The only disappointments: the kid-focused 'DillyDally with Dali' activity room and the introductory film both feel perfunctory.

Excellent, free docent tours occur hourly (on the half hour); these are highly recommended to help crack open the rich symbolism in Dalí's monumental works. Audioguides are also free, but get snapped up fast. To top everything off, there's a Spanish cafe and a first rate gift store. Up to 3000 people have been known to visit in a day, so get here early or suffer waits for everything.

Georgia

The largest state east of the Mississippi River is a labyrinth of geographic and cultural extremes: right-leaning Republican politics rub against liberal idealism; small, conservative towns merge with sprawling, progressive, financially flush cities; northern mountains rise to the clouds and produce roaring rivers, while coastal marshlands teem with fiddler crabs and swaying cordgrass. Georgia's southern beaches and islands are a treat. And so are its restaurant kitchens.

Georgia encompasses two Souths—the Old South of Savannah with its elegant homes, planned squares, and Spanish moss-draped live oaks, and the New South of Atlanta, a bustling high-rise metropolis with enough to keep visitors busy for weeks. For white-columned mansions and romantic visions of the past, look no further than central Georgia. One of the most popular Civil War battlefields is in northern Georgia. There's coastline here, too, with lush barrier islands stretching all the way to Florida.

Sights in Georgia

Wormsloe Plantation Historic Site

Price: adult/senior/6-17yr/1-5yr $10/9/4.50/2

Hours: 9am-5pm Tue-Sun

Contact: http://www.gastateparks.org/Wormsloe

Location: 7601 Skidaway Rd, Savannah, USA

A short drive from downtown, on the beautiful Isle of Hope, this is one of the most photographed sites in town. The real draw is the dreamy entrance through a corridor of mossy, ancient oaks that runs for 1.5 miles, known as the Avenue of the Oaks.

But there are other draws, including an existing antebellum mansion still lived in by the descendants of the original owner, Noble Jones, some old colonial ruins, and a touristy site where you can see folks demonstrate blacksmithing and other bygone trades. There are two flat, wooded walking trails here too.

Martin Luther King Jr National Historic Site

Hours: 9am-5pm

Contact: http://www.nps.gov/malu/index.htm, 404-331-5190

Location: 450 Auburn Ave, Atlanta, USA

The historic site commemorates the life, work and legacy of the civil rights leader and one of the great Americans. The center takes up several blocks.

Stop by the excellent visitor center to get oriented with a map and brochure of area sites, and exhibits that elucidate the context – i.e. the segregation, systematic oppression and racial violence that inspired and fueled King's work. A 1.5-mile landscaped trail leads from here to the Carter Center.

High Museum of Art

Price: adult/child $19.50/12

Hours: 10am-5pm Tue-Thu & Sat, to 9pm Fri, noon-5pm Sun

Contact: http://www.high.org

Location: 1280 Peachtree St NE, Atlanta, USA

Atlanta's modern High Museum was the first to exhibit art lent from Paris' Louvre, and is a destination as much for its architecture as its world-class exhibits. The striking whitewashed multilevel building houses a permanent collection of eye-catching late-19th-century furniture, early American modern canvases from the likes of George Morris and Albert Gallatin, and postwar work from Mark Rothko.

Hawaii

Hawaii overflows with natural beauty. Piercing the surface of the Pacific from the ocean floor, the Hawaiian Islands are garlanded with soft sand beaches and dramatic volcanic cliffs. Long days of sunshine and fairly mild year-round temperatures make this an all-season destination, and the islands' offerings — from urban Honolulu on Oahu to the luxury resorts of Maui to the natural wonders of Kauai and the Big Island—appeal to all kinds of visitors. Less-developed Lanai and Molokai are quieter, but all the islands are rich in Hawaiian culture.

It's easy to see why Hawaii has become synonymous with paradise. Just look at these sugary beaches, Technicolor coral reefs and volcanoes beckoning adventurous spirits.

Hawaii is as proud of its multicultural heritage as it is of island-born US President Barack Obama. On these islands, the descendants of ancient Polynesians, European explorers, American missionaries and Asian plantation immigrants mix and mingle. What's remarkable about contemporary Hawaii is that multiculturalism is the rule, not the exception. Boisterous arts and cultural festivals keep diverse community traditions alive, from Hawaiian hula and outrigger canoe races to Japanese taiko drumming.

Snapshots of these islands scattered in a cobalt blue ocean are heavenly, without the need for any tourist-brochure embellishment. Sunrises and sunsets are so spectacular that they're cause for celebration all by themselves. As tropical getaways go, Hawaii couldn't be easier or more worth the trip, although visiting these Polynesian islands isn't always cheap. Whether you're dreaming of swimming in waterfall pools or lazing on golden-sand beaches, you'll find what you're looking for here.

Floating all by itself in the middle of the Pacific, Hawaii proudly maintains its own identity apart from the US mainland. Spam, shave ice, surfing, ukulele and slack key guitar music, hula, pidgin, 'rubbah slippah' (flip-flops) – these are just some of the touchstones of everyday life, island style. Pretty much everything here feels easygoing, low-key and casual, bursting with genuine aloha and fun. You'll be equally welcome whether you're a globe-trotting surf bum, a beaming couple of fresh-faced honeymooners or a big, multigenerational family with rambunctious kids.

Sights in Hawaii

Hawaiʻi Volcanoes National Park

Price: 7-day entry per car $10

Contact: http://www.nps.gov/havo, 808-985-6000

Location: Hawaiʻi Volcanoes National Park & Around, USA

Even among Hawaii's many wonders, this national park stands out: its two active volcanoes testify to the ongoing birth of the islands. Majestic Mauna Loa (13,677ft) looms like a sleeping giant, while young Kilauea - the world's most active volcano - has been erupting almost continually since 1983. With luck, you'll witness the primal event of molten lava tumbling into the sea. But the park contains much more - overwhelming lava deserts, steaming craters, lava tubes and ancient rainforests. For hikers, it's heaven.

The Road to Hana

With its tumbling waterfalls, lush slopes, and rugged coasts, the Road to Hana is certainly beautiful. But it's the sense of earning the beauty that makes a drive on the road so special. Spanning the northeast shore of Maui, the legendary Hana Hwy ribbons tightly between jungle valleys and towering cliffs. Along the way, 54 one-lane bridges mark nearly as many waterfalls, some tranquil and inviting, others so sheer they kiss you with spray as you drive past. It's ravishingly gorgeous, but certainly not easy.

And there's more to the drive than beauty. When you're ready to get out and stretch your legs the real adventure begins: hiking trails climb into cool forests, short paths lead to Eden-like swimming holes, side roads wind down to sleepy seaside villages. If you've never tried smoked breadfruit, taken a dip in a spring-fed cave or gazed upon an ancient Hawaiian temple, set the alarm early – you've got a big day. As for rental cars, Jeeps and Mustangs look to be the ride of choice on the Hana Hwy.

Once you've left Pa'ia and Ha'iku behind, houses give way to thick jungle, and the scenery gets more dramatic with every mile. Then the road does a sleight-of-hand. After the 16-mile marker on Hwy 36, the Hana Hwy changes numbers to Hwy 360 and the mile markers begin again at zero.

Waikiki Beach

Once a Hawaiian royal retreat, Waikiki is riding high on a new wave of effortlessly chic style these days. No longer just a beach destination for package tourists, this famous strand of sand is flowering, starting with a renaissance of Hawaiian music at beachfront hotels and resorts. In this concrete jungle of modern high-rises, you can, surprisingly, still hear whispers of Hawaii's past, from the chanting of hula troupes at Kuhio Beach to the legacy of Olympic gold medalist Duke Kahanamoku. Take a surfing lesson from a bronzed beach boy, then spend a lazy afternoon lying on Waikiki's golden sands. Before the sun sinks below the horizon, hop aboard a catamaran and sail off toward Diamond Head. Sip a sunset mai tai and be hypnotized by the lilting harmonies of slack key guitar, then mingle with the locals, who come here to party after dark too.

Bishop Museum

Price: adult/child $20/15

Hours: 9am-5pm Wed-Mon

Contact: http://www.bishopmuseum.org, 808-847-3511

Location: 1525 Bernice St, Honolulu, USA

Like Hawaii's version of the Smithsonian Institute in Washington, DC, the Bishop Museum showcases a remarkable array of cultural and natural history exhibits. It is often ranked as the finest Polynesian anthropological museum in the world. Founded in 1889 in honor of Princess Bernice Pauahi Bishop, a descendant of the Kamehameha dynasty, it originally housed only Hawaiian and royal artifacts. These days it honors all of Polynesia.

The recently renovated main gallery, the Hawaiian Hall, resides inside a dignified three-story Victorian building. Displays covering the cultural history of Hawaii include a pili (grass) thatched house, carved ki'i akua (temple images), kahili (feathered royal staffs), shark-toothed war clubs and traditional tapa cloth made by pounding the bark of the paper mulberry tree. Don't miss the feathered cloak once worn by Kamehameha the Great, created entirely of the yellow feathers of the now-extinct mamo – some 80,000 birds were caught and plucked to create this single adornment. Meanwhile, upper-floor exhibits delve further into ali'i (royal) history, traditional daily life and relationships between Native Hawaiians and the natural world.

The fascinating two-story exhibits inside the adjacent Polynesian Hall cover the myriad cultures of Polynesia, Micronesia and Melanesia. You could spend hours gazing at astounding and rare ritual artifacts, from elaborate dance masks and ceremonial costumes to carved canoes. Next door, the Castle Memorial Building displays changing traveling exhibitions.

Across the Great Lawn, the eye-popping, state-of-the-art multisensory Science Adventure Center lets kids walk through an erupting volcano, take a mini submarine dive and play with three floors of interactive multimedia exhibits.

The Bishop Museum is also home to O'ahu's only planetarium, which highlights traditional Polynesian methods of wayfaring (navigation), using wave patterns and the position of the stars to travel thousands of miles across the open ocean in traditional outrigger canoes, as well as modern astronomy and the cutting-edge telescope observatories atop Mauna Kea on the Big Island. Shows usually start at 11:30am, 1:30pm and 3:30pm daily except Tuesday, and are included in the museum admission price.

A gift shop off the main lobby sells books on the Pacific not easily found elsewhere, as well as some high-quality Hawaiian art, crafts and souvenirs. Check the museum website for special events, including popular 'Moonlight Mele' summer concerts, family-friendly Hawaiian cultural festivities and after-dark planetarium shows (buy tickets online or make reservations by calling 808-848-4168 in advance).

From Waikiki or downtown Honolulu, take bus 2 School St-Middle St to the intersection of School St and Kapalama Ave; walk one block makai on Kapalama Ave, then turn right onto Bernice St. By car, take eastbound H-1 Fwy exit 20, turn right on Houghtailing St, then take the second left onto Bernice St. Parking is free.

'Iolani Palace

Price: grounds admission free, adult/child basement galleries $7/3, self-guided audio tour $15/6, guided tour $22/6

Hours: 9am-5pm Mon-Sat, last entry 4pm

Contact: http://www.iolanipalace.org, 808-522-0832

Location: 364 S King St, Honolulu, USA

No other place evokes a more poignant sense of Hawaii's history. The palace was built under King David Kalakaua in 1882. At that time, the Hawaiian monarchy observed many of the diplomatic protocols of the Victorian world. The king traveled abroad meeting with leaders around the globe and received foreign emissaries here. Although the palace was modern and opulent for its time, it did little to assert Hawaii's sovereignty over powerful US-influenced business interests who overthrew the kingdom in 1893.

Two years after the coup, the former queen, Lili'uokalani, who had succeeded her brother David to the throne, was convicted of treason and spent nine months imprisoned in her former home. Later the palace served as the capitol of the republic, then the territory and later the state of Hawaii. In 1969 the government finally moved into the current state capitol, leaving ‘Iolani Palace a shambles. After a decade of painstaking renovations, the restored palace reopened as a museum, although many original royal artifacts had been lost or stolen before work even began.

Visitors must take a docent-led or self-guided tour (no children under age five) to see ‘Iolani’s grand interior, including re-creations of the throne room and residential quarters upstairs. The palace was quite modern by Victorian-era standards. Every bedroom had its own bathroom with flush toilets and hot running water, and electric lights replaced the gas lamps years before the White House in Washington, DC, installed electricity. If you’re short on time, you can independently browse the historical exhibits in the basement, including royal regalia, historical photographs and reconstructions of the kitchen and chamberlain’s office.

The palace grounds are open during daylight hours and are free of charge. The former barracks of the Royal Household Guards, a building that looks oddly like the uppermost layer of a medieval fort, now houses the ticket booth. Nearby, a domed pavilion, originally built for the coronation of King Kalakaua in 1883, is still used for state governor inaugurations. Underneath the huge banyan tree, allegedly planted by Queen Kapi‘olani, the Royal Hawaiian Band gives free concerts on most Fridays from noon to 1pm, weather permitting.

Call ahead to confirm tour schedules and reserve tickets in advance during peak periods.

Pi‘ilanihale Heiau & Kahanu Garden

Price: guided tour adult/child under 13yr $25/free, self-guided tour adult/child under 13yr $10/free

Hours: 9am-2pm Mon-Sat

Contact: http://www.ntbg.org, 808-248-8912

Location: 650 ‘Ula‘ino Rd, ‘Ula‘ino Road, USA

The most significant stop on the entire Road to Hana, this site combines a 294-acre ethnobotanical garden with the magnificent Pi‘ilanihale Heiau, the largest temple in all of Polynesia. A must-do tour provides fascinating details into the extraordinary relationship between the ancient Hawaiians and their environment. This is perhaps the best opportunity in all of Hawaii to really feel what traditional Hawaiian culture was like prior to contact with the West. Amazingly, very few people visit.

Pi'ilanihale Heiau is an immense lava stone platform with a length of 450ft. The history of this astounding temple is shrouded in mystery, but there's no doubt that it was an important religious site. Archaeologists believe construction began as early as AD 1200 and continued in phases. The grand finale was the work of Pi'ilani (the heiau's name means House of Pi'ilani), the 14th-century Maui chief who is also credited with the construction of many of the coastal fishponds in the Hana area.

The temple occupies one corner of Kahanu Garden, near the sea. An outpost of the National Tropical Botanical Garden (which also runs the Allerton and McBryde gardens on Kaua'i), Kahanu Garden contains the largest collection of breadfruit species in the world, with over 127 varieties. Breadfruit is significant because, as its name suggests, its nutritional value makes it a dietary pillar, and hence a weapon to combat global hunger. The garden also contains a living catalog of so-called canoe plants, those essentials of traditional life brought to Hawaii in the canoes of Polynesian voyagers, along with a hand-crafted canoe house that is another step back in time.

The very best way to unlock the relationship between the heiau, the plants, and their beautiful, park-like surroundings, where palms sway in the breeze, is to take a guided tour, something the entire family will enjoy. These are only given Saturdays, at 10am and 1pm, and last two hours. Advance online reservations required. The only other option is a self-guided tour by brochure. The site is located 1.5 miles down 'Ula'ino Rd from the Hana Hwy.

Idaho

It’s been said that "Idaho is as America was"—a western frontier with more wild land than developed, and only 1.5 million people scattered throughout our nation’s 14th-largest state. Its big blue skies, pristine waters, and jagged snowcapped horizons have been largely untouched by the masses, making it an outdoors enthusiast’s paradise. Rafters, kayakers, mountain climbers, backcountry skiers, and backpackers flock to Idaho’s untamed heart—the treacherous 2.3 million acres of the Frank Church River of No Return Wilderness Area (the second-largest protected wilderness in the lower 48 states). Idaho has the most miles of white-water rapids in the continental United States, North America’s deepest gorge, and one of the longest undammed rivers in the country. To the north, in the slim panhandle that touches Canada, are deep wooded hills and huge lakes, while the southern belly is checkered with potato and alfalfa fields along the Snake River Plains. In some of the more picturesque mountain and lake regions, cosmopolitan resort cities are tucked away, with five-star amenities to pamper wealthy vacationers. The state's capitol of Boise is quickly becoming a cultural, commercial, and educational epicenter. But at its heart, the Idaho is still overwhelmingly wild.

Famous for not being particularly famous, the nation's 43rd state is a pristine wilderness of Alaskan proportions, rudely ignored by passing traffic heading west to Seattle or east to Montana. In truth, much of this lightly trodden land is little changed since the days of Lewis and Clark, including a vast 15,000-sq-km 'hole' in the middle of the state and bereft of roads, settlements, or any other form of human interference.

Flatter, dryer southern Idaho is dominated by the Snake River, deployed as a transportation artery by early settlers on the Oregon Trail and tracked today by busy Hwy 84. But, outside of this narrow populated strip, the Idaho landscape is refreshingly free of the soulless strip-mall, fast-food infestations so ubiquitous elsewhere in the US.

Sights in Idaho

Basque Block

Unbeknownst to many, Boise harbors one of the largest Basque populations outside Spain. European émigrés first arrived in the 1910s to work as Idaho shepherds. Elements of their distinct culture can be glimpsed along Grove St between 6th St and Capitol Blvd.

Sandwiched between the ethnic taverns, restaurants and bars is Basque Museum & Cultural Center a commendable effort to unveil the intricacies of Basque culture and how it was transposed 6000 miles west to Idaho. Language lessons in Euskara, Europe's oldest language, are held here, while next door in the Anduiza Fronton Building there's a Basque handball court where aficionados play the traditional sport of pelota.

Boise River & Greenbelt

Laid out in the 1960s, the tree-lined riverbanks of the Boise River protect 30 miles of vehicle-free trails. It personifies Boise's 'city of trees' credentials, with parks, museums and river fun.

The river is insanely popular for its floating and tubing. The put-in point is Barber Park 6 miles east of downtown. It's a 5-mile float to the take-out point at Ann Morrison Park. There are four rest-stops en route and a shuttle bus ($3) runs from the take-out point.

The most central and action-packed space on the Greenbelt, 90-acre Julia Davis Park contains the Idaho State Historical Museum with well thought-out exhibits on Lewis and Clark; and the Boise Art Museum. There's also a pretty outdoor rose garden.

Sawtooth National Recreation Area

Hours: 8am-4:30pm Sep-May, to 5pm Jun-Aug

Contact: 208-727-5000

Location: Hwy 75, Idaho, USA

Following the Salmon River, Hwy 75 north from Ketchum to Stanley is part of the nationally designated Sawtooth Scenic Byway. The 60-mile drive is gorgeous, winding through a misty, thick ponderosa pine forest - where the air is crisp and fresh and smells like rain and nuts - before ascending the 8701ft Galena Summit. From the overlook at the top, there are views of the glacially carved Sawtooth Mountains, part of the 1180-sq-mile Sawtooth National Recreation Area. It is home to 40 peaks over 10,000ft, over 300 high-alpine lakes, 100 miles of streams and 750 miles of trails.

Craters of the Moon National Monument

Price: vehicle/hiker or cyclist $4/2

Hours: 8am-4:30pm Sep-May, to 6pm Jun-Aug

Contact: 208-527-3257

A one-hour drive southeast of Ketchum, Craters of the Moon National Monument is an 83-sq-mile volcanic showcase. Lava flows and tubes and cinder cones are found along the 7-mile Crater Loop Rd, accessible by car or bicycle from April to November. In winter, it's popular with skiers and snowshoers. Short trails lead from Crater Loop Rd to crater edges, onto cinder cones and into tunnels and lava caves. A surreal campground near the entrance station has running water only in summer.

Illinois

Home to Chicago and therefore the de-facto capital of culture for the Midwest, Illinois is much more than its most famous city. Yes, of course, many visitors flock here for the Windy City and its art museums, architecture, blues clubs, comedy shows, and deep-dish pizza, but the rest of the state offers plenty in terms of history, culture, and the great outdoors. Explore the charms of smaller towns like Galena and Evanston, see the houses designed by Frank Lloyd Wright in Oak Park, and learn what makes this the "Land of Lincoln" in Springfield.

Sights in Illinois

Field Museum of Natural History

Price: adult/child $18/13

Hours: 9am-5pm

Contact: http://www.fieldmuseum.org, 312-922-9410

Location: 1400 S Lake Shore Dr, Chicago, USA

The mammoth Field Museum houses everything but the kitchen sink – beetles, mummies, gemstones, Bushman the stuffed ape. The collection's rock star is Sue, the largest Tyrannosaurus rex yet discovered. She even gets her own gift shop. Special exhibits, such as the 3-D movie, cost extra.

The museum's galleries hold some 20 million artifacts, tended by a slew of PhD – wielding scientists, as the Field remains an active research institution.

After communing with Sue, dino lovers should head up to the 'Evolving Planet' exhibit on the second floor, which has more of the big guys and gals. You can learn about the evolution of the species and watch staff paleontologists clean up fossils in the lab.

'Inside Ancient Egypt' is another good exhibit that recreates an Egyptian burial chamber on two levels. The mastaba (tomb) contains 23 actual mummies and is a reconstruction of the one built for Unis-ankh, the son of the last pharaoh of the Fifth dynasty, who died at age 21 in 2407 BC. The relic-strewn bottom level is especially worthwhile.

Other displays that merit your time include the Hall of Gems and its glittering garnets, opals, pearls and deep-blue tanzanite stones (1000 times rarer than diamonds, which you'll also see plenty of). The Northwest Coast and Arctic Peoples totem pole collection got its start with artifacts shipped to Chicago for the 1893 World's Expo. And the largest man-eating lion ever caught is stuffed and standing sentry on the basement floor. Preserved insects and birds are also on display in all their taxidermic glory.

The museum is vast, so get a map at the desk and make a plan of attack or download the museum's free app for curated tours of various collections.

Millennium Park

Hours: 6am-11pm

Contact: http://www.millenniumpark.org, 312-742-1168

Location: 201 E Randolph St, Chicago, USA

The city's showpiece is a trove of free and arty sights. It includes Pritzker Pavilion, Frank Gehry's swooping silver band shell, which hosts free concerts nightly in summer (6:30pm; bring a picnic and bottle of wine); Anish Kapoor's beloved silvery sculpture Cloud Gate, aka the 'Bean'; and Jaume Plensa's Crown Fountain, a de facto water park that projects video images of locals spitting water, gargoyle style.

The McCormick Tribune Ice Rink fills with skaters in winter (and al fresco diners in summer). The hidden Lurie Garden blooms with prairie flowers and tranquility. The Gehry-designed BP Bridge spans Columbus Dr and offers great skyline views, while the Nichols Bridgeway arches from the park up to the Art Institute's small, 3rd-floor sculpture terrace (free to view).

Want more? Free yoga and Pilates classes take place Saturday mornings in summer on the Great Lawn, while the Family Fun Tent provides free kids' activities daily in summer from 10am to 2pm.

Art Institute of Chicago

Price: adult/child $25/free

Hours: 10:30am-5pm Fri-Wed, to 8pm Thu

Contact: http://www.artic.edu, 312-443-3600

Location: 111 S Michigan Ave, Chicago, USA

The second-largest art museum in the country, the Art Institute's collection of impressionist and post-impressionist paintings rivals those in France, and the number of surrealist works is tremendous. Download the free app for DIY tours; it offers 50 jaunts, everything from highlights (Grant Wood's American Gothic, Edward Hopper's Nighthawks) to a 'birthday-suit tour' of naked works. Allow two hours to browse the museum's must-sees; art buffs should allocate much longer.

The main entrance is on Michigan Ave, but you can also enter via the dazzling Modern Wing on Monroe St. Ask at the front desk about free talks and tours once you're inside. Note that the 3rd-floor contemporary sculpture terrace is always free. It has great city views and connects to Millennium Park via the mod, pedestrian-only Nichols Bridgeway.

Indiana

With its feet firmly planted in the heartland, Indiana is like one big small town, where locals take pride in their "Hoosier hospitality." The state is a healthy mix of rural and urban. Indianapolis, the state's largest city, features big-city culture like an opera and symphony orchestra, yet still retains charm and character. Stop and ask for directions and chances are you'll also receive a tip on where to have dinner that night.

One of Indiana's most treasured natural features, the 15-mile stretch of beaches that is now protected as the Indiana Dunes National Lakeshore, is in the thick of an industrial belt, home of behemoth steel mills, refineries, and supporting industries.

To the northeast, in the rolling prairies and lake country of LaGrange and Elkhart counties, the pace is slow, and life is simple. Here is the nation's third-largest concentration of Amish. The Amish began seeking out the wide-open spaces and rich farmland of Indiana in the mid-19th century, and still maintain their horse-drawn buggies and a simple life centered on the farm and home.

The state revs up around the Indy 500 race, but otherwise it's about slow-paced pleasures in corn-stubbled Indiana: pie-eating in Amish Country, meditating in Bloomington's Tibetan temples and admiring the big architecture in small Columbus. For the record, folks have called Indianans 'Hoosiers' since the 1830s, but the word's origin is unknown. One theory is that early settlers knocking on a door were met with 'Who's here?' which soon became 'Hoosier.' It's certainly something to discuss with locals, perhaps over a traditional pork tenderloin sandwich.

Sights in Indiana

Indianapolis Motor Speedway

Price: adult/child $8/5

Hours: 9am-5pm Mar-Oct, 10am-4pm Nov-Feb

Contact: http://www.indianapolismotorspeedway.com, 317-492-6784

Location: 4790 W 16th St, Indianapolis, USA

The Speedway, home of the Indianapolis 500 motor race, is Indy's supersight. The Hall of Fame Museum features 75 racing cars (including former winners), a 500lb. Tiffany trophy and a track tour ($8 extra). OK, so you're on a bus for the latter and not even beginning to burn rubber at 37mph, but it's still fun to pretend.

The big race itself is held on the Sunday of Memorial Day weekend (late May) and attended by 450,000 crazed fans. Tickets can be hard to come by. Try the pre-race trials and practices for easier access and cheaper prices. The track is about 6 miles northwest of downtown.

Indianapolis Museum of Art

Price: adult/child $18/10

Hours: 11am-5pm Tue-Sun, to 9pm Thu

Contact: http://www.imamuseum.org, 317-920-2660

Location: 4000 Michigan Rd, Indianapolis, USA

The museum has a terrific collection of European art (especially Turner and post-Impressionists), African tribal art, South Pacific art and Chinese works. The complex also includes Oldfields – Lilly House & Gardens, where you can tour the 22-room mansion and flowery grounds of the Lilly pharmaceutical family, and Fairbanks Art & Nature Park, with eye-popping mod sculptures set amid 100 acres of woodlands. Fairbanks is free – perfect for those who need an art fix but without the steep admission price.

Indiana Dunes National Lakeshore

The dunes stretch along 15 miles of Lake Michigan shoreline. Swimming is allowed anywhere along the sand. A short walk away from the beaches, several hiking paths crisscross the dunes and woodlands. The best are the Bailly-

Chellberg Trail (2.5 miles) that winds by a still operating 1870s farm, and the Heron Rookery Trail (2 miles), where blue herons flock. Oddly, all this natural bounty lies smack-dab next to smoke-belching factories, which you'll also see at various vantage points.

White River State Park

The expansive park, located at downtown's edge, contains several worthwhile sights. The adobe Eiteljorg Museum of American Indians & Western Art features Native American basketry, pots and masks, as well as several paintings by Frederic Remington and Georgia O'Keeffe. Other park highlights include an atmospheric minor-league baseball stadium, a zoo, a canal walk, gardens, a science museum and a college sports museum.

Kurt Vonnegut Memorial Library

Hours: 11am-6pm Mon, Tue, Thu & Fri, noon-5pm Sat & Sun

Contact: http://www.vonnegutlibrary.org

Location: 340 N Senate Ave, Indianapolis, USA

Author Kurt Vonnegut was born and raised in Indy, and this humble museum pays homage with displays including his Pall Mall cigarettes, droll drawings and rejection letters from publishers. The library also replicates his office, complete with checkerboard carpet, red rooster lamp and blue Coronamatic typewriter. You're welcome to sit at the desk and type Kurt a note; the library tweets the musings.

Iowa

Iowa takes its name from a Native American word meaning "beautiful land," and the soil here, among the most fertile, wisely managed, and lucrative on the planet, is the greatest of many riches in the state. Iowa's 100,000 family farms produce more pork, beef, and grain than any other state in the union. Each year, the average Iowa farm grows enough food to feed 279 people.

Iowa's farm economy is further supported by the state's many small towns. Clean, wide, tree-lined streets, courthouse squares, and corner cafés are omnipresent. The peaceful images captured on canvas by native son Grant Wood are as real today as they were in the 1930s and '40s. Nearly every community can brag about its art center, museum, or community music group. Arts festivals, galleries, and cultural events across the state attract large, appreciative audiences.

Iowans — along with the University of Iowa's sports teams — are known as "Hawkeyes," a name which can be traced rather ironically to the Sauk Indian chief Black Hawk, who led a three-month-long uprising to protest the westward expansion of white settlement in the early 1800s. It was the treaty signed after

Chief Black Hawk's defeat which opened the eastern portion of this "beautiful land" to white settlement.

Sights in Iowa

Effigy Mounds National Monument

Hours: 8am-6pm Jun-Aug, to 4:30pm Sep-May

Contact: http://www.nps.gov/efmo, 563-873-3491

Location: Hwy 76, Iowa Great River Road, USA

Hundreds of mysterious Native American burial mounds sit in the bluffs above the Mississippi River in this gorgeous corner of far northeast Iowa. Listen to songbirds as you hike the lush trails.

Amana Heritage Museum

Price: adult/child $7/free

Hours: 10am-5pm Mon-Sat, noon-4pm Sun Apr-Oct, 10am-5pm Sat Mar, Nov & Dec

Contact: http://www.amanaheritage.org, 319-622-3567

Location: 4310 220th Trail, Amana Colonies, USA

Offers a good overview of the colonies. Ask about the cell phone tours.

Lewis & Clark Interpretive Center

Hours: 9am-5pm Tue-Fri, to 8pm Thu, noon-5pm Sat & Sun

Contact: http://www.siouxcitylcic.com

Location: 900 Larsen Park Rd, Sioux City, IA, Iowa, USA

On August 20, 1804, Sergeant Charles Floyd became the only person to die on the Lewis and Clark expedition team, probably from appendicitis. You can learn much more about this and other aspects of the journey at the beautiful Lewis & Clark Interpretive Center, which is right on the river.

Old Capitol Museum

Hours: 10am-5pm Tue, Wed, Fri & Sat, to 8pm Thu, 1-5pm Sun

Contact: http://www.uiowa.edu/oldcap, 319-335-0548

Location: cnr Clinton St & Iowa Ave, Iowa City, USA

The cute gold-domed building at the heart of the University of Iowa campus is the Old Capitol. Built in 1840, it was the seat of government until 1857 when Des Moines grabbed the reins. It's now a museum with galleries and furnishings from back in its heyday.

Kansas

Wicked witches and yellow-brick roads, pitched battles over slavery and tornadoes powerful enough to pulverize entire towns are some of the more lurid images of Kansas. But the common image – amber waves of grain from north to south and east to west is closer to reality.

There's a simple beauty to the green rolling hills (six states are flatter) and limitless horizons. Places such as Chase County beguile those who value understatement. Gems abound, from the superb space museum in Hutchinson to the indie music clubs of Lawrence. Most importantly, follow the Great Plains credo of ditching the interstate for the two-laners and make your own discoveries.

If you are a traveler who appreciates the simplicity of wide-open spaces, Native American history, or Wild West heritage, you will find much to enjoy in Kansas.

The state was home to legendary lawmen like Wyatt Earp and James Butler "Wild Bill" Hickok, who, along with others, policed once-rowdy railroad and cattle towns like Abilene, Dodge City, and Ellsworth. More infamous Wild

West residents include the Dalton Gang, who fatally sought to rob two banks simultaneously in their hometown of Coffeyville.
Perhaps Kansas's greatest claim to fame, however, is serving as home to Dorothy, Toto, and the great twister in the classic movie The Wizard of Oz, based on L. Frank Baum's book The Wonderful Wizard of Oz. Dorothy and Toto, of course, are fictional, but their story's symbolism can be found in each of the small towns, ranches, farms, and cities that makes up this "land of aaahhs."

Today Kansas's craftspeople are inspired by the vast landscape, whether it's art or food. Small towns are rich in galleries and cafés staffed by locals who carry immense pride for the state.

Sights in Kansas

Kansas Cosmosphere & Space Center

Price: all-attraction pass adult/child $23/21, museum only $12.50/10.50

Hours: 9am-7pm Mon-Sat, noon-7pm Sun

Contact: http://www.cosmo.org, 800-397-0330

Location: 1100 N Plum St, Kansas, USA

Possibly the most surprising sight in Kansas, this amazing museum captures the race to the moon better than any museum on the planet. Absorbing displays and artifacts such as the Apollo 13 command module will enthrall you for hours. The museum is regularly called in to build props for Hollywood movies portraying the space race, including Apollo 13.

The museum's isolated location in Hutchinson is an easy day trip from Wichita or diversion off I-70.

Home on the Range Cabin

Hours: 24hr

Contact: http://www.thehomeontherange.com

Location: Hwy 8, Kansas, USA

The iconic song of the American west, 'Home on the Range,' was written by Brewster M Higley in 1871 at a remote cabin in northern Kansas. Today you can visit the lovely and evocative site of the original cabin where even if you don't see any deer and antelope at play, you'll easily feel the magic that inspired Higley. It's eight sing-posted miles north of a turn off US 36, which is one mile west of Athol.

Brown v Board of Education National Historic Site

Hours: 9am-5pm

Contact: http://www.nps.gov/brvb, 785-354-4273

Location: 1515 SE Monroe St, Topeka, USA

It took real guts to challenge the segregationist laws common in the US in the 1950s and the stories of these courageous men and women are here. Set in Monroe Elementary School, one of Topeka's African American schools at the time of the landmark 1954 Supreme Court decision that banned segregation in US schools, the displays cover the entire Civil Rights movement.

Garden of Eden

Price: adult/child $7/2

Hours: 10am-5pm May-Oct, 1-4pm Mar & Apr, 1-4pm Sat & Sun Nov-Feb

Contact: http://www.garden-of-eden-lucas-kansas.com, 785-525-6395

Location: 301 2nd St, Lucas, USA

In 1907 Samuel Dinsmoor began filling his yard with enormous concrete sculptures reflecting his eccentric philosophies. On a tour you hear some wonderful stories and see his remains in a glass-topped coffin (!).

Kentucky

With an economy based on bourbon, horse racing and tobacco, you might think Kentucky would rival Las Vegas as Sin Central. Well, yes and no. For every whiskey-soaked Louisville bar there's a dry county where you can't get anything stronger than ginger ale. For every racetrack there's a church. Kentucky is made of such strange juxtapositions. A geographic and cultural crossroads, the state combines the friendliness of the South, the rural frontier history of the West, the industry of the North and the aristocratic charm of the East. Every corner is easy on the eye, but there are few sights more heartbreakingly beautiful than the rolling limestone hills of horse country, where thoroughbred breeding is a multimillion-dollar industry. In spring the pastures bloom with tiny azure buds, earning it the moniker 'Bluegrass State.'

Kentucky has an extensive system of state parks for boating, fishing, hiking, and other outdoor recreation. The Daniel Boone National Forest occupies hundreds of thousands of acres in the eastern part of the state. Among the many sites are the Cumberland Gap in the southeast corner (through which Daniel Boone led the first pioneer settlers); the mansions, horse farms, and bourbon distilleries of the central Bluegrass region; and the Native American burial mounds in the western lowlands where the Ohio and Mississippi rivers meet. The state is also known for Mammoth Cave; with its 340 miles of mapped passages, it's the longest cave system in the world. Scores of antebellum and Victorian inns are scattered throughout Kentucky, providing you with a taste of real Southern hospitality, as well as traditional regional cooking.

Sights in Kentucky

Churchill Downs

Contact: http://www.churchilldowns.com

Location: 700 Central Ave, Louisville, USA

On the first Saturday in May, a who's who of upper-crust America puts on their seersucker suits and most flamboyant hats and descends for the 'greatest two minutes in sports': the Kentucky Derby, the longest-running consecutive sporting event in North America.

After the race, the crowd sings 'My Old Kentucky Home' and watches as the winning horse is covered in a blanket of roses. Then they party. Actually, they've been partying for a while. The Kentucky Derby Festival, which includes a balloon race, a marathon, and the largest fireworks display in North America, starts two weeks before the big event. Most seats at the derby are by invitation only or have been reserved years in advance. On Derby Day, $60 gets you into the infield, which is a debaucherous rave with no seats, as well as the classier Paddock Area, where you can see the horses getting ready for each race. It's crowded and it was previously hard to see races, but the newly-installed 4K video board (the world's largest) has alleviated that minor detail. If you are a connoisseur of the thoroughbreds, warm-ups and other races take place from April to June and again in September and November, where it's possible to snag $3 seats.

Headley-Whitney Museum

Price: adult/child $10/7

Hours: 10am-5pm Tue-Fri, noon-5pm Sat & Sun

Contact: http://www.headley-whitney.org

Location: 4435 Old Frankfort Pike, Lexington, USA

This marvelously old place holds the private collection of the late George Headley, a jewelry designer whose gemstone trinkets and handmade dollhouses are on display, along with a truly bizarre garage turned 'seashell grotto.'

Creation Museum

Price: adult/child $30/16

Hours: 10am-6pm Mon-Fri, from 9am Sat, from noon Sun

Contact: http://www.creationmuseum.org

Location: 2800 Bullittsburg Church Rd, Louisville, USA

Fact: nearly half of Americans don't believe in evolution. Hence the popularity of Petersburg, Kentucky's multimillion-dollar Creation Museum, an interactive tour through a biblical interpretation of history. The scientific-minded will fume at what may be seen as an anti-rational message. Still, that doesn't mean they won't enjoy the walk-through Noah's Ark, animatronic dinosaurs (creationists believe they coexisted with humans), and the zonkeys (zebra-donkey hybrids) in the petting zoo. Oh, and it's pricey. But who said faith was free?

Still, that doesn't mean they won't enjoy the walk-through Noah's Ark, animatronic dinosaurs (creationists believe they coexisted with humans), and the zonkeys (zebra-donkey hybrids) in the petting zoo. Oh, and it's pricey. But who said faith was free?

Mammoth Cave National Park

Price: tours adult $5-55, child $3.50-20

Hours: 8am-6pm, to 6:30pm summer

Contact: http://www.nps.gov/maca

Location: 1 Mammoth Cave Pkwy, Central Kentucky, USA

With the longest cave system on earth, Mammoth Cave National Park has some 400 miles of surveyed passageways. Mammoth is at least three times bigger than any other known cave, with vast interior cathedrals, bottomless pits, and strange, undulating rock formations.

The caves have been used for prehistoric mineral gathering, as a source of saltpeter for gunpowder and as a tuberculosis hospital. Tourists started visiting around 1810 and guided tours have been offered since the 1830s. The area became a national park in 1926 and now brings nearly two million visitors each year.

Louisiana

Bordered to the south by the Gulf of Mexico, Louisiana is a mix of swampland and farm country as well as a melting pot of French, African and American cultures. Its capital, Baton Rouge, is home to the USS Kidd Navy destroyer, while its largest city, New Orleans, is famous for its colonial-era French Quarter and festive Mardi Gras, a raucous, city-wide party celebrated with a colorful parades, loud music and outlandish floats. Louisianans share an appreciation for the good things in life as well as an outspoken enthusiasm for their state's Creole heritage.

Louisiana runs deep: a French colony turned Spanish protectorate turned reluctant American purchase; a southern fringe of swampland, bayou and alligators dissolving into the Gulf of Mexico; a northern patchwork prairie of heartland farm country; and everywhere, a population tied together by a deep, unshakable appreciation for the good things in life: food and music.

New Orleans, its first city, lives and dies by these qualities, and its restaurants and music halls are second to none. But everywhere, the state shares a love for this joie de vivre. We're not dropping French for fun, by the way; while the language is not a cultural component of North Louisiana, near I-10 and below it is a generation removed from the household – if it has been removed at all.

Sights in Louisiana

National WWII Museum

Price: adult/child/senior $23/14/20, plus 1/2 films $5/10

Hours: 9am-5pm

Contact: http://www.nationalww2museum.org, 504-528-1944

Location: 945 Magazine St, New Orleans, USA

This extensive, heart-wrenching museum presents an admirably nuanced and thorough analysis of the biggest war of the 20th century. And its exhibits, which are displayed in three grand pavilions, are amazing. Wall-sized photographs capture the confusion of D-Day. Riveting oral histories tell remarkable stories of survival. A stroll through the snowy woods of Ardennes feels eerily cold. The experience is personal, immersive and educational. Don't miss it.

How did this fascinating place land in New Orleans, not Washington, DC? The reconstructed LCVP or 'Higgins boat,' on display in the Louisiana Pavilion, provides the link. Originally designed by local entrepreneur Andrew Jackson Higgins for commercial use on Louisiana's bayous, these flat-bottomed amphibious landing craft moved tens of thousands of soldiers onto Normandy's beaches during the D-Day invasion on June 6, 1944.

The museum continues to open in several stages across three pavilions. The new Campaigns of Courage Pavilion spotlights the European and Pacific theaters. Inside, the new Road to Berlin galleries cover European battlefronts. A reconstructed Quonset hut – with a bombed-out roof – brings the air war powerfully close. The Road to Tokyo galleries, opening in December 2015, will highlight the Pacific theater. Visitors can personalize their explorations by registering for a dog tag, which connects them with the same WWII participant at various exhibits.

The Louisiana Memorial Pavilion covers D-Day in four galleries: The Home Front, Planning for D-Day, The D-Day Beaches and The D-Day Invasion in the Pacific. Don't miss the German Enigma machine. A restored Boeing B-17 bomber is visible from catwalks in the US Freedom Pavilion: The Boeing Center. Here you can join an immersive submarine experience inspired by the last patrol of the USS Tang.

Across the street, the movie Beyond all Boundaries takes a 4-D look at America's involvement in the war on a 120ft-wide screen. Get ready for rumbling seats and a dusting of snowflakes!

Lafayette Cemetery No 1

Hours: 7am-2:30pm Mon-Fri, to noon Sat

Location: Washington Ave, New Orleans, USA

Shaded by groves of lush greenery, this cemetery exudes a strong sense of Southern subtropical gothic. Built in 1833, it is divided by two intersecting footpaths that form a cross. Look out for the crypts built by fraternal organizations such as the Jefferson Fire Company No 22, which took care of their members and their families in large shared tombs. Some of the wealthier family tombs were built of marble, with elaborate details, but most were constructed simply of inexpensive plastered brick.

You'll notice many German and Irish names on the above-ground graves, testifying that immigrants were devastated by 19th-century yellow-fever epidemics. Not far from the entrance is a tomb containing the remains of an entire family that died of yellow fever.

The cemetery was filled to capacity within decades of its opening, and before the surrounding neighborhood reached its greatest affluence. By 1872 the prestigious Metairie Cemetery in Mid-City had opened and its opulent grounds appealed to those with truly extravagant and flamboyant tastes.

In July 1995 author Anne Rice staged her own funeral here. She hired a horse-drawn hearse and a brass band to play dirges, and wore an antique wedding dress as she laid down in a coffin. The event coincided with the release of one of Rice's novels.

Ogden Museum of Southern Art

Price: adult/child 5-17yr/student $10/5/8

Hours: 10am-5pm Wed-Mon, plus 5:30-8pm Thu

Contact: http://www.ogdenmuseum.org, 504-539-9650

Location: 925 Camp St, New Orleans, USA

One of our favorite museums in the city manages to be beautiful, educational and unpretentious all at once. New Orleans entrepreneur Roger Houston Ogden has assembled one of the finest collections of Southern art anywhere, which includes huge galleries ranging from impressionist landscapes to outsider folk-art quirkiness, to contemporary installation work.

On Thursday nights, pop in for Ogden after Hours, when you can listen to great Southern musicians and sip wine with a fun-loving, arts-obsessed crowd in the midst of the masterpieces.

The glass-and-stone Stephen Goldring Hall, with its soaring atrium, provides an inspiring welcome to the grounds. The building, which opened in 2003, is home to the museum's 20th- and 21st-century exhibitions as well as the Museum Store and its Center for Southern Craft & Design. 'Floating' stairs between floors will lead you to select pieces from regional artists as well as Southern landscapes, ceramics, glasswork and eye-catching works from self-taught artists. The Ogden's 18th-, 19th- and early-20th-century collections will be showcased in the Patrick F Taylor Library and the Clementine Hunter Education Wing, both under renovation.

City Park

Contact: http://www.neworleanscitypark.com, 504-482-4888

Location: Esplanade Ave & City Park Ave, New Orleans, USA

Live oaks, Spanish moss and lazy bayous frame this masterpiece of urban planning. Three miles long and 1 mile wide, dotted with gardens, waterways, bridges and home to a captivating art museum, City Park is bigger than Central Park in NYC, and it's New Orleans' prettiest green space. It's also a perfect expression of a local 'park,' in the sense that it is an only slightly tamed expression of the forest and Louisiana wetlands that are the natural backdrop of the city.

Art- and nature-lovers could easily spend a day exploring the park. Anchoring the action is the stately New Orleans Museum of Art, which spotlights regional and American artists. From there, stroll past the whimsical creations in the Sydney & Walda Besthoff Sculpture Garden then check out the lush Botanical Gardens. Kids in tow? Hop the rides at Carousel Gardens; climb the fantastical statuary inside Storyland; play mini-golf at City Putt; or rent a bike or paddleboat at Wheel Fun Rentals beside Big Lake. Across Big Lake, don't miss the Singing Oak and its wind chimes.

Maine

With more lobsters, lighthouses and charming resort villages than you can shake a selfie stick at, Maine is New England at its most iconic. The sea looms large here, with mile upon mile of jagged sea cliffs, peaceful harbors and pebbly beaches. Eat and drink your way through food- and beer-crazed Portland, one of America's coolest small cities. Explore the historic shipbuilding villages of the Midcoast. Hike through Acadia National Park, a spectacular island of mountains and fjord-like estuaries. Let the coastal wind whip through those cobwebs and inhale the salty air. Venture into the state's inland region, a vast wilderness of pine forest and snowy peaks.

Outdoor adventurers can race white-water rapids, cycle the winding shore roads or kayak beside playful harbor seals. For slower-paced fun, there are plenty of antique shops, cozy lobster shacks, charming inns and locally brewed beer on hand.

Classic townscapes, rocky shorelines punctuated by sandy beaches, and picturesque downtowns draw vacationing New Englanders to Maine like a magnet. Counting all its nooks, crannies, and crags, Maine's coast would stretch for thousands of miles if you could pull it straight. The Southern Coast is the most visited section, stretching north from Kittery to just outside Portland, but don't let that stop you from heading farther "Down East" (this nautical term is Maine-speak for "up the coast"), where you'll be rewarded with the majestic mountains and rugged coastline of popular Acadia National Park. Slow down to explore the museums, galleries, and shops in the larger towns and cities, like Portland, and the antiques and curio shops and harbor side lobster shacks in the smaller towns and fishing villages. Despite the cold North Atlantic waters, beachgoers enjoy miles of sandy—or, more frequently, rocky—beaches, with sweeping views of lighthouses, forested islands, and the wide-open sea. The most visited areas in inland Maine are the Western Lakes and Mountains—stretching west and north from the New Hampshire border—and the North Woods — extending north from central Maine. This area attracts skiers, hikers, campers, canoeists, anglers, and other outdoors enthusiasts

Sights in Maine

Old Port District

Handsome 19th-century brick buildings line the streets of the Old Port, with Portland's most enticing shops, pubs and restaurants located within this five-square-block district. By night, flickering gas lanterns add to the atmosphere. What to do here? Eat some wicked-fresh seafood, down a local microbrew, buy a nautical-themed T-shirt from an up-and-coming designer or peruse the many local art galleries. Don't forget to wander the authentically stinky wharfs, ducking into a fishmonger's to order some lobsters to ship home.

Farnsworth Art Museum

Price: adult/child $15/free

Hours: 10am-5pm Jun-Oct, closed Mon Jan-Apr, May, Nov & Dec, plus Tue Jan-Mar

Contact: http://www.farnsworthmuseum.org, 207-596-6457

Location: 16 Museum St, Rockland, USA

One of the country's best small regional museums, the Farnsworth houses a collection spanning 200 years of American art. Artists who have lived or worked in Maine are the museum's definite strength – look for works by the Wyeth family (Andrew, NC and Jamie), Edward Hopper, Louise Nevelson,

Rockwell Kent and Robert Indiana. Exhibits on the Wyeth family continue in the Wyeth Center, in a renovated church across the garden from the main museum (open in summer).

LL Bean Flagship Store

Hours: 24hr

Contact: http://www.llbean.com, 877-755-2326

Location: 95 Main St, Freeport, Portland, USA

A 10ft-tall Bean Boot sits outside the flagship LL Bean store. Although a hundred other stores have joined it in Freeport, the wildly popular LL Bean is still the epicenter of town and one of the most popular tourist attractions in Maine. It's part store, part outdoor-themed amusement park, with an archery range, an indoor trout pond and coffee shops.

Surrounding it is a small campus of LL Bean stores (one dedicated to hunting and fishing; another to bike, boat and ski, etc).

Coastal Maine Botanical Gardens

Price: adult/child $16/8

Hours: 9am-5pm

Contact: http://www.mainegardens.org, 207 633 8000

Location: 132 Botanical Gardens Dr, off Barters Island Rd, Boothbay Harbor, USA

These magnificent gardens are one of the state's most popular attractions. The verdant waterfront kingdom has 270 acres, with groomed trails winding through forest, meadows and ornamental gardens blooming with both native and exotic plant species. The storybook-themed children's garden offers interactive fun, and visitors with kids in town shouldn't miss the daily story time, puppet theater or chicken-feeding (daily from mid-June to early September).

Take the Shoreline Trail to the riverside Landing (about a 20-minute walk from the visitor center), where in summer there are kayaks and stand-up paddleboards for rent, and the chance to join a three-hour kayaking tour (departs 9:30am, tour excluding garden admission $60). One-hour electric boat cruises also leave from the Landing up to five times daily in summer (cruises including garden admission adult/child $36/20).

A free garden-highlight walking tour leaves daily at 11am (May to October) from the visitor center, which also houses a cafe and gift shop.

The website outlines details of events and tours, including the gorgeous 'Gardens Aglow' event, which lights up chilly nights in the six weeks preceding Christmas.

Maine Maritime Museum

Price: adult/child $15.50/10

Hours: 9:30am-5pm

Contact: http://www.mainemaritimemuseum.org, 207-443-1316

Location: 243 Washington St, Bath & Around, USA

On the western bank of the Kennebec River, this wonderful museum preserves the Kennebec's long shipbuilding tradition with paintings, models and hands-on exhibits that tell the tale of the past 400 years of seafaring. One highlight is the remains of the Snow Squall, a three-mast 1851 clipper ship. The on-site 19th-century Percy & Small Shipyard, preserved by the museum, is America's only remaining wooden-boat shipyard. There's also a life-size sculpture of the Wyoming, the largest wooden sailing vessel ever built.

In summer, the museum offers a variety of boat trips (per person $32 to $50, including museum admission), taking in assorted lighthouses and bird-rich bays. It also has a popular trolley tour ($30) that gives an insider's perspective of the Bath Iron Works (reservations recommended). See details and schedules on the website.

Fort Williams Park

Hours: sunrise-sunset

Contact: http://www.fortwilliams.org

Location: 1000 Shore Rd, Portland, USA

Four miles southeast of Portland on Cape Elizabeth, 90-acre Fort Williams Park is worth visiting simply for the panoramas and picnic possibilities. Stroll around the ruins of the fort, a late-19th-century artillery base, checking out the WWII bunkers and gun emplacements that still dot the rolling lawns (a German U-boat was spotted in Casco Bay in 1942). The fort actively guarded the entrance to Casco Bay until 1964. A favorite feature of the park is the Portland Head Light; the oldest of Maine's 52 functioning lighthouses, it was commissioned by President George Washington in 1791.

Look out for the much-loved Bite into Maine (www.biteintomaine.com) food truck that sets up in the park and serves delicious lobster rolls from May to October (see the website for hours).

Maryland

Maryland's mythic hero — its cowboy, if you will — is the waterman, who prowls the Chesapeake in his skipjack, dredging oysters. Today the waterman is a symbol of contemporary Maryland: not in the manner in which he works, but in the variety of his catch. Maryland has always been a land of diversity, and from its rich Civil War history to the contemporary appeal of Baltimore's Inner Harbor, Maryland casts a wide net.

Maryland is often described as 'America in Miniature,' and for good reason: this small state possesses all of the best bits of the country, from the Appalachian Mountains in the west to sandy white beaches in the east. A blend of Northern streetwise and Southern down-home gives this most osmotic of border states an appealing identity crisis. Its main city, Baltimore, is a sharp, demanding port town; the Eastern Shore jumbles art-and-antique-minded city refugees and working fishermen; while the DC suburbs are packed with government and office workers seeking green space, and the poor seeking lower rents. Yet it all somehow works – scrumptious blue crabs, Natty Boh beer and lovely Chesapeake country being the glue that binds all. This is also an extremely diverse and progressive state, and was one of the first in the country to legalize gay marriage.

Sights in Maryland

American Visionary Art Museum

Price: adult/child $16/10

Hours: 10am-6pm Tue-Sun

Contact: http://www.avam.org, 410-244-1900

Location: 800 Key Hwy, Baltimore, USA

Housing a jaw-dropping collection of self-taught (or 'outsider' art), AVAM is a celebration of unbridled creativity utterly free of arts-scene pretension. You'll find broken-mirror collages, homemade robots and flying apparatuses, elaborately sculptural works made of needlepoint, and gigantic model ships painstakingly created from matchsticks.

Evergreen Museum

Price: adult/child $8/5

Hours: 11am-4pm Tue-Fri, noon-4pm Sat & Sun

Contact: http://museums.jhu.edu, 410-516-0341

Location: 4545 N Charles St, Baltimore, USA

Well worth the drive out, this grand 19th-century mansion provides a fascinating glimpse into upper-class Baltimore life of the 1800s. The house is packed with fine art and masterpieces of the decorative arts – including paintings by Modigliani, glass by Louis Comfort Tiffany and exquisite Asian porcelain – not to mention the astounding rare book collection, numbering some 32,000 volumes.

More impressive than the collection, however, is the compelling story of the Garrett family, who were world travelers (John W was an active diplomat for some years) and astute philanthropists, as well as lovers of the arts, if not always successful performers in their own right – though that didn't stop Alice from taking the stage (her own, which you'll see in the intimate theater below the house).

Walters Art Museum

Hours: 10am-5pm Wed-Sun, to 9pm Thu

Contact: http://www.thewalters.org, 410-547-9000

Location: 600 N Charles St, Baltimore, USA

Don't pass up this excellent, eclectic gallery: it spans more than 55 centuries, from ancient to contemporary, with excellent displays of Asian treasures, rare and ornate manuscripts and books, and a comprehensive French paintings collection.

Antietam National Battlefield

Price: 3-day pass per person/family $4/6

Hours: 8:30am-6pm, visitor center 9am-5pm

Contact: http://www.nps.gov/anti, 301-432-5124

Location: 5831 Dunker Church Rd, Sharpsburg, MD, Western Maryland, USA

The site of the bloodiest day in American history is now, ironically, supremely peaceful, quiet and haunting – uncluttered save for plaques and statues. On September 17, 1862, General Robert E Lee's first invasion of the North was stalled here in a tactical stalemate that left more than 23,000 dead, wounded or missing – more casualties than America had suffered in all her previous wars combined. Poignantly, many of the battlefield graves are inscribed with German and Irish names, a roll call of immigrants who died fighting for their new homeland.

The visitor center shows a short film (playing on the hour and half-hour) about the events that transpired here. It also sells books and materials, including self-guided driving and walking tours of the battlefield.

Massachusetts

The history is legendary – Plymouth, where the Pilgrims landed; Boston, where the first shots of the American Revolution rang out; and Nantucket, whose whaling ships swarmed the oceans. But there's a lot more than landmark sights in this old state. Fast forward to the present: Boston and neighboring Cambridge have blossomed into spirited college towns, Provincetown's a gay-extravaganza whirl, and those whales – a major attraction in their own right – are now followed by affectionate sightseers on whale-watching cruises. By all means start in Boston, the state's busy hub, where you can mix colonial sights and museum strolls with sizzling nightlife and pub crawls. Then move further afield, to the woodsy Berkshires and the dunes and beaches of Cape Cod and Martha's Vineyard.

Massachusetts's state capital, Boston, is New England's largest and most cosmopolitan city. It is the region's hub for modern commerce, education, and culture, and the early history of the United States is never far from view. The 50-acre Boston Common is the oldest public park in the nation and the 2.5-mile Freedom Trail winds past 16 of the city's most historic landmarks such as the USS Constitution ("Old Ironsides") and the Old North Church (of "one if by land, two if by sea" fame). This is the cradle of American democracy, a place where soaring skyscrapers cast shadows on Colonial graveyards. Nearby

Boston, great beaches, delicious seafood, and artisan-filled shopping districts await in scenic Cape Cod, chic Martha's Vineyard, and cozy Nantucket. In Western Massachusetts, the mountainous Berkshires live up to the storybook image of rural New England. Staying at a bed-and-breakfast, taking in the local arts scene in quaint towns like Stockbridge and Lenox, and leaf peeping in the fall are all part of the experience. Farther east, the Pioneer Valley is home to a string of historic settlements, and artsy and thriving college towns like Amherst and Northampton.

Sights in Massachusetts

Massachusetts State House

Hours: 9am-5pm, tours 10am-3:30pm Mon-Fri

Contact: http://www.sec.state.ma.us

Location: cnr Beacon & Bowdoin Sts, Boston, USA

High atop Beacon Hill, Massachusetts' leaders and legislators attempt to turn their ideas into concrete policies and practices within the State House. John Hancock provided the land (previously part of his cow pasture); Charles Bulfinch designed the commanding state capitol; but it was Oliver Wendell Holmes who called it 'the hub of the solar system' (thus earning Boston the nickname 'the Hub'). Free 40-minute tours cover the history, artwork, architecture and political personalities of the State House.

Tours start in the Doric Hall, the columned reception area directly below the dome. Once the main entryway to the State House, these front doors are now used only by a visiting US president or by a departing governor taking 'the long walk' on his last day in office.

The nearby Nurses Hall is named for the moving statue of a Civil War nurse tending to a fallen soldier. The circular Memorial Hall, known as the Hall of Flags, honors Massachusetts soldiers by displaying some of the tattered flags that have been carried to battle over the years. Finally, the impressive marble Great Hall is hung with 351 flags, representing all the cities and towns in Massachusetts.

Upstairs, visitors can see both legislative chambers: The House of Representatives, also home of the famous Sacred Cod; and the Senate Chamber, residence of the Holy Mackerel. The Governor's office is also here, though it's not open to the public.

On the front lawn, statues honor important Massachusetts figures, among them orator Daniel Webster, Civil War general Joseph Hooker, religious martyrs Anne Hutchinson and Mary Dyer, President John F Kennedy, and educator Horace Mann. Unfortunately, these lovely grounds are closed to the public, so you'll have to peek through the iron fence to catch a glimpse.

Fenway Park

Price: tours adult/child $18/12, premium tour $30

Hours: 9am-5pm

Contact: http://www.redsox.com

Location: 4 Yawkey Way, Boston, USA

What is it that makes Fenway Park 'America's Most Beloved Ballpark'? It's not just that it's the home of the Boston Red Sox. Open since 1912, it is the oldest operating baseball park in the country. As such, the park has many quirks that make for a unique experience. See them all on a ballpark tour. (Avoid afternoon tours on game days; crowds are huge and tours shortened.)

The Green Monster, the 37ft-high wall in left field, is the most famous feature at Fenway Park. It's only 310ft away from home plate (compared to the standard 325ft). That makes it a popular target for right-handed hitters, who can score an easy home run with a high hit to left field. On the other hand, a powerful line drive – which might normally be a home run – bounces off the Monster for an off-the-wall double. As all Red Sox fans know, 'the wall giveth and the wall taketh away.'

The Green Monster was painted green only in 1947. But since then, it has become a patented part of the Fenway experience. Literally. The color is officially known as Fence Green and the supplier will not share the recipe.

The Pesky Pole, Fenway's right-field foul pole, is named for former shortstop Johnny Pesky. 'Mr Red Sox' Johnny Pesky has been associated with the team for 15 years as a player and 45 years as a manager or coach.

The Triangle, in the deepest darkest corner of center field where the walls form a triangle, is – at 425ft – the furthest distance from home plate.

The bleachers at Fenway Park are green, except for the lone red seat: seat 21 at section 42, row 37. This is supposedly the longest home run ever hit at Fenway Park – officially 502ft, hit by Ted Williams in 1946.

Museum of Fine Arts

Price: adult/child $25/free

Hours: 10am-5pm Sat-Tue, to 10pm Wed-Fri

Contact: http://www.mfa.org

Location: 465 Huntington Ave, Boston, USA

Since 1876, the Museum of Fine Arts has been Boston's premier venue for showcasing art by local, national and international artists. Nowadays the museum's holdings encompass all eras, from the ancient world to contemporary times, and all areas of the globe, making it truly encyclopedic in scope. Most recently, the museum has added gorgeous new wings dedicated to the Art of the Americas and to contemporary art, contributing to Boston's emergence as an art center in the 21st century.

The centerpiece of the MFA is the four-story Americas wing, which includes 53 galleries exhibiting art from the pre-Columbian era up through the 20th century. The 2nd level is, perhaps, the richest part of the wing. An entire gallery is dedicated to John Singer Sargent, including his iconic painting The Daughters of Edward Darley Boit.

Located in the museum's northern wing, the MFA's collection of European art spans the centuries from the Middle Ages to the 20th century. The highlight of the European exhibit is no doubt the Impressionists and post-Impressionists, with masterpieces by Degas, Gauguin, Renoir and Van Gogh, as well as the largest collection of Monets outside Paris.

In the southwestern wing, the collection of Asian art includes the exhibits in the serene Buddhist Temple room. In the southeastern part of the museum, the MFA's ancient-art collection also covers a huge geographic spectrum, including two rooms of mummies in the Egyptian galleries.

The Linde Wing for Contemporary Art is full of surprises. The darling of museum patrons is Black River, a fantastic woven tapestry of discarded bottle caps by Ghanaian artist El Anatsui.

Michigan

Flanked by four Great Lakes and with 2,000 miles of shoreline (even more than California), Michigan is divided into two peninsulas—the Lower, which resembles a mitten and is the more densely populated, and the Upper, which is more rugged and rural. Ask a Michigander where he or she lives, and directions will likely be given using the palm of their hand, with the south-central part of the state known as "the Thumb."

Lakes play a part both in the state's psyche and its recreational possibilities, which are both legendary and numerous. In summer, popular choices include canoeing, fishing, swimming, sailing, scuba diving, water skiing, and camping. In winter, trails welcome snowmobilers, skiers, snowshoers, and dogsledders. The state is also blessed with dramatic topography, including waterfalls in the Upper Peninsula and towering dunes near Lake Michigan. Growing wine-country regions exist near Traverse City and Grand Rapids.
Lovely resort towns, from Traverse City to Saugatuck, overflow with lakeside inns, boutiques, and antiques shops. Yet Michigan has its share of big cities, too, including the Furniture City (Grand Rapids), the Capital City (Lansing),

and the better-known Motor City (Detroit). All have vibrant arts and culture, excellent restaurants, neighborhoods with character, and tourist attractions.

More, more, more – Michigan is the Midwest state that cranks it up. It sports more beaches than the Atlantic seaboard. More than half the state is covered by forests. And more cherries and berries get shoveled into pies here than anywhere else in the USA. Plus its gritty city Detroit is the Midwest's rawest of all – and we mean that in a good way.

Michigan occupies prime real estate, surrounded by four of the five Great Lakes – Superior, Michigan, Huron and Erie. Islands – Mackinac, Manitou and Isle Royale – freckle its coast and make top touring destinations. Surfing beaches, colored sandstone cliffs and trekkable sand dunes also woo visitors.

The state consists of two parts split by water: the larger Lower Peninsula, shaped like a mitten; and the smaller, lightly populated Upper Peninsula, shaped like a slipper. They are linked by the gasp-worthy Mackinac Bridge, which spans the Straits of Mackinac (pronounced mac-in-aw).

Sights in Michigan

Eastern Market

Contact: http://www.easternmarket.com

Location: Adelaide & Russell Sts, Detroit, USA

Produce, cheese, spice and flower vendors fill the large halls on Saturday, but you also can turn up Monday through Friday to browse the specialty shops (props to the peanut roaster) and cafes that flank the halls on Russell and Market Sts. In addition, from June through October there's a scaled-down market on Tuesdays and a Sunday craft market with food trucks.

Detroit Institute of Arts

Price: adult/child $8/4

Hours: 9am-4pm Tue-Thu, to 10pm Fri, 10am-5pm Sat & Sun

Contact: http://www.dia.org, 313-833-7900

Location: 5200 Woodward Ave, Detroit, USA

The cream of the museum crop. The centerpiece is Diego Rivera's mural Detroit Industry, which fills an entire room and reflects the city's blue-collar labor history. Beyond it are Picassos, suits of armor, mod African American paintings, puppets and troves more.

Fort Mackinac

Price: adult/child $12/7

Hours: 9:30am-6pm Jun-Aug, to 5pm May & Sep–mid-Oct

Contact: http://www.mackinacparks.com, 906-847-3328

Fort Mackinac sits atop limestone cliffs near downtown. Built by the British in 1780, it's one of the best-preserved military forts in the country. Costumed interpreters and cannon and rifle firings (every half-hour) entertain the kids.

Stop into the tearoom for a bite and million-dollar view of downtown and the Straits of Mackinac from the outdoor tables.

The fort admission price also allows you entry to five other museums in town along Market St, including the Dr Beaumont Museum (where the doctor performed his famous digestive tract experiments) and Benjamin Blacksmith Shop.

Pictured Rocks National Lakeshore

Stretching along prime Lake Superior real estate, Pictured Rocks National Lakeshore is a series of wild cliffs and caves where blue and green minerals have streaked the red and yellow sandstone into a kaleidoscope of color. Rte 58 (Alger County Rd) spans the park for 52 slow miles from Grand Marais in the east to Munising in the west.

Top sights (from east to west) include Au Sable Point Lighthouse (reached via a 3-mile round-trip walk beside shipwreck skeletons), agate-strewn Twelvemile Beach, hike-rich Chapel Falls and view-worthy Miners Castle Overlook.

Minnesota

Minnesota's 11,842 lakes offer more shoreline than Florida, California, and Hawaii combined. One out of every six people in Minnesota owns a boat, the highest ratio in the country. Minnesota also ranks as number one in the per-capita rate of fishing-license purchases. And fishing isn't just a warm-weather activity, either. Every winter, little heated shacks pop up on thousands of lakes. Inside, you'll find anglers huddling over holes in the ice, hoping to hook a lunker.

While the state's outdoor attractions lure boaters, hikers, cross-country skiers, and snowmobilers, the Twin Cities of Minneapolis and St. Paul feature a variety of entertainment opportunities, including theater, music, shopping, and spectator sports.

If you travel all of Minnesota's 406 miles, from Canada to Iowa, you'll see three distinct kinds of terrain. To the west and south you'll find grassland plains and prairies. Much of this land has been converted to agricultural use, but some still remains in its native state. The eastern part of the state, once known as the "Big Woods," is the natural home of hardwood forests.

Sights in Minnesota

Minneapolis Sculpture Garden

Hours: 6am-midnight

Location: 725 Vineland Pl, Minneapolis, USA

The 11-acre garden, studded with contemporary works such as the oft-photographed Spoonbridge & Cherry by Claes Oldenburg, sits beside the Walker Art Center. The Cowles Conservatory, abloom with exotic hothouse flowers, is also on the grounds. In summer a trippy mini-golf course amid the sculptures adds to the fun ($12 for adults, $9 for kids). Note the garden will be closed through 2016 as it gets an ecofriendly facelift.

Endless Bridge

Hours: 8am-8pm, to 11pm on performance days

Location: 818 2nd St S, Minneapolis, USA

Head inside the cobalt-blue Guthrie Theater and make your way up the escalator to the Endless Bridge, a far-out cantilevered walkway overlooking the Mississippi River. You don't need a theater ticket, as it's intended as a public space. The theater's 9th floor Amber Box provides another knockout view.

Walker Art Center

Price: adult/child $14/free, admission free Thu evening & 1st Sat of month

Hours: 11am-5pm Tue, Wed & Fri-Sun, to 9pm Thu

Contact: http://www.walkerart.org, 612-375-7622

Location: 1750 Hennepin Ave, Minneapolis, USA

The first-class center has a strong permanent collection of 20th-century art and photography, including big-name US painters and great US pop art. On Monday evenings from late July to late August, the museum hosts free movies and music across the pedestrian bridge in Loring Park that are quite the to-do.

Minneapolis Institute of Arts

Hours: 10am-5pm Tue-Sat, to 9pm Thu, 11am-5pm Sun

Contact: http://www.artsmia.org, 612-870-3131

Location: 2400 3rd Ave S, Minneapolis, USA

This museum is a huge trove housing a veritable history of art. The modern and contemporary collections astonish, while the Asian galleries (2nd floor) and Decorative Arts rooms (3rd floor) are also highlights. Allot at least a few hours to visit. The museum is a mile south of downtown via 3rd Ave S.

Mississippi

The state named for the most vital waterway in North America encompasses, appropriately enough, a long river of identities. Mississippi features palatial mansions and rural poverty; haunted cotton flats and lush hill country; honey-dipped sand on the coast and serene farmland in the north. Oft mythologized and misunderstood, this is the womb of some of the rawest history – and music – in the country.

Today's Mississippi is a multifaceted landscape of rich history, legendary musical heritage, mouthwatering culinary delights, and adventurous outdoor recreation. From the natural splendor of the Hills region to the mighty Mississippi River to the sandy beaches of the Gulf Coast, Mississippi celebrates diversity and creativity through her people, geography, sights, and sounds. Journey along miles of hiking and biking trails inside the vast acreage of state parks and national forests. Relish authentic sounds of blues, country, or rock 'n' roll in the birthplace of it all along the Mississippi Blues and Country Music Trails. Experience the state's history by touring antebellum homes during spring and fall pilgrimages. Meander through one of Mississippi's state-of-the-art museums. Or explore civil rights history along the Mississippi Freedom Trail.

Indulge in a little retail therapy at the many antiques shops and cozy boutiques on a nearby town square. Dine on Southern classics like fresh Gulf seafood, hot tamales or fried pickles, or one-of-a-kind entrées with a modern twist. Whether you fly or drive to get here, you can celebrate a Mississippi tradition year-round at any of the state's plethora of festivals and fairs.

Sights in Mississippi

Vicksburg National Military Park

Price: per car/individual $8/4

Hours: 8am-5pm

Contact: http://www.nps.gov/vick, 601-636-0583

Location: Clay St, Vicksburg, USA

Vicksburg controlled access to the Mississippi River, and it's seizure was one of the turning points of the Civil War. A 16-mile driving tour passes historic markers explaining battle scenarios and key events from the city's long siege, when residents lived like moles in caverns to avoid Union shells. Plan on staying for at least 90 minutes. If you have your own bike, cycling is a fantastic way to tour the place. Locals use the scenic park for walking and running.

Rowan Oak

Price: adult/child $5/free

Hours: 10am-4pm Tue-Sat, 1-4pm Sun, from Jun-Aug 10am-6pm Tue-Sat, 1-6pm Sun

Contact: http://www.rowanoak.com, 662-234-3284

Location: Old Taylor Rd, Oxford, USA

Literary pilgrims head directly here, to the graceful 1840s home of William Faulkner. He authored many brilliant and dense novels set in Mississippi, and his work is celebrated in Oxford with an annual conference in July. Tours of Rowan Oak – where Faulkner lived from 1930 until his death in 1962, and which may reasonably be dubbed, to use the author's own elegant words, his 'postage stamp of native soil' – are self-guided.

Natchez Trace Parkway

The Natchez Trace Parkway winds 444 miles from Pasquo, Tennessee southwest to Natchez, Mississippi. This northern section is one of the most attractive stretches of the entire route, with broad-leafed trees leaning together to form an arch over the winding road. Along the way, you are treated to a wide panoply of Southern landscapes: thick, dark forests, soggy wetlands, gentle hill country and wide swathes of farmland.

Walter Anderson Museum

Price: adult/child $10/5

Hours: 9:30am-4:30pm Mon-Sat, from 12:30pm Sun

Contact: http://www.walterandersonmuseum.org, 228-872-3164

Location: 510 Washington St, Gulf Coast, USA

A consummate artist and lover of Gulf Coast nature, Walter Anderson suffered from mental illness, which spurred his monastic existence and fueled his life's work: in his own words, being one of 'those who have brought nature and art together into one thing.' After he died, the beachside shack where he lived on Horn Island was discovered to be painted in mind-blowing murals, which you'll see here.

Missouri

The most populated state in the Plains, Missouri likes to mix things up, serving visitors ample portions of both sophisticated city life and down-home country sights. St Louis and Kansas City are the region's most interesting cities and each is a destination in its own right. But, with more forest and less farm field than neighboring states, Missouri also cradles plenty of wild places and wide-open spaces, most notably the rolling Ozark Mountains, where the winding valleys invite adventurous exploration or just some laid-back meandering behind the steering wheel. Maybe you'll find an adventure worthy of Hannibal native Mark Twain as you wander the state.

Missouri sits where the Midwest meets the South, and the state's central location—along with its great rivers—has made it an important hub for explorers and pioneers over the centuries. The Missouri River carried Lewis and Clark north as they began their great expedition; soon after, its banks saw the rise of the 19th-century wagon trails heading west. Once frequented by steamboats, both the Missouri and the Mississippi are now home to riverboat gambling, a controversial part of the state's tourism industry. Elsewhere in Missouri, a wealth of lakes, rivers, and caves provide plenty of opportunities for outdoor recreation.

Sights in Missouri

Gateway Arch & Jefferson National Expansion Memorial

Price: tram ride adult/child $10/5

Hours: 8am-10pm Jun-Aug, 9am-6pm Sep-May, last tram 1hr before closing

Contact: http://www.gatewayarch.com, 314-655-1700

Location: St Louis, USA

As a symbol for St Louis, the Arch has soared above any expectations its backers could have had in 1965 when it opened. The centerpiece of this National Park Service property, the silvery, shimmering Gateway Arch is the Great Plains' own Eiffel Tower. It stands 630ft high and symbolizes St Louis' historical role as 'Gateway to the West.' The tram ride takes you to the tight confines at the top.

Book tickets in advance on the NPS website.

A massive project has transformed the area around the Arch in time for its 50th birthday. A large plaza now covers I-70 and connects the Arch and its park directly to the Old Courthouse and the rest of downtown. It's a huge and welcome improvement. Note that some portions of the upgrade, which includes all of the parks, won't be complete until 2017. Find out more at www.cityarchriver.org.

Truman Home

Price: tours adult/child $5/free

Hours: 9am-4:30pm, closed Mon Nov-May

Contact: http://www.nps.gov/hstr

Location: 219 N Delaware St, Independence, USA

See the simple life Harry and Bess lived in this basic but charming wood house. It is furnished with their original belongings and you fully expect the couple to wander out and say hello.

Tour tickets are sold at the visitor center. Ask for directions to the Truman Family Farm, where the future president 'got his common sense.'

Truman lived here from 1919 to 1972 and in retirement entertained visiting dignitaries in his strictly pedestrian front room – he's said to have hoped none of the callers would linger more than 30 minutes.

Forest Park

Hours: 6am-10pm

Contact: 314-289-5300

Location: bounded by Lindell Blvd, Kingshighway Blvd & I-64, St Louis, USA

New York City may have Central Park, but St Louis has the bigger (by 528 acres) Forest Park. The superb, 1371-acre spread was the setting of the 1904 World's Fair. It's a beautiful place to escape to and is dotted with attractions, many free. Two walkable neighborhoods, The Loop and Central West End, are close.

The Visitor and Education Center is in an old streetcar pavilion and has a cafe. Free walking tours leave from here, or you can borrow an iPod audio tour.

National WWI Museum

Price: adult/child $14/8

Hours: 10am-5pm, closed Mon Sep-May

Contact: http://www.theworldwar.org, 816-888-8100

Location: 100 W 26th St, Kansas City, USA

Enter this impressive modern museum on a glass walkway over a field of red poppies, the symbol of the trench fighting. Through detailed and engaging displays, learn about a war that is almost forgotten by many Americans. The only quibble is that military hardware and uniforms take precedence over the horrible toll. The museum is crowned by the historic Liberty Memorial, which has sweeping views over the city.

Montana

Big Sky Country is more than just a nickname: Montana has huge expanses of rugged country. It's a place to discover how beautiful the night sky can be and what "dark" truly is with limited city lights. But in addition to the natural beauty—stunning glaciers and ski slopes, trout-filled streams and high plains—you'll also find a welcoming place full of locals who love to share their state's natural beauty, mining history, and thriving cultural communities with others.

Maybe it's the independent frontier spirit, wild and free and oh-so-American, that earned Montana its 'live and let live' state motto. The sky seems bigger and bluer. The air is crisp and pine-scented. From mountains that drop into undulating ranchlands to brick brewhouses and the shaggy grizzly found lapping at an ice-blue glacier lake, Montana brings you to that euphoric place, naturally. And then it remains with you long after you've left its beautiful spaces behind.

Sights in Montana

Logan Pass

Location: Glacier National Park, USA

Perched above the tree line, atop the wind-lashed Continental Divide, and blocked by snow for most of the year, 2026m (6646ft) Logan Pass – named for William R Logan, Glacier's first superintendent – is the park's highest navigable point by road. Two trails, Hidden Lake Overlook (which continues on to Hidden Lake itself) and Highline, lead out from here. Views are stupendous; the parking situation, however, is not – you might spend a lot of time searching for a spot during peak hours.

Museum of the Rockies

Price: adult/child $14.50/9.50

Hours: 8am-8pm Jun-Aug, 9am-5pm Mon-Sat, noon-5pm Sun Sep-May

Contact: http://www.museumoftherockies.org, 406-994-2251

Location: 600 W Kagy Blvd, Bozeman, USA

Montana State University's museum is the most entertaining in Montana and shouldn't be missed, with stellar dinosaur exhibits, early Native American art and laser planetarium shows, as well as a living-history outdoors section (closed in winter) and various temporary exhibits. Guided tours happen more or less constantly and are recommended for families with young children, as they let kids get more interactive with some of the displays.

Grizzly & Wolf Discovery Center

Price: adult/child 5-12yr $11.50/6.50

Hours: 8:30am-8:30pm, closes earlier in winter

Contact: http://www.grizzlydiscoveryctr.org, 406-646-7001

Location: 201 S Canyon, West Yellowstone, USA

Offering an afterlife to 'pest' grizzlies facing extermination, this nonprofit center grants a chance to see captive wolves and bears if you failed to see any in the park. The indoor bear exhibit is good, and there is an information wall with clippings of recent bear encounters, as well as the latest wolf-pack locations. The daily programs on hiking safely in bear country and using bear spray are excellent primers for the park.

The twice-daily 'Keeper Kids' program even allows kids to hide food in the enclosures and then watch the bears sniff them out – fun! Check the website for timings. Admission is good for two days. Here's an interesting fact: faced with a regular supply of food, the bears here don't hibernate.

St Mary Lake

Location: Glacier National Park, USA

Located on the park's dryer eastern side, where the mountains melt imperceptibly into the Great Plains, St Mary Lake lies in a deep, glacier-carved valley famous for its astounding views and ferocious winds. Overlooked by the tall, chiseled peaks of the Rockies and still dramatically scarred by the landscape-altering effects of the 2006 Red Eagle Fire, the valley is spectacularly traversed by the Going-to-the-Sun Rd and punctuated by numerous trailheads and viewpoints.

St Mary's gorgeous turquoise sheen, easily the most striking color of any of Glacier's major bodies of water, is due to the suspension of tiny particles of glacial rock in the lake's water that absorbs and reflects light.

Nebraska

Those who just see Nebraska as 480 miles of blandness along I-80 are missing out on a lot. The Cornhusker State (they do grow a lot of ears) has beautiful river valleys and an often-stark bleakness that is entrancing. Its links to the past – from vast fields of dinosaur remains to Native American culture to the toils of hardy settlers – provides a dramatic storyline. Alongside the state's sprinkling of cute little towns, Nebraska's two main cities, Omaha and Lincoln, are vibrant and artful.

The key to enjoying this long stoic stretch of country is to take the smaller roads, whether it's US 30 instead of I-80, US 20 to the Black Hills, or the lonely and magnificent US 2.

Nebraska has everything from city sophistication to country charm. There are places so rugged and wild they still conjure images of the Old West frontier, and there are cosmopolitan cities with fabulous shopping and superb restaurants. The terrain varies from the rolling hill country along the Missouri River, where foliage is lush and varied, to the grasslands of the Sandhills, to the Panhandle's rough breaks with their bluffs and buttes. Nebraska was declared part of the "Great American Desert" by government explorer Stephen Long in 1820. But the state actually has 23,000 miles of rivers and streams and 246 public lakes and reservoirs that also attract an estimated 10 million ducks and 2 million snow geese.

European emigrants homesteaded the state at the turn of the 20th century; today Nebraska has an "Irish Capital" (O'Neill), a "Czech Capital" (Wilber), and a "Danish Capital" (Dannebrog). This is a state where you can still find a hamburger for a couple of bucks, and where a fried chicken dinner is likely to be served family-style: a platter of chicken, a bowl of potatoes, and a pitcher of gravy.

Sights in Nebraska

Durham Museum

Price: adult/child $9/6

Hours: 10am-8pm Tue, to 5pm Wed-Sat, 1-5pm Sun

Contact: http://www.durhammuseum.org, 402-444-5071

Location: 801 S 10th St, Omaha, USA

The soaring art-deco Union Station train depot houses a remarkable museum. Covering local history from the Lewis and Clark expedition to the Omaha stockyards to the trains that once called here, the Durham makes the most of its beautiful surrounds. The soda fountain still serves hot dogs and phosphate sodas.

The museum offers themed historic tours ($25) of Omaha several days a week in summer.

Agate Fossil Beds National Monument

Hours: 9am-5pm Jun-Aug, 8am-4pm Sep-May

Contact: http://www.nps.gov/agfo, 308-668-2211

Location: River Rd, Nebraska Panhandle, USA

Some 20 million years ago, this part of Nebraska was like the Serengeti in Africa today: a gathering place for a rich variety of creatures. Today the bones of thousands of these ancient dinosaurs are found at this isolated site. Displays and walks detail the amazing – and ongoing – finds. Don't miss the Bone Cabin and the burrowing beaver plus the Native American exhibits.

Scotts Bluff National Monument

Price: per car $5

Hours: visitor center 8am-7pm Jun-Aug, to 5pm Sep-May

Contact: http://www.nps.gov/scbl, 308-436-9700

Location: Hwy 92, Nebraska Panhandle, USA

Scotts Bluff has been a beacon to travelers for centuries. Rising 800ft above the flat plains of western Nebraska, it was an important waypoint on the Oregon Trail in the mid-19th century. You can still see wagon ruts today. The visitor center has displays and can guide you to walks and drives. It's south of Scottsbluff town.

Union Pacific Railroad Museum

Hours: 10am-4pm Tue-Sat

Contact: http://www.uprrmuseum.org

Location: 200 Pearl St, Omaha, USA

Just across the river in the cute little downtown area of Council Bluffs, IA, this grand museum tells the story of the world's most profitable railroad and the company that rammed the transcontinental line west from here in the 1860s. Look for the pictures of Ronald Reagan and his chimp-pal Bonzo aboard a train.

Nevada

Nevada is a vast state with most of its population clustered in a certain Sin City in the southwest corner, where more than 40 million people visit annually. Stark desert beauty and a bit of the Wild West is found in much of the rest of Nevada, particularly in Great Basin National Park, where high desert meets alpine forest. Straddling the California/Nevada state line is the Sierra Nevada resort region of Lake Tahoe and Reno, which beckons naturalists, campers, boaters, and those looking for similar action to Las Vegas in a more local setting.

From ski boots to stilettos, Nevada is a paradox, a place of contrasts and contradictions, which could make packing tricky. Vast, empty and the driest state in the nation, it's only recently coming into its own as an outdoors destination. Three-quarters of the population surrounds the desert star of Las Vegas, a glittering world unto itself.

In this libertarian state, freedom rules. Rural brothels coexist with Mormon churches, slot machines and Basque cowboy culture. The ghost of the Wild West persists in old silver mining towns, while Vegas polishes its own brand of modern-day lawlessness.

Seeking thrills? Start on the Vegas Strip, but don't hesitate to step into Nevada's wide wilderness. The cobalt lakes and snowy mountains around Reno and Tahoe are a world away from the Great Basin expanses and the lonely curves of Highway 50, where fighter jets pierce the sky… or was that alien spacecraft?

Sights in Nevada

Hoover Dam

Price: admission & 30min tour adult/child 4-16yr $15/12; with 1hr tour $30

Hours: 9am-6pm Apr-Oct, to 5pm Nov-Mar

Contact: http://www.usbr.gov/lc/hooverdam, 702-494-2517

Location: off Hwy 93, Lake Mead & Hoover Dam, USA

Straddling the Arizona–Nevada border, the graceful concrete curve of the art deco-style Hoover Dam redefines the stark landscape. The massive 726ft structure is one of the world's tallest dams. Originally named Boulder Dam, this New Deal public works project, completed ahead of schedule and under budget in 1936, was the Colorado River's first major dam.

At the height of the Depression, thousands of men and their families migrated here to build the dam. They worked in excruciating conditions, dangling hundreds of feet above the canyon in 120°F (about 50°C) desert heat. Hundreds lost their lives.

Guided tours begin at the visitor center, with a video of original construction footage. An elevator takes visitors 50 stories below to view the dam's massive generators, which could each could power a city of 100,000 people.

Children under 8 are not permitted on the more extensive dam tour (one hour) that visits the dam passageways. Parking at the site costs $10.

Mob Museum

Price: adult/child 11-17yr $20/14

Hours: 9am-9pm

Contact: http://www.themobmuseum.org, 702-229-2734

Location: 300 Stewart Ave, Las Vegas, USA

It's hard to say what's more impressive: the museum's physical location in a historic federal courthouse where mobsters sat for federal hearings in 1950–51, the fact that the board of directors is headed up by a former FBI Special Agent, or the thoughtfully curated exhibits telling the story of organized crime in America. In addition to hands-on FBI equipment and mob-related artifacts, the museum boasts a series of multimedia exhibits featuring interviews with real-life Tony Sopranos.

Opened to great fanfare on February 14, 2012 – the 83rd anniversary of the notorious St Valentine's Day Massacre in Chicago – the museum is officially known as the National Museum of Organized Crime & Law Enforcement. Check the website for special events like book signings and mob history talks.

Parking in the adjacent lot costs $5.

CityCenter

Contact: http://www.citycenter.com

Location: 3780 Las Vegas Blvd S, Las Vegas, USA

We've seen this symbiotic relationship before (think giant hotel anchored by a mall 'concept') but the way that this futuristic-feeling complex places a small galaxy of hypermodern, chichi hotels in orbit around the glitzy Crystals shopping center is a first. The uber-upscale spread includes the subdued, stylish Vdara, the hush-hush opulent Mandarin Oriental and the dramatic architectural showpiece Aria, whose sophisticated casino provides a fitting backdrop to its many drop-dead gorgeous restaurants.

Golden Nugget

Hours: 24hr

Contact: http://www.goldennugget.com, 702-385-7111

Location: 129 E Fremont St, Las Vegas, USA

Check out the polished brass and white leather seats in the casino: day or night, the Golden Nugget is downtown's poshest address. With classy eateries and a swimming pool famous for its shark tank, the Golden Nugget outshines the competition. This swank carpet joint rakes in a moneyed downtown crowd with a 38,000-sq-ft casino populated by table games and slot machines with the same odds as at Strip megaresorts. The nonsmoking poker room hosts daily tournaments.

Wunderkind entrepreneurs Tim Poster and Thomas Breitling bought this vintage Veges casino hotel. which was once owned by none other than casino impresario Steve Wynn, in 2003. The duo catapulted the Nugget into the national limelight on the Fox reality-TV series Casino, but then sold it off to Landry's Inc.

One of the Golden Nugget's claims to fame is the Tank, an outdoor pool featuring a three-story waterslide through a 200,000-gallon shark tank.

Swimmers can press their faces against the glass to come face-to-face with six species of sharks, rays and tropical fish. If you want to get up close to the fish without getting wet (or being a hotel guest), take a behind-the-scenes tour ($30) or stop for a drink at Chart House, a seafood restaurant where you can perch at the bar encircling a 75,000-gallon tropical aquarium.

Another of the Nugget's famous attractions is the Hand of Faith, the world's largest single gold nugget still in existence. Discovered in Australia and weighing a massive 61lb, it's on display under glass near the North Tower elevators. Taking photos is not permitted in most casinos for security reasons, but the Golden Nugget smiles benignly upon wide-eyed visitors who photograph the mighty rock.

New Hampshire

New Hampshire bleeds jagged mountains, scenic valleys and forest-lined lakes – they lurk in every corner of this rugged state. It all begs you to embrace the outdoors, from kayaking the hidden coves of the Lakes Region to trekking the upper peaks surrounding Mt Washington. Each season yields a bounty of adrenaline and activity: skiing and snowshoeing in winter, magnificent walks and drives through autumn's fiery colors, and swimming in crisp mountain streams and berry-picking in summer. Jewel-box colonial settlements like Portsmouth buzz a sophisticated tune, while historic attraction and small-town culture live on in pristine villages like Keene and Peterborough.

But there's a relaxing whiff in the air too – you're encouraged to gaze out at a loon-filled lake, recline on a scenic railway trip or chug across a waterway on a sunset cruise – all while digging into a fried-clam platter or a lobster roll, of course.

New Hampshire's mountain peaks, clear air, and sparkling lakes have attracted trailblazers and artists (and untold numbers of tourists) for centuries. The state's varied geography—not to mention the range of outdoor activities its mountains, lakes, and forests support—is part of the attraction, but hospitality and friendliness are major factors, too: visitors tend to feel quickly at home in this place of beauty and history. Whether you're an outdoors enthusiast seeking adventure or just want to enjoy a good book on the porch swing of a century-old inn, you'll find plenty of opportunities to fulfill your heart's desire.

Ralph Waldo Emerson, Henry David Thoreau, Nathaniel Hawthorne, and Louisa May Alcott all visited and wrote about the state, sparking a fervent literary tradition that continues today. It also has a strong political history: this was the first colony to declare independence from Great Britain, the first to adopt a state constitution, and the first to require its constitution be referred to the people for approval.

The state's diverse terrain makes it popular with everyone from avid adventurers to young families looking for easy access to nature. You can hike, climb, ski, snowboard, snowshoe, and fish, as well as explore on snowmobiles, sailboats, and mountain bikes. New Hampshirites have no objection to others enjoying the beauty here as long as they leave a few dollars behind: the state has long resisted both sales and income taxes, so tourism brings in much-needed revenue.

With several cities consistently rated among the most livable in the nation, New Hampshire has seen considerable growth over the past decade. Longtime residents worry that the state will soon develop two distinct personalities: one characterized by rapid urbanization in the southeast and the other by quiet village life in the west and north. Although newcomers have brought change, the free-spirited sensibility of the Granite State remains intact, as does its natural splendor.

Sights in New Hampshire

Frost Place

Price: adult/child $5/3

Hours: 1-5pm Thu-Sun Jun, 1-5pm Wed-Mon Jul–mid-Sep, 10am-5pm Wed-Mon mid-Sep–mid-Oct

Contact: http://www.frostplace.org, 603-823-5510

Location: 158 Ridge Rd, Franconia Town & Around, USA

Robert Frost (1874–1963) was America's most renowned and best-loved poet in the mid-20th century. For several years he lived with his wife and children on a farm near Franconia, now known as Frost Place. Many of his best and most famous poems describe life on this farm and the scenery surrounding it, including 'The Road Not Taken' and 'Stopping by Woods on a Snowy Evening,' and the years spent here were some of the most productive and inspired of his life.

The farmhouse has been kept as faithful to the period as possible, with numerous exhibits of Frost memorabilia.

In the forest behind the house there is a 0.5-mile nature trail. Frost's poems are mounted on plaques in sites appropriate to the things the poems describe, and in several places the plaques have been erected at the exact spots where Frost was inspired to compose the poems. To find Frost's farm, follow NH 116 south from Franconia. After exactly a mile, turn right onto Bickford Hill Rd, then left onto unpaved Ridge Rd. It's a short distance along on the right.

Baker Berry Library

Hours: 8am-2am Mon-Fri, 10am-2am Sat & Sun, teatime 4pm Mon-Fri

Contact: http://dartmouth.edu/education/libraries, 603-646-2560

Location: 25 N Main St, Hanover & Around, USA

On the north side of the green is Dartmouth College's central Baker Berry Library. The reserve corridor on the lower level houses an impressive mural called Epic of American Civilization, by José Clemente Orozco (1883–1949). The renowned Mexican muralist taught and painted at Dartmouth from 1932 to 1934. The mural follows the course of civilization in the Americas from the time of the Aztecs to the present.

Go upstairs and enjoy the view of the campus from the Tower Room on the 2nd floor. This collegiate wood-paneled room is one of the library's loveliest.

The adjacent Sanborn House also has ornate woodwork, plush leather chairs and books lining the walls, floor to ceiling, on two levels. It is named for Professor Edwin Sanborn, who taught for almost 50 years in the Department of English. This is where students (and you!) can enjoy a traditional teatime each afternoon.

Conway Scenic Railroad

Price: Notch Train coach/1st class/dome car $62/76/90, Valley Train coach/1st class/dome/dining car from $17/21/25.50/36.50

Hours: mid-Jun–Oct

Contact: http://www.conwayscenic.com, 603-356-5251

Location: 38 Norcross Circle, North Conway & Around, USA

The Notch Train, dating to 1874, offers New England's most scenic rail journey, a slow but spectacular 5½-hour out-and-back trip from North Conway to Crawford Notch. Accompanying live commentary recounts the railroad's history and folklore. Reservations are required.

The same company operates the antique steam-powered Valley Train, which makes a shorter journey through Mt Washington Valley, stopping in Conway and Bartlett. Sunset trains, dining trains and other special events are all available. Fares are reduced for kids aged 12 and under.

Both offer the option of 1st-class or dome car seats for an extra $10 to $30. It's only worth the extra on the Valley Train: 1st-class seats are in a perfectly restored Pullman observation car, which features wicker chairs, mahogany woodwork and an open observation platform.

Hood Museum of Art

Hours: 10am-5pm Tue & Thu-Sat, to 9pm Wed, noon-5pm Sun

Contact: http://hoodmuseum.dartmouth.edu, 603-646-2808

Location: 6 E Wheelock St, Hanover & Around, USA

Shortly after the college's founding in 1769, Dartmouth began to acquire artifacts of artistic or historical interest. Since then the collection has expanded to include nearly 70,000 items, which are housed at the Hood Museum of Art. The collection is particularly strong in American pieces, including Native American art. One of the highlights is a set of Assyrian reliefs from the Palace of Ashurnasirpal that date to the 9th century BC. Special exhibitions often feature contemporary artists.

In mid-2016 the museum initiated a $50 million renovation and expansion project, with an anticipated completion date of summer 2019.

New Jersey

Everything you've seen on TV, from the McMansions of Real Housewives of New Jersey to the thick accents of The Sopranos, is at least partially true. But Jersey (natives lose the 'New') is at least as well defined by its high-tech and banking headquarters, and a quarter of it is lush farmland (hence the Garden State nickname). And on the 127 miles of beautiful beaches, you'll find, yes, the guidos and guidettes of Jersey Shore, but also many other oceanfront towns, each with a distinct character.

The New Jersey "Garden State" has the third-largest state park system in the country and is almost entirely bordered by water—the Atlantic Ocean (and the famous Jersey Shore) to the east, the Delaware River to the west, and the Delaware Bay to the south. Along the Hudson River run the famous Palisades, with its heart-stopping views of the Manhattan skyline. The Pinelands, a national Biosphere Reserve, is in the middle of the state: it's a sandy-soiled area with unique flora and fauna. Several mountain chains also run through New Jersey, including the Appalachians in the northeast and the Kittatinny Mountains along the northwest corner (from the New York border to the Delaware Water Gap).

Sights in New Jersey

Princeton University Art Museum

Hours: 10am-5pm Tue-Sat, to 10pm Thu, 1-5pm Sun

Contact: http://www.princetonartmuseum.org, 609-258-3788

Location: McCormick Hall, New Jersey, USA

This wide-ranging collection is particularly strong on antiquities, Asian art and photography.

The Boardwalk in Atlantic City

Atlantic City's famous Boardwalk was the first in the world, built in 1870 by local business owners who wanted to cut down on sand being tracked into hotel lobbies by guests returning from the beach. Alexander Boardman came up with the idea, and the long stretch of planks became known as Boardman's Walk - later shortened to 'Boardwalk'.

The Boardwalk is still the lifeline of the city and the path that leads to all doors. It runs along an 8mi (13km) stretch of beach where visitors sunbathe, picnic and swim.

If you're interested in losing some serious currency or just want to check out the grand gambling halls, there are several along the Boardwalk. Showboat Casino Hotel has a riverboat-themed interior, while the super-extravagant Trump Taj Mahal boasts nine gigantic limestone elephants to greet its guests. It is easily recognized by the 70 bright minarets crowning the rooftops. If you're new to the roulette wheel, try Claridge Casino Hotel, which has low-stakes tables and is just one block west of the Boardwalk.

Sandy Hook Gateway National Recreation Area

Price: parking $15 summer

Contact: http://www.nps.gov/gate, 718-354-4606

In Sandy Hook Gateway National Recreation Area, you'll find the nation's oldest lighthouse; excellent birding in a holly forest; outstanding views of Manhattan's skyline on clear days; beautiful white dunes; and even a nude beach alongside a gay beach (area G).

Best of all, you can get here via a ferry from Lower Manhattan in a cool and salty 45 minutes. Bring your bike along for the ride, and you can enjoy the paved bike paths through the dunes and pedal on to the nearby towns of Atlantic Highlands and Highlands.

Cape May Point State Park

Contact: 884-2159

Location: 707 E Lake Dr, Cape May, USA

The 190-acre Cape May Point State Park, just off Lighthouse Ave, has 2 miles of trails, plus the famous Cape May Lighthouse. Built in 1859, the 157ft lighthouse recently underwent a $2 million restoration, and its completely reconstructed light is visible as far as 25 miles out to sea. You can climb the 199 stairs to the top in the summer months. Hours change daily; call for details.

New Mexico

They call this the 'Land Of Enchantment' for a reason. Maybe it's the drama of sunlight and shadow playing out across juniper-speckled hills; or the traditional mountain villages of horse pastures and adobe homes; or the centuries-old towns on the northern plateaus, overlooked by the magnificent Sangre de Cristos; or the volcanoes, canyons and vast desert plains spread beneath an even vaster sky. The beauty casts a powerful spell. Mud-brick churches filled with sacred art; ancient Indian pueblos; real-life cowboys and legendary outlaws; chile-smothered enchiladas – all add to the pervasive sense of otherness that often makes New Mexico feel like a foreign country.

Maybe the state's all-but-indescribable charm is best expressed in the iconic paintings of Georgia O'Keeffe. The artist herself exclaimed, on her very first visit: 'Well! Well! Well!... This is wonderful! No one told me it was like this.'

But seriously, how could they?

Albuquerque is New Mexico's welcoming gateway, and its residents — like its food and art — reflect a confluence of Native American, Hispanic, and Anglo culture. Santa Fe is surrounded by mind-expanding mountain views and is filled with streets characterized by low-slung adobe architecture. Venture beyond New Mexico's cities and you'll discover a land of exceptionally diverse scenery, from the natural formations of Carlsbad Caverns, to river gorges with sheer basalt walls, to the aspen-covered slopes of the Sangre de Cristo mountains.

Sights in New Mexico

Carlsbad Caverns National Park

Price: adult/child $10/free

Hours: caves 8:30am-5pm late May-early Sep, 8:30am-3:30pm early Sep-late May

Contact: http://www.nps.gov/cave, 505-785-3012

Drive for hours across the desert just to see a cave? But it's not just any cave; it's a truly astonishing and immense system of caves, one of the world's greatest. Once visitors get a glimpse, even the most skeptical are impressed. A visit is, without a doubt, a highlight of any Southwestern journey. But wait, there's more. The cave's other claim to fame is the 250,000-plus Mexican free-tail bat colony that roosts here from April through to October. Visitors flock here at sunset to watch them fly out to feast on a smorgasbord of bugs. The park covers 73 sq. miles and includes almost 100 caves. Visitors can take a 2-mile subterranean walk from the cave mouth to an underground chamber 1800ft long, 255ft high and over 800ft below the surface. Exploration for experienced spelunkers only continues at the awe-inspiring Lechugilla Cave. With a depth of 1567ft and a length of about 60 miles, it's the deepest cave and third-longest limestone cave in North America. The park entrance is 23 miles southwest of Carlsbad. A three-day pass for self-guided tours to the natural entrance and the Big Room (send a postcard from the lunchroom, 829ft below the surface!) costs $6 for adults and $3 for children. The park also has a spectrum of ranger-led tours ($7); call for advance reservations. If you want to scramble to lesser-known areas, ask about Wild Cave tours. The last tickets are sold two to 3½ hours before the visitor center closes. Wilderness backpacking trips into the desert are allowed by permit (free); the visitor center sells topographical maps of the 50-plus miles of hiking trails.

White Sands

Price: adult/under 16yr $3/free

Hours: 7am-9pm Jun-Aug, to sunset Sep-May

Contact: http://www.nps.gov/whsa, 575-479-6124

Slide, roll and slither through brilliant, towering sand hills. Sixteen miles southwest of Alamogordo (15 miles southwest of Hwy 82/70), gypsum covers 275 sq. miles to create a dazzling white landscape at this crisp, stark monument. These captivating windswept dunes are a highlight of any trip to New Mexico.

Georgia O'Keeffe Museum

Price: adult/child $12/free

Hours: 10am-5pm, to 7pm Fri

Contact: http://www.okeeffemuseum.org, 505-946-1000

Location: 217 Johnson St, Santa Fe, USA

With 10 beautifully lit galleries in a rambling 20th-century adobe, this museum boasts the world's largest collection of O'Keeffe's work. She's best known for her luminous New Mexican landscapes, but the changing exhibitions here range through her entire career, focusing for example on her years in New York. Major museums worldwide own her most famous canvases, so you may not see familiar paintings, but you're sure to be bowled over by the thick brushwork and transcendent colors on show.

Visit the museum website to reserve a tour of O'Keeffe's former home, in the village of Abiquiú, 50 miles northwest of Santa Fe.

Roswell Museum & Art Center

Hours: 9am-5pm Mon-Sat, 1-5pm Sun

Contact: http://www.roswellmuseum.org, 575-624-6744

Location: 100 W 11th St, Roswell, USA

Roswell's excellent museum deserves a visit. Seventeen galleries showcase Southwestern artists including Georgia O'Keeffe, Peter Hurd and Henriette Wyeth, along with an eclectic mix of Native American, Hispanic and Anglo artifacts that illustrate the domestic and spiritual lives of the region's inhabitants. There's also a fascinating display on local rocket pioneer Robert H Goddard, who launched the first successful liquid fuel rocket in 1926. The adjoining Goddard Planetarium was only open for special events at the time of research.

New York

Say the words "New York" and icons like Times Square and the Museum of Modern Art may be the first things that pop to mind but the state is also very much a destination for appreciating the outdoors, in every season. Across New York, from Niagara Falls to the tip of Long Island, there are breathtaking hiking trails, lakes and rivers for fishing and boating, mountains for skiing, and lovely ocean beaches for relaxing. And with historical mansions, Revolutionary War sites, stunning mountain lodges, renowned B&Bs, and some of the country's best wineries, there's something for just about everyone.

Upstate New York – anywhere outside the city, essentially – and downstate share virtually nothing but a governor and dysfunctional legislature in the capital, Albany. This incongruity produces political gridlock, but it's a blessing for those who cherish a hike up a mountaintop as much as a bar crawl around the Lower East Side. Upstate is defined largely by its inland waterways. The Hudson River heads straight north from NYC, like an escape route. From Albany, the 524-mile Erie Canal cuts due west to Lake Erie, by the world-famous Niagara Falls and Buffalo, a lively city despite its epic winters. And the St Lawrence River forms the border with Canada in the under-the-radar Thousand Islands area. Another patch of water is the Finger Lakes region, and the college town of Ithaca, known for its wines. Add in the rugged backcountry of the Adirondack mountains and the lush farms of the Catskills, plus miles and miles of sandy beaches along Long Island, it's easy to understand why people leave the city, never to return.

Sights in New York State

Cathedral Church of St John the Divine

Price: suggested donation $10, highlights tour $12, vertical tour $20

Hours: 7:30am-6pm, highlights tour 11am & 2pm Mon, 11am & 1pm Tue-Sat, 1pm on selected Sun, vertical tour noon Wed & Fri, noon & 2pm Sat

Contact: http://www.stjohndivine.org, 212-316-7540

Location: 1047 Amsterdam Ave, New York City, USA

The largest place of worship in the US has yet to be completed – and probably won't be any time soon. But this storied Episcopal cathedral nonetheless commands attention with its ornate Byzantine-style facade, booming vintage organ and extravagantly scaled nave – twice as wide as Westminster Abbey in London. Aside from a one-hour highlights tour, the cathedral also offers a one-hour vertical tour, taking you on a steep climb to the top of the Cathedral (bring your own flashlight).

Prayer services are held four times daily (three times on Saturday; see the website for the schedule). Two special services worth seeing are the annual Blessing of the Animals, a pilgrimage for pet owners held on the first Sunday of October, and the Blessing of the Bikes, held on May 1, when local riders tool in on everything from sleek 10-speeds to clunky cruisers.

The cathedral itself was founded in the 19th century by Bishop Horatio Potter, with the first cornerstone laid on St John's Day in 1892. The construction, however, was hardly a breeze. Engineers had to dig 70ft in order to find bedrock to which they could anchor the building. Architects died and were fired. And in 1911, the initial Romanesque design was exchanged for something bigger and more Gothic. Construction has been halted on countless occasions (whenever funds run out). To this day, the north tower remains unbuilt, and a 'temporary' domed roof, constructed out of terra-cotta tile in 1909, still shelters the Crossing. In 2001, there was a raging fire to contend with, too. Much of the church has since been restored, but the north transept, which was severely damaged, has not been rebuilt. If it is ever completed, the 601ft-long Cathedral will rank as the third-largest church in the world, after St Peter's Basilica in Rome and Basilica of Our Lady of Peace at Yamoussoukro in Côte d'Ivoire. Just don't count on this happening any time soon.

Framing the western entrance are two rows of Gothic-inspired sculptures that were carved in the 1980s and '90s by British artist Simon Verity (b 1945). On the central pillar stands St John the Divine himself, author of the Book of Revelation. (Note the Four Horsemen of the Apocalypse under his feet.) Flanking him are various biblical figures, including Moses, John the Baptist and Noah. Themes of devastation are rife, but most unnerving is the statue of Jeremiah (third on the right), which stands on a base that shows the New York City skyline – Twin Towers included – in the process of being destroyed.

The nave is laid out west to east. Lining this monumental passageway are two magisterial sets of 17th century tapestries. The Barberini Tapestries from Italy depict scenes from the life of Christ, while the Mortlake Tapestries, based on cartoons by Raphael, show the Acts of the Apostles. Installed in 1932, the largest stained glass window in the country contains more than 10,000 individual pieces of glass. The design features a red-robed image of Christ at the center, from which trumpet-bearing angels radiate outward to the prophets.

One of the most powerful organs in the world, the Great Organ was originally installed in 1911 and then enlarged and rebuilt in 1952. It contains 8035 pipes arranged in 141 ranks. The 2001 fire damaged the instrument, but a careful five-year restoration brought it back. You can hear it roar during services and concerts. Behind the choir is the silver triptych 'Life of Christ,' carved by '80s pop artist Keith Haring (1958–90). It's one of the last works of art he produced prior to succumbing to an AIDS-related illness at the age of 31.

The Cathedral is situated on a lovely 11-acre plot. On the south side of the building, you'll find the whimsical Children's Sculpture Garden (check out the bizarre Peace Fountain, which shows the archangel Michael and Satan doing battle) and the Biblical Garden, containing plants mentioned in the Bible.

Central Park

Hours: 6am-1am

Contact: http://www.centralparknyc.org

Location: 59th & 110th Sts, New York City, USA

One of the world's most renowned green spaces, Central Park spreads across 843 acres of rolling meadows, boulder-studded outcroppings, elm-lined walkways, manicured European-style gardens, a lake and a reservoir — not to mention an outdoor theater, a memorial to John Lennon, an idyllic waterside eatery (the Loeb Boathouse) and one very famous statue of Alice in Wonderland. Highlights include Sheep Meadow, where thousands of people lounge and play on warm days; Central Park Zoo; and the forest-like paths of the Ramble.

Like the city's subway system, the vast and majestic Central Park, a rectangle of open space in the middle of Manhattan, is a great class leveler – which is exactly what it was envisioned to be. Created in the 1860s and '70s by Frederick Law Olmsted and Calvert Vaux on the marshy northern fringe of the city, the immense park was designed as a leisure space for all New Yorkers, regardless of color, class or creed. And it's an oasis from the insanity: the lush lawns, cool forests, flowering gardens, glassy bodies of water and meandering, wooded paths providing the dose of serene nature that New Yorkers crave.

Olmsted and Vaux (who also created Prospect Park in Brooklyn) were determined to keep foot and road traffic separate and cleverly designed the cross-town transverses under elevated roads to do so. That such a large expanse of prime real estate has survived intact for so long again proves that nothing eclipses the heart, soul and pride that forms the foundation of New York City's greatness.

Today, this 'people's park' is still one of the city's most popular attractions, beckoning throngs of New Yorkers with free outdoor concerts on the Great Lawn, precious animals at the Central Park Wildlife Center and top-notch drama at the annual Shakespeare in the Park productions, held each summer at the open-air Delacorte Theater. Other recommended stops include the ornate Bethesda Fountain, which edges the Lake and its Loeb Boathouse, where you can rent rowboats or enjoy lunch at an outdoor cafe; the Shakespeare Garden, on the west side between 79th and 80th Sts, with its lush plantings and excellent skyline views; and the Ramble, a wooded thicket that's popular with bird-watchers. While parts of the park swarm with joggers, in-line skaters, musicians and tourists on warm weekends, it's quieter on weekday afternoons, especially in less well-trodden spots above 72nd St such as the Harlem Meer and the North Meadow (north of 97th St).

Folks flock to the park even in winter, when snowstorms inspire cross-country skiing and sledding or just a simple stroll through the white wonderland, and crowds turn out every New Year's Eve for a midnight run. The Central Park Conservancy offers ever-changing guided tours of the park, including ones that focus on public art, wildlife and places of interest to kids.

Metropolitan Museum of Art

Price: suggested donation adult/child $25/free

Hours: 10am-5.30pm Sun-Thu, to 9pm Fri & Sat

Contact: http://www.metmuseum.org, 212-535-7710

Location: 1000 Fifth Ave, New York City, USA

This sprawling encyclopedic museum, founded in 1870, houses one of the biggest art collections in the world. Its permanent collection has more than two million individual objects, from Egyptian temples to American paintings. Known colloquially as 'The Met,' the museum attracts over six million visitors a year to its 17 acres of galleries – making it the largest single-site attraction in New York City. In other words, plan on spending some time here. It is B-I-G.

The museum has an unrivaled collection of ancient Egyptian art, some of which dates back to the Paleolithic era. Located to the north of the Great Hall, the 39 Egyptian galleries open dramatically with one of the Met's prized pieces: the Mastaba Tomb of Perneb (c 2300 BC), an Old Kingdom burial chamber crafted from limestone.

On the museum's 2nd floor, the European Paintings' galleries display a stunning collection of masterworks. The 'New Galleries for the Art of the Arab Lands, Turkey, Iran, Central Asia, and Later South Asia' are comprised of 15 incredible rooms that showcase the museum's extensive collection of art from the Middle East and Central and South Asia.

In the northwest corner, the American galleries showcase a wide variety of decorative and fine art from throughout US history. The 27 galleries devoted to classical antiquity are another Met doozy, some of which are dramatically illuminated by natural daylight.

The most popular galleries with children are generally the Egyptian, African and Oceania galleries (great masks) and the collection of medieval arms and armor – all of which are on the 1st floor. The Met hosts plenty of kid-centric happenings (check the website) and distributes a special museum brochure and map made specifically for the tykes.

One of the best spots in the entire museum is the roof garden, which features rotating sculpture installations by contemporary and 20th century artists. (Jeff Koons, Andy Goldsworthy and Imran Qureshi have all shown here.) But its best feature are the views it offers of the city and Central Park. It's also home to the Roof Garden Café & Martini Bar, the best place in the museum for a sip — especially at sunset. The roof garden is open from April to October.

A desk inside the Great Hall has audio tours in several languages ($7), though you can access audio tours for free if you have a smartphone. Docents also offer guided tours of specific galleries (free with admission). Check the website or information desk for details. If you can't stand crowds, avoid weekends.

Studio Museum in Harlem

Price: suggested donation $7, Sun free

Hours: noon-9pm Thu & Fri, 10am-6pm Sat, noon-6pm Sun

Contact: http://www.studiomuseum.org, 212-864-4500

Location: 144 W 125th St, New York City, USA

This small, cultural gem has been exhibiting the works of African American artists for more than four decades. While its rotating exhibition program is always fascinating, the museum is not just another art display center. It is an important point of connection for Harlem cultural figures of all stripes, who arrive to check out a rotating selection of shows, attend film screenings or sign up for gallery talks.

Founded in 1968, the museum originally came to life in a small loft space off 125th St that was sandwiched between a couple of garment factories and a supermarket. But it quickly became known for its thoughtful, contemporary-minded exhibits and vibrant event programming, which included concerts, poetry readings and lectures. Roughly a dozen years after its establishment, it moved to its present location, a renovated bank building that offered more room for exhibits, archives and the growing permanent collection. You'll also find the Harlem Visitor Information Kiosk located here.

The permanent collection is small (just under 2000 objects), but it is rich. The Studio Museum has been an important patron to African American artists and the collection features work by more than 400 of them. This includes important pieces by painter Jacob Lawrence, photographer Gordon Parks and collagist Romare Bearden – all of whom are represented in major museum collections in the US.

In addition, its photography holdings include an extensive archive of work by James VanDerZee (1886–1983), an unparalleled chronicler of early 20th century Harlem life. He shot portraits of prominent entertainers and black nationalists, and continued to take pictures well into his nineties. One well-known snap shows Jean-Michel Basquiat, the '80s graffiti artist and painter, sitting pensively with a Siamese cat on his lap.

The museum's long-running artist-in-residence program has provided crucial support to a long list of well-known artists, including conceptualist David Hammons, figurative painter Mickalene Thomas and portraitist Kehinde Wiley, and the venue hosts regular special events, including artist talks and workshops (check the website).

When visiting, make sure to look up on your way in. One of the museum's most iconic works hangs right outside the front door: Hammons' 1990 piece 'African-American Flag' replaces the traditional red, white and blue of the Stars and Stripes with the red, green and black of the pan-African flag. It is a sly comment on the African American presence in the US.

North Carolina

The conservative Old South and the liberal New South are jostling for political dominance in the fast-growing Tar Heel State, home to hipsters, hog farmers, hi-tech wunderkinds and an increasing number of craft brewers. For the most part, though, from the ancient mountains in the west to the sandy barrier islands of the Atlantic, the various cultures and communities here coexist.

From the Outer Banks' secluded barrier islands to the Smoky Mountains' majestic peaks, North Carolina is an outdoor enthusiast's dream. There are championship golf courses, beautiful gardens, scenic drives along the Blue Ridge Parkway, and numerous opportunities for hiking, biking, and fishing. Urban adventures include hip Asheville, host to America's largest private home, Biltmore Estate, and university-centric cities like Raleigh, Durham, and Chapel Hill.

Agriculture is an important economic force, and there are 52,200 farms across the state. North Carolina leads the nation in tobacco production and is the second-largest producer of pigs. But new technologies also drive the economy, and more than 190 businesses operate in Research Triangle Park alone. Other important industries include finance, nanotechnology, and Christmas trees. Craft brewers have contributed nearly $800 million to the economy.

Though the bulk of North Carolinians live in the business-oriented urban centers of the central Piedmont region, most travelers stick to the scenic routes along the coast and through the Appalachian Mountains.

So come on down, grab a platter of barbecue and watch the Duke Blue Devils battle the Carolina Tar Heels on the basketball court. College hoops rival Jesus for Carolinians' souls.

Sights in North Carolina

Biltmore Estate

Price: adult/child 10-16yr $60/30

Hours: house 9am-4:30pm

Contact: http://www.biltmore.com, 800-411-3812

Location: 1 Approach Rd, Asheville, USA

The country's largest privately-owned home, and Asheville's number-one tourist attraction, the Biltmore was built in 1895 for shipping and railroad heir George Washington Vanderbilt II. He modeled it after the grand chateaux he'd seen on his various European jaunts. Viewing the estate and its 250 acres of gorgeously manicured grounds and gardens takes several hours.

Tours of the house are self-guided. To get the most out of your visit, pay an extra $10 for the informative audio tour. Also available is a behind-the-scenes guided tour ($17) covering the servants, guest rooms and parties. In summer, children visiting with an adult are free.

Beyond the house, there are numerous cafes, a gift shop the size of a small supermarket, a hoity-toity hotel, and an award-winning winery with free tastings. In Antler Village, the new Biltmore Legacy exhibit, 'The Vanderbilts at Home and Abroad' provides a more personal look at the family.

Duke Lemur Center

Price: adult/child $10/7

Contact: http://www.lemur.duke.edu, 919-489-3364

Location: 3705 Erwin Rd, Durham, USA

The secret is out: the Lemur Center is the coolest attraction in Durham. Located about two miles from the main campus, this research and conservation center is home to the largest collection of endangered prosimian primates outside their native Madagascar. Only a robot could fail to melt at the sight of these big-eyed fuzzy-wuzzies. Visits are by guided tour only. To guarantee a tour spot, make your reservation well ahead of your visit.

Call at least three weeks in advance for weekdays, and one to two months ahead for weekends.

North Carolina Museum of Art

Hours: 10am-5pm Tue-Thu, Sat & Sun, 10am-9pm Fri, park dawn-dusk

Contact: http://www.ncartmuseum.org

Location: 2110 Blue Ridge Rd, Raleigh, USA

The light-filled glass-and-anodized-steel West Building won praise from architecture critics nationwide when it opened in 2010. The fine and wide-ranging collection, with everything from ancient Greek sculptures to commanding American landscape paintings to elaborate African masks, is worthy as well. Short on time? Then stretch your legs on the winding outdoor sculpture trail. It's a few miles west of downtown.

Fort Raleigh National Historic Site

Hours: grounds dawn-dusk, visitor center 9am-5pm

Contact: http://www.nps.gov/fora

Location: 1401 National Park Dr, Manteo, Outer Banks, USA

In the late 1580s, three decades before the Pilgrims landed at Plymouth Rock, a group of 116 British colonists disappeared without a trace from their Roanoke Island settlement. Were they killed off by drought? Did they run away with a Native American tribe? The fate of the 'Lost Colony' remains one of America's greatest mysteries. Explore their story in the visitor center. One of the site's star attractions is the beloved musical the Lost Colony Outdoor Drama (www.thelostcolony.org), which is staged between late May and August.

The play, from Pulitzer Prize-winning North Carolina playwright Paul Green, dramatizes the fate of the colonists and will celebrate its 80th anniversary in 2017. It plays at the Waterside Theater throughout summer.

Other attractions include exhibits, artifacts, maps and a free film to fuel the imagination, hosted at the visitor center. The 16th-century-style Elizabethan Gardens include a Shakespearian herb garden and rows of beautifully manicured flower beds. A commanding statue of Queen Elizabeth I stands guard at the entrance.

North Dakota

'Magnificent desolation' – Buzz Aldrin used it to describe the moon, and it applies just as well in North Dakota. Fields of grain – green in the spring and summer, bronze in the fall, and white in winter – stretch beyond every horizon. Except for the rugged 'badlands' of the far west, geographic relief is subtle; more often it is the collapsing remains of a failed homestead that breaks up the vista.

North Dakota is a massive expanse of rolling prairies under intense blue skies, much of it unchanged since the expeditions led by Lewis and Clark in 1804 and 1806. This rectangular state straddles the Canadian border between Minnesota and Montana. The eastern edge, marked by the Red River, is rich soil on land so flat you can see the horizon as an uninterrupted straight line.

The Badlands are home to Theodore Roosevelt National Park, a remarkable area that's been described both as "the Grand Canyon in miniature" and "hell with the fires put out." Nearby Medora is a frontier town famous for its cowboy music festival in summer, museums, and quaint shops. The biggest city in the state, Fargo, has plenty of museums and family attractions. The state capital of Bismarck is a short drive from national historic sites and has a few attractions of its own.

Isolated in the far north, this is one of the least-visited states in the US. But that just means that there's less traffic as you whiz along. This is a place to get lost on remote two-lane routes and to appreciate the beauty of raw land. And don't forget to pause to marvel at the songs of meadowlarks.

Note that despite those seemingly endless summer fields of grain, the state's economy is tied to large oil deposits in the west. Soaring energy prices turned once-moribund towns such as Williston and Watford City into boomtowns, with vast trailer encampments for oil-field workers, roads clogged – and battered – by huge trucks, and constant parades of tanker trains filled with flammable petroleum. However, with recent downturns in prices, the boom may turn to bust.

Sights in North Dakota

Fargo Woodchipper

Hours: 7:30am-8pm Mon-Fri, 10am-6pm Sat & Sun Jun-Aug, 8am-5pm Mon-Fri, 10am-4pm Sat Sep-May

Contact: http://www.fargomoorhead.org, 800-235-7654

Location: 2001 44th St, Fargo, USA

Fargo's embrace of its namesake film is on full display at the town's visitor center, which houses the actual wood chipper used for the scene where Gaear feeds the last of Carl's body into its maw and is discovered by Marge. You can reenact the scene – although not the results – while wearing Fargo-style hats and jamming in a fake leg (both provided!).

North Dakota Heritage Center

Hours: 8am-5pm Mon-Fri, 10am-5pm Sat & Sun

Contact: http://www.history.nd.gov, 701-328-2666

Location: 612 East Boulevard Ave, Bismarck, USA

Behind the Sacagawea statue, the North Dakota Heritage Center has details on everything from Norwegian bachelor farmers to the scores of nuclear bombs perched on missiles in silos across the state. Four new galleries have doubled its size.

Theodore Roosevelt National Park

Price: 7-day pass per vehicle $20

Contact: http://www.nps.gov/thro, 701-623-4466

A tortured region known as the 'badlands' whose colors seem to change with the moods of nature, Theodore Roosevelt National Park is the state's natural highlight. Bizarre rock formations, streaked with a rainbow of red, yellow, brown, black and silver minerals, are framed by green prairie. The park is vast, with only the rush of rivers and the distant hoof beat of animals to interrupt the silence.

Wildlife abounds: mule deer, wild horses, bighorn sheep, elk, bison, around 200 bird species and, of course, sprawling subterranean prairie-dog towns.

The park is divided into two sections. Most visitors to the South Unit opt for the 36-mile scenic drive that begins in Medora, an enjoyable town with motels just off I-94; prairie dogs are a highlight. The North Unit gets few visitors, but is well worth the journey for the 14-mile drive to the Oxbow Overlook, with its wide views into the vast and colorfully striated river canyon. The verdant surrounds are protected as the Little Missouri National Grassland, and bison are everywhere. It is 68 miles north of I-94 on US 85.

Hikers can explore 85 miles of backcountry trails. For a good adventure, hike or cycle the 96-mile Maah Daah Hey Trail between the park units. Driving, continue north on US 85 to Fort Buford.

The park has three visitor centers, including the South Unit Visitor Center, with Theodore Roosevelt's old cabin out back. The park has two simple campgrounds (sites $7 to $14) and free backcountry camping (permit required).

Lewis & Clark Interpretive Center

Price: adult/child $7.50/3

Hours: 9am-5pm daily Jun-Aug, 9am-5pm Mon-Sat, noon-5pm Sun Sep-May

Contact: http://www.fortmandan.com, 701-462-8535

Location: junction US 83 & ND Hwy 200A, North Dakota, USA

At this impressive center you can learn about the duo's epic expedition and the Native Americans who helped them. Check out the beautiful drawings from George Catlin's portfolio.

The same ticket gets you into Fort Mandan, a replica of the fort built by Lewis and Clark, 2.5 miles west (10 miles downstream from the flooded original site). It sits on a lonely stretch of the Missouri River marked by a monument to Seaman, the expedition's dog.

Inside the small but worthwhile information building, look for the display on period medicine, including Dr Rush's 'Thunderclappers.'

Ohio

All right, time for your Ohio quiz. In the Buckeye State you can 1) buggy-ride through the nation's largest Amish community; 2) lose your stomach on one of the world's fastest roller coasters; 3) suck down a dreamy creamy milkshake fresh from a working dairy; or 4) examine a massive, mysterious snake sculpture built into the earth. And the answer is…all of these. It hurts locals' feelings when visitors think the only thing to do here is tip over cows, so c'mon, give Ohio a chance. Besides these activities, you can partake in a five-way in Cincinnati and rock out in Cleveland.

A New Yorker or Californian who's never been to Ohio likely conjures up an image with plenty of barn silos, a dairy cow in every backyard, and perhaps a smoky skyline or two. That's not surprising, given that for centuries Ohio has been known as the "Gateway to the West." In truth the Buckeye State, which has reinvented itself over the last 40 years, is a beautifully balanced blend of not only everything Midwestern but also everything American.

From college and pro sports to ballet and theater, Ohio's got a lot to entice folks from out of town. There are history, science, art, and children's museums; and water parks north and south. There are gardens sheltering colorful butterflies and hundreds of varieties of roses. Food lovers relish the many ethnic eateries.

Indoor and outdoor concerts pull in the biggest names around, while riverboats and dining cruises entertain you with games of chance and stage shows. Natural attractions and outdoor activities can be found in parks and along lakes and rivers throughout the state. Across the state each year, nearly 100 county and independent fairs and festivals make for even more fun.

Sights in Ohio

National Museum of the US Air Force

Hours: 9am-5pm

Contact: http://www.nationalmuseum.af.mil, 937-255-3286

Location: 1100 Spaatz St, Dayton & Yellow Springs, USA

Located at the Wright-Patterson Air Force Base, 6 miles northeast of Dayton, the huuuuge museum has everything from a Wright Brothers 1909 Flyer to a Sopwith Camel (WWI biplane) and the 'Little Boy' type atomic bomb (decommissioned and rendered safe for display) dropped on Hiroshima. The hangars hold miles of planes, rockets and aviation machines. A spiffy new building adds space craft and presidential planes starting in summer 2016. Download the audio tour from the website before arriving. Plan on three or more hours here.

Cleveland Museum of Art

Hours: 10am-5pm Tue-Sun, to 9pm Wed & Fri

Contact: http://www.clevelandart.org, 216-421-7340

Location: 11150 East Blvd, Cleveland, USA

Fresh off a whopping expansion, the art museum houses an excellent collection of European paintings, as well as African, Asian and American art. Head to the 2nd floor for rock-star works from Impressionists, Picasso and surrealists. Interactive touchscreens are stationed throughout the galleries and provide fun ways to learn more. Gallery One, near the entrance, holds a cool quick hit of museum highlights.

Vent Haven Museum

Price: adult/child $10/5

Hours: by appt May-Sep

Contact: http://www.venthavenmuseum.com, 859-341-0461

Location: 33 W Maple Ave, Cincinnati, USA

Jeepers creepers! When you first glimpse the roomful of goggle-eyed wooden heads staring mutely into space, try not to run screaming for the door. (If you've seen the film Magic, you know what dummies are capable of.) Local William Shakespeare Berger started the museum after amassing a collection of some 700 dolls. Today Jacko the red-fezzed monkey, white-turtleneck-clad Woody DeForest and the rest of the crew sit silently throughout three buildings.

Rock and Roll Hall of Fame & Museum

Price: adult/child $22/13

Hours: 10am-5:30pm, to 9pm Wed year-round, to 9pm Sat Jun-Aug

Contact: http://www.rockhall.com, 216-781-7625

Location: 1100 E 9th St, Cleveland, USA

Cleveland's top attraction is like an overstuffed attic bursting with groovy finds: Jimi Hendrix's Stratocaster, Keith Moon's platform shoes, John Lennon's Sgt Pepper suit and a 1966 piece of hate mail to the Rolling Stones from a cursive-writing Fijian. It's more than memorabilia, though. Multimedia exhibits trace the history and social context of rock music and the performers who created it.

Why is the museum in Cleveland? Because this is the hometown of Alan Freed, the disk jockey who popularized the term 'rock 'n' roll' in the early 1950s, and because the city lobbied hard and paid big. Be prepared for crowds (especially thick until 1pm or so).

Oklahoma

Oklahoma is the geographical and cultural crossroads of America, where the green mountains of the East dissolve into the golden prairies of the West. A dozen ecosystems blanket the state, which cradles 200 man-made lakes, more than 1 million surface-acres of water, and 2,000 more miles of shoreline than the Atlantic and Gulf coasts combined. With deep ties to Native Americans, Oklahoma (derived from the combination of two Choctaw words meaning "red people") is home to 39 tribal headquarters.

But Oklahoma is more than just a metaphorical crossroads. Five cattle trails that crossed this territory after the Civil War left behind a still-vibrant Western heritage that is most evident in a thriving agricultural and ranching economy, with more horses per capita than any other state. Visitors benefit from frequent rodeos, superb trail-riding facilities, and some of the best Western art collections in the world.

Today, Oklahoma is crossed by two transcontinental highways, Interstate 40 and Interstate 35, although the state is probably best known for its 420-mile drive along Route 66. Once known as "America's Main Street," the nostalgic highway is a vibrant thoroughfare for one of Oklahoma's chief charms: its small towns, where you'll find saddle shops and hardware stores bellied up next to espresso bars and art galleries.

Oklahoma gets its name from the Choctaw name for 'Red People.' One look at the state's vividly red earth and you'll wonder if the name is more of a sartorial than an ethnic comment. Still, with 39 tribes located here, it is a place with deep Native American significance. Museums, cultural displays and more abound.

The other side of the Old West coin, cowboys, also figure prominently in the Sooner State. Although pickups have replaced horses, there's still a great sense of the open range, interrupted only by urban Oklahoma City and Tulsa. Oklahoma's share of Route 66 links some of the Mother Road's iconic highlights and there are myriad atmospheric old towns.

Sights in Oklahoma

Washita Battlefield National Historic Site

Hours: site dawn-dusk, visitor center 9am-5pm

Contact: http://www.nps.gov/waba, 580-497-2742

Location: Hwy 47A, Western Oklahoma, USA

On November 27, 1868, George Custer's troops launched a dawn attack on the peaceful village of Chief Black Kettle. It was a slaughter of men, women, children and domestic animals, an act some would say led to karmic revenge on Custer eight years later. Trails traverse the site of the killings, which is remarkably unchanged. An excellent visitor center 0.7 miles away contains a good museum; seasonal tours and talks are worthwhile.

The site is 2 miles west of Cheyenne, 30 miles north of I-40 via US 283.

Oklahoma Jazz Hall of Fame

Price: Sun jazz concerts adult/child $15/5

Hours: 9am-5pm Mon & Wed-Fri, to 9pm Tue, noon-7pm Sun, live music 5:30-8pm Tue

Contact: http://www.okjazz.org, 918-928-5299

Location: 111 E 1st St, Tulsa, USA

Tulsa's beautiful Union Station is filled with sound again, but now it's melodious as opposed to cacophonous. During the first half of the 20th century, Tulsa was literally at the crossroads of American music with performers both homegrown and from afar. Learn about greats like Charlie Christian, Ernie Fields Senior and Wallace Willis in detailed exhibits. Sunday jazz concerts are played in the once-segregated grand concourse. On Tuesday nights there are free jam sessions.

Oklahoma City National Memorial Museum

Price: adult/student $15/12

Hours: 9am-6pm Mon-Sat, noon-6pm Sun

Contact: http://www.oklahomacitynationalmemorial.org

Location: 620 N Harvey Ave, Oklahoma City, USA

The story of America's worst incident of domestic terrorism is told at this poignant museum, which avoids becoming mawkish and lets the horrible events speak for themselves. The outdoor Symbolic Memorial has 168 empty chair sculptures for each of the people killed in the attack (the 19 small ones are for the children who perished in the day-care center).

Woody Guthrie Center

Price: adult/child $8/6

Hours: 10am-6pm Tue-Sun

Contact: http://www.woodyguthriecenter.org, 918-574-2710

Location: 102 E Brady St, Tulsa, USA

Woody Guthrie gained fame for his 1930s folk ballads that told stories of the Dust Bowl and the depression. His life and music are recalled in this impressive new museum, where you can listen to his music and explore his legacy via the works of Dylan and more.

Oregon

It's hard to slap a single characterization onto Oregon's geography and people. Its landscape ranges from rugged coastline and thick evergreen forests to barren, fossil-strewn deserts, volcanoes and glaciers. As for its denizens, you name it – Oregonians run the gamut from pro-logging conservatives to tree-hugging liberals, and everything in between. What they have in common is an independent spirit, a love of the outdoors and a fierce devotion to where they live.

It doesn't usually take long for visitors here to feel a similar devotion. Who wouldn't fall in love with the spectacle of glittering Crater Lake, or the breathtaking colors of the Painted Hills in John Day, or the hiking trails through deep forests and over stunning mountain passes? And then there are the towns: you can eat like royalty in funky Portland, see top-notch dramatic productions in Ashland, or sample an astounding number of brewpubs in Bend.

Rugged beauty, locavore cuisine, and indie spirit are just some of Oregon's charms. The Pacific Northwest darling is home to hip Portland, whose happening foodie and arts scenes are anchored by an eco-friendly lifestyle. Smaller cities draw you in, too: you can sample microbrews in Bend, see top-notch theater in Ashland, and explore maritime history in Astoria. Miles of bike paths, hikes up Mt. Hood, and rafting in the Columbia River Gorge thrill outdoor enthusiasts. For pure relaxation, taste award-winning Willamette Valley wines and walk windswept Pacific beaches.

Sights in Oregon

Cape Perpetua Scenic Area

Price: day-use fee $5

Location: Hwy 101, Yachats, USA

Located 3 miles south of Yachats, this volcanic remnant was sighted and named by England's Captain James Cook in 1778. Famous for dramatic rock formations and crashing surf, the area contains numerous trails that explore ancient shell middens, tide pools and old-growth forests. Views from the cape are incredible, taking in coastal promontories from Cape Foulweather to Cape Arago.

The visitor center details human and natural histories, and has displays on the Alsi tribe.

For spectacular ocean views, head up Overlook Rd to the Cape Perpetua day-use area.

Deep fractures in the old volcano allow waves to erode narrow channels into the headland, creating effects such as Devil's Churn, about a half-mile north of the visitors center. Waves race up this chasm, shooting up the 30ft inlet to explode against the narrowing sides of the channel. For an easy hike, take the paved Captain Cook Trail (1.2 miles round-trip) down to tide pools near Cooks Chasm, where at high tide the geyser-like spouting horn blasts water out of a sea cave.

The Giant Spruce Trail (2 miles round-trip) leads up Cape Creek to a 500-year-old Sitka spruce with a 15ft diameter. The Cook's Ridge-Gwynn Creek Loop Trail (6.5 miles round-trip) heads into deep old-growth forests along Gwynn Creek; follow the Oregon Coast Trail south and turn up the Gwynn Creek Trail, which returns via Cook's Ridge.

Maryhill Museum of Art

Price: adult/child $9/3

Hours: 10am-5pm mid-Mar–mid-Nov

Contact: http://www.maryhillmuseum.org, 509-773-3733

Location: 35 Maryhill Museum Dr, WA, Eastern Gorge, USA

If you've ever wondered about that expression, 'What in Sam Hill?,' here's your answer: this museum in a hilltop mansion was founded by Sam Hill (1857–1931), one of the great innovators in Northwest history. An exhibit in the museum's permanent collection tells his story. The collection also includes sculpture and drawings by Auguste Rodin, art-nouveau glass, and various American and European paintings. There's a newly updated Native American gallery, plus a series of temporary exhibits.

Spectacularly located on a bluff above the Columbia, this old mansion also boasts a seal intestine parka and carved walrus tusks, a large and amazing collection of chess sets and a variety of French fashion mannequins. Outside are garden sculptures and picnic tables with fine views. There's also a cafe on premises.

In 2012 the Maryhill opened a new wing, adding more collection rooms, educational and research spaces and outdoor areas with expansive views of the gorge.

The museum is in Washington, just across the Columbia; cross The Dalles bridge and head west for 3 miles.

Pioneer Courthouse Square

Contact: http://www.thesquarepdx.org

Location: Portland, USA

The heart of downtown Portland, this brick plaza is nicknamed 'Portland's living room' and is the most-visited public space in the city. When it isn't full of Hacky Sack players, sunbathers or office workers lunching, the square hosts concerts, festivals, rallies, farmers' markets, and even summer Friday-night movies (aka 'Flicks on the Bricks').

One of Portland's grandest Victorian hotels once stood here, but it fell into disrepair and was torn down in 1951. Later the city decided to build Pioneer Courthouse Sq, and grassroots support resulted in a program that encouraged citizens to buy and personalize the bricks that eventually built the square. Names include Sherlock Holmes, William Shakespeare and Elvis Presley.

Across 6th Ave is the Pioneer Courthouse. Built in 1875, this was the legal center of 19th-century Portland.

Tom McCall Waterfront Park

Location: Naito Pkwy, Portland, USA

This popular riverside park, which lines the west bank of the Willamette River, was finished in 1978 after four years of construction. It replaced an old freeway with 1.5 miles of paved sidewalks and grassy spaces, and attracts heaps of joggers, in-line skaters, strollers and cyclists. During summer the park is perfect for hosting large outdoor events such as the Oregon Brewers Festival. Walk over the Steel and Hawthorne bridges to the Eastbank Esplanade, making a 2.6-mile loop.

Salmon Street Springs Fountain, in the park at Salmon St, draws a crowd on a hot day. North of Burnside Bridge is the Japanese American Historical Plaza, a memorial to Japanese Americans who were interned by the US government during WWII.

Pennsylvania

More than 300 miles across, stretching from the East Coast to the edge of the Midwest, Pennsylvania contains multitudes. Philadelphia, once the heart of the British colonial empire, is very much a part of the east, a link on the Boston-Washington metro corridor. Outside the city, though, the terrain turns pastoral, emphasized by the Pennsylvania Dutch – that is, Mennonite, Amish and others – who tend their farms by hand, as if it were still the 18th century. West of here, the Appalachian mountains begin, as do the so-called Pennsylvania Wilds, a barely inhabited patch of deep forest. In the far west edge of the state, Pittsburgh, the state's only other large city and once a staggeringly wealthy steel manufacturing center, is fascinating in its combination of rust-belt decay and new energy.

From the dramatic hills of Pittsburgh across rolling farmland and majestic forest to the narrow streets of colonial Philadelphia, Pennsylvania provides a wide range of experiences. The state reflects a rich history—from halcyon days as the seat of the American Revolution and a fledgling nation's first capital through its role as a leader in the country's transformation into an industrial powerhouse—

and its role today as a leader in the health-care and pharmaceutical industries, a center for the arts, and a burgeoning tourist destination.

Pennsylvania has fascinating contrasts. A mostly rural state, it is home to two large cities: Philadelphia, the nation's fifth largest and the regional center for the eastern portion of the state; and Pittsburgh, the focus for the western portion. Within a few hours' drive of the worldliness and sophistication of these cities, you can return to a simpler way of life. The winding country lanes and now-silent battlefields conjure up images of the Civil War, while in Lancaster, the horse and buggy is still a viable means of transportation, as today's Pennsylvania Dutch hew to the traditions of their ancestors.

Sights in Pennsylvania

Barnes Foundation

Price: adult/child $25/10

Hours: 10am-5pm Wed-Mon

Contact: http://www.barnesfoundation.org, 215-278-7200

Location: 2025 Benjamin Franklin Pkwy, Philadelphia, USA

In the first half of the 20th century, collector and educator Albert C Barnes amassed a remarkable trove of artwork by Cézanne, Degas, Matisse, Renoir, Van Gogh and other European stars. Alongside, he set beautiful pieces of folk art from Africa and the Americas – an artistic desegregation that was shocking at the time. Today's Barnes Foundation is a modern shell, inside which is a faithful reproduction of Barnes's original mansion (still in the Philadelphia suburbs).

The art is hung according to his vision, a careful juxtaposition of colors, themes and materials. In one room, all the portraits appear to be staring at a central point. Even more remarkable: you've likely never seen any of these works before, because Barnes' will limits reproduction and lending.

Philadelphia Museum of Art

Price: adult/child $20/free

Hours: 10am-5pm Tue, Thu, Sat & Sun, to 8:45pm Wed & Fri

Contact: http://www.philamuseum.org, 215-763-8100

Location: 2600 Benjamin Franklin Pkwy, Philadelphia, USA

To many, this building is simply the steps Sylvester Stallone ran up in the 1976 flick Rocky. But well beyond that, this is one of the nation's finest treasure troves, featuring excellent collections of Asian art, Renaissance masterpieces, post-impressionist works and modern pieces by Picasso, Duchamp and Matisse. Especially neat are the complete rooms: a medieval cloister, a Chinese temple, an Austrian country house.

There's so much to see that a ticket gives admission for two days, here and at the separate Perelman Building, two nearby historic homes and the Rodin Museum. Wednesday and Friday nights are pay-what-you-wish (but note the Perelman is closed).

Monongahela & Duquesne Inclines

Price: one-way adult/child $2.50/1.25

Hours: 5:30am-12:45am Mon-Sat, from 7am Sun

Contact: http://www.duquesneincline.org

Location: Pittsburgh, USA

These two funiculars, built in the late 19th century, are Pittsburgh icons, zipping up the steep slope of Mt Washington every five to 10 minutes. They provide commuters a quick connection and they give visitors great city views, especially at night. You can make a loop, going up one, walking along aptly named Grandview Ave (about 1 mile, or take bus 40) and coming down the other.

If you ride just one, make it the Duquesne (du-kane). At the top, you can pay 50¢ to see the gears and cables at work. Outside the station, Altius restaurant is a good place to enjoy the view over a drink.

Independence National Historic Park

Hours: visitor center & most sites 9am-5pm

Contact: http://www.nps.gov/inde, +1 215 965 2305

Location: 3rd & Chestnut Sts, Philadelphia, USA

This L-shaped park, along with Old City, has been dubbed 'America's most historic square mile.' Once the backbone of the United States government, it has become the backbone of Philadelphia's tourist trade. Stroll around and you'll see storied buildings in which the seeds for the Revolutionary War were planted and the US government came into bloom. You'll also find beautiful, shaded urban lawns dotted with plenty of squirrels, pigeons and costumed actors.

Rhode Island

Rhode Island, the smallest of the US states, isn't actually an island. Although it takes only 45 minutes to traverse, this little wonder packs in over 400 miles of coastline with some of the finest white-sand swimming beaches in the northeast, deserted coves, rugged seaside cliffs and isolated lighthouses.

Hugging the shoreline before heading inland, delightful resorts, quaint colonial villages and extravagant mansions give way to lush fields of berry farms, vineyards, and the horse studs of Middletown and Portsmouth. Rhode Island's two cities, Providence, of working-class roots, and Newport, born of old money the likes of which most cannot conceive, are each among New England's finest, brimming with fantastic museums, neighborhoods boasting utterly gorgeous historic homes, and an urban fabric of top-notch restaurants and seriously cool bars. It's no wonder the nouveau riche continue to flock here for summer shenanigans.

"Rhode Island: 3% Bigger at Low Tide," reads a locally made T-shirt—an exaggeration, of course: the state geologist calculates it's actually more like 0.5%. But the smallest state's size is a source of pride, given all there is to do within its 1,500 square miles. You may find it hard to choose among so many experiences: historic walks, fine dining, and the WaterFire display in Providence; apple picking and riverboat cruises in the Blackstone Valley; fishing trips and beach excursions in South County and Block Island; pedaling along Bristol's bike path; and taking sunset sails in Newport and touring the Gilded Age mansions.

Rhode Island and Providence Plantations, the state's official name, has a long history of forward thinking and a spirit of determination and innovation embodied in the 11-foot-tall bronze Independent Man atop the marble-domed State House. The first of the 13 colonies to declare independence from Britain can also claim the first successful textile mill (in Pawtucket), America's oldest synagogue (in Newport), and the first lunch wagon (in Providence). A state founded on the principle of religious liberty drew Baptists, Jews, Quakers, and others throughout the 17th and 18th centuries, then flourished with factories, silver foundries, and jewelry companies, which brought workers from French Canada, Italy, Ireland, England, Portugal, and Eastern Europe.

Rhode Island remains an attractive, spirited place to live or visit. A public works project has opened up the river in Downtown Providence; infrastructural improvements at Fort Adams State Park in Newport allow it to host international yacht-racing events; extended commuter rail service makes it easier to travel between Providence, T. F. Green Airport, and Wickford; and bike-path expansions allow cyclists to traverse South County, East Bay, and Blackstone Valley. Rhode Island's 39 cities and towns—none more than 50 miles apart—offer natural beauty, inspired culinary artistry, and many opportunities to relax and enjoy its scenic vistas.

Sights in Rhode Island

WaterFire

Hours: dates vary

Contact: http://www.waterfire.org

Over 15 summer nights, beginning at sunset, Providence's landscaped riverfront promenades spring to life with scheduled (and unscheduled) street performers, vendors, food trucks and throngs of onlookers who come to view the spectacle of 100 anchored, flaming braziers illuminating the water, marking the convergence of the Providence, Moshassuck and Woonasquatucket Rivers.

Created by Barnaby Evans in 1994, WaterFire has become locals' most loved annual event, celebrating the resurrection of sections of the river and Providence's phoenix-like transformation from a once certain fate of death by industry.

Check the homepage for upcoming dates.

Rough Point

Price: adult/child $25/free

Hours: 10am-2pm Thu-Sat mid-Apr–mid-May, 10am-3:45pm Tue-Sun mid-May–mid-Nov

Contact: http://www.newportrestoration.com, 401-849-7300

Location: 680 Bellevue Ave, Newport, USA

While the peerless position and splendor of the grounds alone are worth the price of admission, this faux-English manor house also contains heiress and philanthropist Doris Duke's impressive art holdings, including medieval tapestries, furniture owned by French emperors, Ming dynasty ceramics, and paintings by Renoir and Van Dyck.

Built in 1889 by Frederick W Vanderbilt on a rocky bluff jutting out into the ocean, Rough Point was later purchased by tobacco baron James B Duke, and passed to his only daughter, Doris (then aged 12), in 1925 along with his $80 million fortune. Throughout her teenage years Doris spent her summers here, and as an adult Rough Point was one of her favorite houses.

The contents of the house are exactly as she left them at the time of her death in 1993, when she bequeathed the house to the Newport Restoration Society (which she founded) with the directive that it be opened as a museum. Particularly interesting is a glassed-in sunroom containing just about the only pedestrian furniture (the couch appears to be from a department store). Also on hand are mannequins wearing some of Duke's eight decades of bizarre clothing.

Rhode Island State House

Hours: tours by appointment

Contact: http://www.rilin.state.ri.us, 401-222-2357

Location: 82 Smith St, Providence, USA

Designed by McKim, Mead and White in 1904, the Rhode Island State House rises above the Providence skyline, easily visible from miles around. Modeled in part on St Peter's Basilica in Vatican City, it has the world's fourth-largest self-supporting marble dome and houses one of Gilbert Stuart's portraits of George Washington, which you might want to compare to a dollar bill from your wallet.

Inside the public halls are the battle flags of Rhode Island military units and a Civil War cannon, which sat here for a century loaded and ready to shoot until someone thought to check whether it was disarmed. The giant half-naked guy standing on top of the dome is The Independent Man, continuously struck by lightning.

Rhode Island School of Design

Contact: http://www.risd.edu, 401-454-6300

Location: 20 N Main St, Providence, USA

Perhaps the top art school in the USA, RISD's imprint on Providence is easily felt, with students' creativity extending across the cityscape. Open to the public, the extraordinary collections of the Museum of Art include 19th-century French paintings; classical Greek, Roman and Etruscan art; medieval and Renaissance works; and examples of 19th- and 20th-century American painting, furniture and decorative arts.

Kids love staring at the mummy, while others will be impressed to see the works of Manet, Matisse and Sargent. The museum stays open until 9pm on the third Thursday of the month, when admission is free after 5pm. It's also free the last Saturday of the month and Sunday from 10am to 1pm.

Breakers

Price: adult/child $21/7

Hours: 9am-5pm Apr–mid-Oct, hours vary mid-Oct–Mar

Contact: http://www.newportmansions.org, 401-847-1000

Location: 44 Ochre Point Ave, Newport, USA

A 70-room Italian Renaissance mega-palace inspired by 16th-century Genoese palazzos, Breakers is the most magnificent Newport mansion. At the behest of Cornelius Vanderbilt II, Richard Morris Hunt did most of the design (though craftsmen from around the world perfected the decorative program). The building was completed in 1895 and sits at Ochre Point, on a grand oceanside site. The furnishings, most made expressly for the Breakers, are all original. Don't miss the Children's Cottage on the grounds.

Admission also includes entry into the Breakers' Stable & Carriage House, also designed by Hunt, on the west side of Bellevue Ave.

South Carolina

Moss-draped oaks. Stately mansions. Wide beaches. Rolling mountains. And an ornery streak as old as the state itself. Ah yes, South Carolina, where the accents are thicker and the traditions more dear. From its Revolutionary War patriots to its 1860s secessionist government to its current crop of outspoken legislators, the Palmetto State has never shied away from a fight.

From the silvery sands of the Atlantic Coast, the state climbs westward from the Coastal Plain across the Piedmont and up into the Blue Ridge Mountains. Most travelers stick to the coast, with its splendid antebellum cities and palm-tree-studded beaches. But the interior has a wealth of sleepy old towns, wild and undeveloped state parks and spooky black-water swamps. Along the sea islands you hear the sweet songs of the Gullah, a culture and language created by former slaves who held onto many West African traditions through the ravages of time.

From well-bred, gardenia-scented Charleston to bright, tacky Myrtle Beach, South Carolina is always a fascinating destination.

South Carolina's crown jewel is the port city of Charleston. It's one of the South's best preserved cities with beautifully restored homes and churches, cobblestone streets, hidden gardens, and a thriving culinary scene. The South Carolina coast also includes family-friendly Myrtle Beach and the gracious Grand Strand. Hilton Head Island's exclusive resorts, excellent golfing, and genteel good life make it one of the coast's most popular getaways. Inland, South Carolina has small-town charm with antique shops and shady town squares.

Sights in South Carolina

Middleton Place

Price: gardens adult/child 6-13yr $28/10, house museum tour adult & child extra $15

Hours: 9am-5pm

Contact: http://www.middletonplace.org, 843-556-6020

Location: 4300 Ashley River Rd, Ashley River Plantations, USA

Designed in 1741, this plantation's vast gardens are the oldest in the US. One hundred slaves spent a decade terracing the land and digging the precise geometric canals for the owner, wealthy South Carolina politician Henry Middleton. The bewitching grounds are a mix of classic formal French gardens and romantic woodland, bounded by flooded rice paddies and rare-breed farm animals. Union soldiers burned the main house in 1865; a 1755 guest wing, now housing the house museum, still stands.

The on-site inn is a series of ecofriendly modernist glass boxes overlooking the Ashley River. Enjoy a traditional Lowcountry plantation lunch of she-crab soup and hoppin' john at the highly regarded cafe.

Gateway Walk

Location: Charleston, USA

Long a culturally diverse city, Charleston gave refuge to persecuted French Protestants, Baptists and Jews over the years and earned the nickname the 'Holy City' for its abundance of houses of worship. The Gateway Walk, a little-known garden path between Archdale St and Philadelphia Alley, connects four of the city's most beautiful historic churches: the white-columned St John's Lutheran Church; the Gothic Revival Unitarian Church; the striking Romanesque Circular Congregational Church, originally founded in 1681; and St Philip's Church, with its picturesque steeple and 17th-century graveyard, parts of which were once reserved for 'strangers and transient white persons.'

Table Rock State Park

Price: adult/child 6-15yr $5/3 Jun-Nov, adult/child under 16yr $2/free Dec-May

Hours: 7am-7pm Sun-Thu, to 9pm Fri & Sat, extended hours mid-May–early Nov

Contact: http://www.southcarolinaparks.com, 864-878-9813

Location: 158 Ellison Ln, Greenville & The Upcountry, USA

The Upcountry's marquee natural attraction is Table Rock Mountain, a 3124ft-high mountain with a striking granite face. The 7.2-mile round trip hike to its summit is a popular local challenge. For overnight stays, camping is available (campsites tent/RV from $17/25), as are cabins built by the Civilian Conservation Corps ($95 to $250).

Cabins are a choice of 1- to 3-bedrooms and come with air-conditioning, kitchenettes and coffeemakers. Campers have their choice of 93 campsites with water and hookups, spread across two separate wooded camping areas, plus six primitive trailside sites.

Fort Sumter

Location: Charleston

The first shots of the Civil War rang out at Fort Sumter, on a pentagon-shaped island in the harbor. A Confederate stronghold, the fort was shelled to bits by Union forces from 1863 to 1865. A few original guns and fortifications give a feel for the momentous history. The only way to get here is by boat tour, which depart from 340 Concord St at 9:30am, noon and 2:30pm in summer (less frequently in winter) and from Patriot's Point in Mt Pleasant, across the river, at 10:45am, 1:30pm and 4pm from mid-March to late August (less frequently the rest of the year).

South Dakota

Marked by windswept prairies, rugged badlands, and an emerald oasis known as the Black Hills, South Dakota is a state of rugged beauty. The chiseled spires, ragged ridges, and steep-sided canyons of Badlands National Park are awe-inspiring, while the Black Hills, with its imposing peaks and the famed Mount Rushmore monument, attracts sizable crowds in summer.

Gently rolling prairies through shallow fertile valleys mark much of this endlessly attractive state. But head southwest and all hell breaks loose – in the best possible way. The Badlands National Park is the geologic equivalent of fireworks. The Black Hills are like opera: majestic, challenging, intriguing and even frustrating. Mt Rushmore matches the Statue of Liberty for five-star icon status

Sights in South Dakota

Wounded Knee Massacre Site

Location: Hwy 27, Pine Ridge Indian Reservation, USA

The massacre site, 16 miles northeast of Pine Ridge town, is marked by a faded sign. It helps to read up on the events before you arrive. The mass grave, often frequented by people looking for donations, sits atop the hill near a church. Small memorials appear daily amid the stones listing dozens of names such as Horn Cloud. It's a desolate place, with sweeping views. An ad hoc timeline on a pillar lists acts of genocide against Native Americans.

Wall Drug

Hours: 6:30am-8pm May-Sep, to 6pm Oct-Apr

Contact: http://www.walldrug.com, 605-279-2175

Location: 510 Main St, Wall, USA

Hyped for hundreds of miles, Wall Drug is a surprisingly enjoyable stop. It really does have 5¢ coffee, free ice water, good donuts and enough diversions and come-ons to warm the heart of schlock-lovers everywhere. But amid the fudge in this faux frontier complex is a superb bookstore with a great selection of regional titles. Out back, ride the mythical jackalope and check out the historical photos.

Mount Moriah Cemetery

Price: adult/child $1/50¢, tours $9/5

Hours: 8am-8pm Jun-Aug, to 5pm Sep-May

Location: Mt Moriah Dr, Deadwood, USA

Calamity Jane (born Martha Canary; 1850–1903) and Wild Bill Hickok (1847–76) rest side by side up on Boot Hill at the very steep cemetery. Entertaining bus tours leave hourly from Main St.

Tennessee

Most states have one official state song. Tennessee has seven. And that's not just a random fact – Tennessee has music deep within its soul. Here, the folk music of the Scots-Irish in the eastern mountains combined with the bluesy rhythms of the African Americans in the western Delta to give birth to the modern country music that makes Nashville famous.

These three geographic regions, represented by the three stars on the Tennessee flag, have their own unique beauty: the heather-colored peaks of the Great Smoky Mountains; the lush green valleys of the central plateau around Nashville; and the hot, sultry lowlands near Memphis.

In Tennessee you can hike shady mountain trails in the morning, and by evening whoop it up in a Nashville honky-tonk or walk the streets of Memphis with Elvis' ghost.

Tennessee's music, scenic beauty, and history are top reasons the state continues to attract, entertain, and charm the masses. Several genres of American music have their roots and branches here: bluegrass and Appalachian music in the eastern parts of the state; country, Americana, and pop in Nashville; and blues, soul, and rock 'n' roll in Memphis. Elvis Presley recorded his early hits at Sun Studio in Memphis and most of his No. 1 records at Studio B in Nashville. Popular recording artists Sheryl Crow, Jack White, Taylor Swift, and the Black Keys, who all live in Nashville now, thrive on its reputation as "Music City," as do world-famous music attractions that include the Grand Ole Opry, Honky Tonk Row, and Country Music Hall of Fame & Museum. Enduring entertainment attractions like Dollywood in Pigeon Forge, the historic Ryman Auditorium in Nashville, and the newly opened Discovery Park of America in Union City demonstrate Tennessee's popularity with diverse audiences.

In East Tennessee, the Great Smoky Mountains National Park is a world biosphere and Eden for nature lovers, attracting more visitors than any other park in the federal system. Long before there was a park, however, Tennessee was part of the American frontier, where Davy Crockett, Daniel Boone, and U.S. presidents Andrew Jackson, James K. Polk, and Andrew Johnson lived.

The Civil War is commemorated at Shiloh National Military Park, the geographical setting for one of the war's bloodiest battles. An additional 270 Civil War sites are marked along Tennessee's Civil War Trail, one of 16 self-driving trails in the Discover Tennessee Trails & Byways system, comprising all 95 counties in the state.

Sights in Tennessee

Graceland

Price: tours house only adult/child $36/16, expanded tours from $40/19

Hours: 9am-5pm Mon-Sat, to 4pm Sun, shorter hours & closed Tue Dec

Contact: http://www.graceland.com, 901-332-3322

Location: Elvis Presley Blvd/US 51, Memphis, USA

If you only make one stop in Memphis, it should be here: the sublimely kitschy, gloriously bizarre home of the King of Rock and Roll. Though born in Mississippi, Elvis Presley was a true son of Memphis, raised in the Lauderdale Courts public housing projects, inspired by blues clubs on Beale St, and discovered at Sun Studio. In the spring of 1957, the already-famous 22-year-old spent $100,000 on a Colonial-style mansion, named Graceland by its previous owners.

The King himself had the place, ahem, redecorated in 1974. With a 15ft couch, fake waterfall, yellow vinyl walls and green shag-carpet ceiling – it's a virtual textbook of ostentatious '70s style. You'll begin your tour at the visitor plaza on the other side of Elvis Presley Blvd. Book ahead in the busy season (June to August and important Elvis dates) to ensure a prompt tour time. The basic self-guided mansion tour comes with an engaging multimedia iPad narration. Pay just $4 extra to see the car museum, and $9 extra to tack on the two custom planes (check out the blue-and-gold private bathroom on the Lisa Marie, a Convair 880 Jet).

Priscilla Presley (who divorced Elvis in 1973) opened Graceland to tours in 1982, and now millions come here to pay homage to the King who died here (in the upstairs bathroom) from heart failure in 1977. Throngs of fans still weep at his grave, next to the swimming pool out back. Graceland is nine miles south of Downtown on US 51, also called 'Elvis Presley Blvd.' A free shuttle runs from Sun Studio. Parking costs $10.

Sun Studio

Price: adult/child $12/free

Hours: 10am-6:15pm

Contact: http://www.sunstudio.com, 800-441-6249

Location: 706 Union Ave, Memphis, USA

This dusty storefront is ground zero for American rock and roll music. Starting in the early 1950s, Sun's Sam Phillips recorded blues artists such as Howlin' Wolf, BB King and Ike Turner, followed by the rockabilly dynasty of Jerry Lee Lewis, Johnny Cash, Roy Orbison and, of course, the King himself (who started here in 1953).

Packed 40-minute guided tours (no children under five allowed; hourly from 10:30am to 5:30pm) through the tiny studio offer a chance to hear original tapes of historic recording sessions. Guides are full of anecdotes; you can pose for photos on the 'X' where Elvis once stood, or buy a CD of the 'Million Dollar Quartet,' Sun's spontaneous 1956 jam session between Elvis, Johnny Cash, Carl Perkins and Jerry Lee Lewis. From here, hop on the studio's free shuttle (hourly, starting at 11:15am), which does a loop between Sun Studio, Beale St and Graceland.

Country Music Hall of Fame & Museum

Price: adult/child $25/15, with audio tour $27/18, with Studio B 1hr tour $40/30

Hours: 9am-5pm

Contact: http://www.countrymusichalloffame.com

Location: 222 5th Ave S, Nashville, USA

Following a $100-million expansion in 2014, this monumental museum, reflecting the near-biblical importance of country music to Nashville's soul, is a must-see, whether you're a country music fan or not. Gaze at Carl Perkins' blue suede shoes, Elvis' gold Cadillac (actually white) and gold piano (actually gold) and Hank Williams' western-cut suit with musical note appliqués.

Highlights of the ambitious 210,000-square-foot expansion include the 800-seat CMA Theater, the Taylor Swift Education Center and the relocation of the legendary letterpress operation of Hatch Show Print. Written exhibits trace country's roots, computer touch screens access recordings and photos from the enormous archives, and the fact- and music-filled audio tour is narrated by contemporary stars.

National Civil Rights Museum

Price: adult $15, student & senior $14, child $12

Hours: 9am-5pm Mon & Wed-Sat, 1-5pm Sun Sep-May, to 6pm Jun-Aug

Contact: http://www.civilrightsmuseum.org

Location: 450 Mulberry St, Memphis, USA

Housed across the street from the Lorraine Motel, where the Reverend Dr Martin Luther King Jr was fatally shot on April 4, 1968, is the gut-wrenching National Civil Rights Museum. Five blocks south of Beale St, this museum's extensive exhibits and detailed timeline chronicle the struggle for African American freedom and equality. Both Dr King's cultural contribution and his assassination serve as prisms for looking at the Civil Rights movement, its precursors and its continuing impact on American life.

The turquoise exterior of the 1950s motel and two preserved interior rooms remain much as they were at the time of King's death.

Texas

Texas is big and bold. The sheer diversity of the state allows you to combine specific interests into a customized itinerary based on your personal preferences, time, and budget: outdoor adventures in more than 90 state parks, Wild West lifestyle experiences at dozens of guest ranches, and evolving Western art and culinary traditions in Texas's premier cities. Wherever you travel in the state's seven distinct regions, you'll find dramatic culture and a myriad of opportunities to explore Texas history and heritage. Weather varies according to geography, but is generally mild under clear blue skies with abundant sunshine. August and September temperatures can climb into the upper 90s; December and January dip down into the 30s.

A darn sight bigger than a whole heap of countries, Texas is largely diverse: big-city lights to small-town simplicity; white-sand beaches to high-country hikes.

Bright lights, big cities? Check, Texas has them. Dallas and Houston both boast rich arts and culture districts to explore by day, as well as active nightlife. If you really want to party, Austin is the place – with endless live-music concerts and an outdoorsy, alternative vibe. San Antonio may seem a bit more sedate, but once evening falls on the Riverwalk there's a fiesta every night. City life is fun, but don't stop there; Texas also has countless small towns with brick building–lined courthouse squares, landmark cafes and eclectic antiques and boutiques to explore at a much slower pace.

Sights in Texas

Sixth Floor Museum

Price: adult/child $16/13

Hours: 10am-6pm Tue-Sun, noon-6pm Mon

Contact: http://www.jfk.org

Location: Book Depository, 411 Elm St, Dallas, USA

No city wants the distinction of being the site of an assassination – especially if the victim happens to be President John F Kennedy. But rather than downplay the events that sent the city reeling in 1963, Dallas gives visitors a unique opportunity to delve into the world-altering events unleashed by an assassin in the former Texas School Book Depository. Fascinating multimedia exhibits (plus the included audio guide) give an excellent historical context of JFK's time, as well as his life and legacy.

And while any museum dedicated to the subject could have reconstructed the historical event using footage, audio clips and eyewitness accounts, this museum offers you a goosebump-raising view through the exact window from which Lee Harvey Oswald fired upon the motorcade. (If that last statement raises your hackles, not to worry: the displays don't shy away from conspiracy theories, either.)

The museum also offers an interesting self-guided Cell Phone Walking Tour (one hour; $2.50) of Dealey Plaza and other JFK assassination sites.

Sabal Palm Sanctuary

Price: adult/child $5/3

Hours: 7am-5pm

Contact: http://www.sabalpalmsanctuary.org, 956-541-8034

Location: Sabal Palm Rd, Brownsville, USA

The only palm tree native to Texas grows at this 557-acre sanctuary, operated by a foundation for the National Audubon Society. It sits in a bend of the Rio Grande River that was never plowed under. It's a lush, beautiful and peaceful place with excellent nature hikes.

Although closed for several years by border politics, an agreement keeps the US border fence open during the day so that you can access this lost oasis on US soil. A highlight is the Rabb Plantation House, the 1892 mansion of the original owner. It's being restored and will house a visitors center. Among the good hikes is the 0.4-mile-long Forest Trail.

Sabal palms reach 20ft to 48ft high and have feathery crowns and thick, bristly trunks. They once lined the Rio Grande, covering an area of nearly 63 sq. miles. In the past 150 years, most have been cut down, first by early settlers who needed lumber and later by those clearing land for agriculture.

The preserve is 6 miles east of Brownsville off FM 1419 (also called Southmost Rd).

River Walk

Contact: http://www.thesanantonioriverwalk.com

Location: San Antonio, USA

A little slice of Europe in the heart of downtown San Antonio, the River Walk is an essential part of the San Antonio experience. This is no ordinary riverfront, but a charming canal and pedestrian street that is the main artery at the heart of San Antonio's tourism efforts. For the best overview, hop on a Rio San Antonio river cruise.

You can meander past landscaped hotel gardens and riverside cafes, and linger on the stone footbridges that stretch over the water. During summer it gets mighty crowded, but at peaceful times (and as you get away from downtown) it's a lovely place to stroll – especially during the holidays when it's bedecked with twinkling lights.

The Riverwalk used to be just a downtown thing, but a $358-million project completed in 2013 expanded it to include 15 miles of paths. You can now walk south to the King William district and beyond to the Spanish missions, or north to the San Antonio Art Museum and even up to the Pearl Brewery complex.

McDonald Observatory

Price: daytime pass adult/child 6-12yr/under 12yr $8/7/free, star parties adult/child $12/8

Hours: visitor center 10am-5pm

Contact: http://www.mcdonaldobservatory.org, 432-426-3640

Location: 3640 Dark Sky Dr, Fort Davis & Davis Mountains, USA

Away from all the light pollution of the big cities, the middle of west Texas has some of the clearest and darkest skies in North America, making it the perfect spot for an observatory. They have some of the biggest telescopes in the world here, perched on the peak of 6791ft Mt Locke and so enormous you can spot them from miles away.

A day pass gets you a guided tour (11am and 2pm) that includes close-up peeks at – but not through – the 2.7m Harlan J Smith Telescope and the 11m Hobby-Eberly Telescope, as well as a solar viewing, where you get to stare at the sun without scorching your eyeballs. On Tuesday, Friday and Saturday nights, the star parties help you see the night sky in a whole new way. Call ahead: reservations are required for all programs.

The observatory is 19 miles northwest of Fort Davis. Allow 30 minutes to drive from town.

Utah

Welcome to nature's most perfect playground. From red-rock mesas to skinny slot canyons, powder-bound slopes and slick rock trails, Utah's diverse terrain will stun you. The biking, hiking and skiing are world-class. And with more than 65% of the state lands public, including 12 national parks and monuments, the access is simply superb.

From mountain-biking on slickrock to hiking past dinosaur fossils, Utah has thrilling adventures for everyone. The world-class ski resorts of the Wasatch Mountains are a haven for those seeking perfect powder, and national parks such as Arches and Zion offer colorful geology lessons with natural arches, hoodoos, and mesas in brilliant ocher and red. History lovers can ponder petroglyphs made by the earliest inhabitants or explore the Mormons' pioneer past in Salt Lake City. At the end of the day's activities, a hot tub and plush bed await.

Southern Utah is defined by red-rock cliffs, sorbet-colored spindles and seemingly endless sandstone desert. The pine-forested and snow-covered peaks of the Wasatch Mountains dominate northern Utah. Interspersed are old pioneer remnants, ancient rock art and ruins, and traces of dinosaurs.

Mormon-influenced rural towns can be quiet and conservative, but the rugged beauty has attracted outdoorsy progressives as well. Salt Lake City (SLC) and Park City, especially, have vibrant nightlife and progressive dining scenes. So pull on your boots and stock up on water: Utah's wild and scenic hinterlands await.

Sights in Utah

Natural History Museum of Utah

Price: adult/child $11/9

Hours: 10am-5pm Thu-Tue, to 9pm Wed

Contact: http://nhmu.utah.edu

Location: 301 Wakara Way, Salt Lake City, USA

The stunning architecture of the Rio Tinto Center forms a multistory indoor 'canyon' that showcases exhibits to great effect. Walk up through the layers as you explore both indigenous peoples' cultures and natural history. Past Worlds paleontological displays are the most impressive – an incredible perspective from beneath, next to and above a vast collection of dinosaur fossils offers the full breadth of pre-history.

Antelope Island State Park

Price: day-use per vehicle $10; tent & RV sites without hookups $15

Hours: 7am-10pm Jul-Sep, to 7pm Oct-Jun

Contact: http://stateparks.utah.gov, 801-773-2941

Location: Antelope Dr, Salt Lake Region, USA

White-sand beaches, birds and buffalo are what attract people to the pretty, 15-mile-long Antelope Island State Park. That's right, the largest island in the Great Salt Lake is home to a 600-strong herd of American bison, or buffalo. The November roundup, for veterinary examination, is a thrilling wildlife spectacle. And then there are the hundreds of thousands of migratory birds that descend on the park to feast on tiny brine shrimp along the Great Salt Lake's shore en route to distant lands during fall (September to November) and spring (March to

May) migrations. The island is a year-round home to burrowing owls and raptors as well as namesake antelope, bighorn sheep and deer. Nineteen miles of hiking trails provide many opportunities to view wildlife; however, some trails are closed during mating and birthing seasons. Rangers lead hikes and star parties from the visitor center (open 9am-5pm). At the end of an 11-mile paved road, several short nature trails lead off from Fielding Garr Ranch. There's also a small marina and a simple restaurant (801-776-6734; lunch & dinner May-Sep). There's also a small marina and simple restaurant on the island. Bridger Bay Campground (800-322-3770; campsites $13) has water and pit toilets. The white, sandy beach nearby has showers and flushing toilets that both swimmers (more like floaters with all that salt) and campers use. To get to the park (25 miles north of Salt Lake City, 10 miles south of Ogden), head west from I-15 exit 335 and follow the signs; a 7-mile causeway leads to the island.

Valley of the Gods

Location: Bluff

Up and over, through and around: the 17-mile unpaved road (County Rd 242) that leads through Valley of the Gods is like a do-it-yourself roller coaster amid some mind-blowing scenery. In other states, this incredible butte-filled valley would be a national park, but such are the riches of Utah that here it is merely a BLM-administered area (www.blm.gov). The field office in Monticello puts out a BLM pamphlet, available online, identifying a few of the sandstone monoliths and pinnacles, including Seven Sailors, Lady on a Tub and Rooster Butte.

Locals call it 'mini–Monument Valley'.

Free, dispersed camping among the rock giants is a dramatic – if shadeless – prospect. In such an isolated, uninhabited place, the night sky is incredible. Or splurge for a secluded refuge at Valley of the Gods B&B, a 1930s homestead with giant beam-and-post ceilings, stone showers and off-the-grid charm. Homemade breakfasts are monumental and the owners are happy to share hiking and travel tips. It's 6.5 miles north of Hwy 163. Water is trucked in, biofuels are used and solar power is harnessed out of necessity (leave your hair dryer at home).

A high-clearance vehicle is advised for driving the Valley of the Gods. A rental car can make it on a very dry day, but don't go without a 4WD if it has rained recently. Allow an hour for the 17-mile loop connecting Hwys 261 and 163. The nearest services are in Mexican Hat, 7 miles southwest of the Hwy 163 turnoff.

Goblin Valley State Park

Price: per car $10

Hours: park 6am-10pm, visitor center 8am-5pm

Contact: http://www.stateparks.utah.gov/parks/goblin-valley, 435-275-4584

Location: Goblin Valley Rd, Green River, USA

A Salvador Dali-esque melted-rock fantasy, a valley of giant stone mushrooms, an otherworldly alien landscape or the results of a cosmological acid trip? No matter what you think the stadium-like valley of stunted hoodoos resembles, one thing's for sure – the 3654-acre Goblin Valley State Park is just plain fun.

A few trails lead down from the overlooks to the valley floor, but after that there's no path to follow. You can climb down, around and even over the evocative 'goblins' (2ft- to 20ft-tall formations). Kids and photographers especially love it.

A 19-site campground books up on most weekends. There are small shade shelters and picnic tables, as well as water and no-charge showers, but no hookups. The new 8-person yurts are popular, so reserve well ahead. West of the park off Goblin Valley Rd is BLM land, with good, free dispersed camping, but no services (stay on designated roads).

Twenty miles further south on Hwy 24 is Hanksville (population 350, elevation 4300ft); if you don't need gas, there's little reason to stop. It's better to stay in Green River, Torrey or at Lake Powell, depending on where you're headed. The BLM Field Office has maps and information for surrounding lands, particularly the Henry Mountains. Before continuing south, fill up your car and carry your own food and water. There are no more services until you get to Bullfrog Marina (70 miles) or Mexican Hat (130 miles).

Vermont

Vermont is a land of hidden treasures and unspoiled scenery. Wander anywhere in the state — nearly 80% is forest — and you'll find pristine countryside dotted with farms and framed by mountains. Tiny towns with picturesque church steeples, village greens, and clapboard Colonial-era houses are perfect for exploring.

Sprawl has no place here. Highways are devoid of billboards by law, and on some roads cows still stop traffic twice a day en route to and from pasture. In spring, sap boils in sugarhouses, some built generations ago, while up the road a chef trained at the New England Culinary Institute in Montpelier might use the syrup to glaze a pork tenderloin.

It's the landscape, for the most part, that attracts people to Vermont. Rolling hills belie rugged terrain underneath the green canopy of forest growth. In summer, clear lakes and streams provide ample opportunities for swimming, boating, and fishing; hills attract hikers and mountain bikers. The more than 14,000 miles of roads, many of them only intermittently traveled by cars, are great for biking. In fall the leaves have their last hurrah, painting the mountainsides in yellow, gold, red, and orange. Vermont has the best ski resorts in the eastern United States, centered along the spine of the Green Mountains running north to south, and the traditional heart of skiing here is the town of Stowe. Almost anywhere you go, no matter what time of year, the Vermont countryside will make you reach for your camera.

Although Vermont may seem locked in time, technological sophistication appears where you least expect it: wireless Internet access in a 19th-century farmhouse-turned-inn and cell phone coverage from the state's highest peaks. Like an old farmhouse under renovation, though, the state's historic exterior is still the main attraction.

Whether seen under blankets of snow, patchworks of blazing fall leaves or the exuberant greens of spring and summer, Vermont's blend of bucolic farmland, mountains and picturesque small villages make it one of America's most uniformly appealing states. Hikers, bikers, skiers and kayakers will find four-season bliss here, on the expansive waters of Lake Champlain, the award-winning Kingdom Trails Network, the 300-mile Long and Catamount Trails, and the fabled slopes of Killington, Stowe and Sugarbush.

Foodies will love it here: small farmers have made Vermont a locavore paradise, complemented by America's densest collection of craft brewers. But most of all, what sets Vermont apart is its independent spirit: the first state to endorse same-sex civil unions, the only one to elect a socialist senator in the 21st century and the only one without a McDonald's in its capital city, it remains a haven of quirky creativity unlike anyplace else in America.

Sights in Vermont

Shelburne Museum

Price: adult/child/teen $24/12/14

Hours: 10am-5pm daily May-Dec, 10am-5pm Wed-Sun Jan-Apr

Contact: http://www.shelburnemuseum.org, 802-985-3346

Location: 6000 Shelburne Rd/US 7, Burlington, USA

This extraordinary 45-acre museum, 9 miles south of Burlington, showcases the priceless Americana collections of Electra Havemeyer Webb (1888–1960) and her parents – 150,000 objects in all. The mix of folk art, decorative arts and more is housed in 39 historic buildings, most of them moved here from other parts of New England to ensure their preservation.

Structures include a sawmill (1786), a one-room brick schoolhouse (1840), a covered bridge (1845), a lighthouse (1871), a luxury rail coach (1890), a classic round barn (1901), a railroad station (1915), the Lake Champlain side-wheeler steamship Ticonderoga (1906) and a 1920s carousel. There's also an entire building (Owl Cottage) filled with books, games and activities for kids. Allow at least half a day for your visit.

Billings Farm & Museum

Price: adult/child $14/8

Hours: 10am-5pm daily May-Oct, to 4pm Sat & Sun Nov-Feb, closed Mar & Apr

Contact: http://www.billingsfarm.org, 802-457-2355

Location: 5302 River Rd, Woodstock & Quechee Village, USA

A mile north of Woodstock's village green, this historic farm founded by 19th-century railroad magnate Frederick Billings delights children with hands-on activities related to old-fashioned farm life. Farm animals, including pretty cows descended from Britain's Isle of Jersey, are abundant. Family-friendly seasonal events include wagon and sleigh rides, pumpkin and apple festivals, and old-fashioned Halloween, Thanksgiving and Christmas celebrations.

Hildene

Price: adult/child $20/5, guided tours $7.50/2

Hours: 9:30am-4:30pm

Contact: http://www.hildene.org, 802-362-1788

Location: 1005 Hildene Rd/VT 7A, Manchester, USA

Outside Manchester, the 24-room Georgian Revival mansion of Robert Todd Lincoln, son of Abraham and Mary Lincoln, is a national treasure. Lincoln family members lived here until 1975, when it was converted into a museum and filled with many of the family's personal effects and furnishings. These include the hat Abraham Lincoln probably wore when he delivered the Gettysburg Address, and remarkable brass casts of his hands, the right one swollen from shaking hands while campaigning for the presidency.

Visitors can take a self-guided tour of the mansion any time of year. Guided tours are also available (for an additional fee) from June to mid-September at 11am and 1pm, and from November to May (by reservation only) at 1pm; there are no guided tours between mid-September and October.

The museum ticket includes access to the surrounding grounds, which are home to 8 miles of walking, skiing and snowshoeing trails, an observatory with a telescope, the Cutting and Kitchen Garden (a pretty herb and vegetable garden), the Hoyt Formal Garden (an exquisite flower garden designed to resemble a stained-glass window) and an agricultural center with a solar-powered barn where you can see the goats that produce Hildene cheese (watch it being made here, and purchase it at the museum gift shop).

Hildene also has a packed calendar of concerts and lectures; check its website for up-to-date listings.

Merck Forest & Farmland Center

Hours: visitor center 9am-4pm

Contact: http://www.merckforest.org, 802-394-7836

Location: 3270 VT 315, Manchester, USA

Encompassing over 2700 acres of high-country meadow and forest, this sprawling farm and environmental education center is a blissful place to experience Vermont's natural beauty and agricultural heritage. The park's centerpiece is a working organic farm with animals, vegetable gardens, renewable-energy installations and a sugar house where you can watch maple syrup being produced during sugaring season. It's hidden away on a gorgeous hilltop, only 25 minutes from Manchester but a world apart from the village hustle and bustle.

The center offers a wide range of hikes, environmental education programs and such events as sheepdog trials. It also rents out cabins and tent sites, which are spread all over the property. Sales of produce and syrup, coupled with voluntary contributions, help sustain the nonprofit foundation at the heart of it all. To get here from Manchester, take VT 30 northwest 8 miles to East Rupert, then turn left on VT 315, travel 2 miles and look for signs on your left at the top of the hill.

Quechee Gorge

Location: US 4, Woodstock & Quechee Village, USA

Lurking beneath US 4, less than a mile east of Quechee Village, the gorge is a 163ft-deep scar that cuts about 3000ft along a stream that you can view from a bridge or easily access by footpaths from the road. A series of well-marked, undemanding trails, none of which should take more than an hour to cover, lead down into the gorge.

Just upstream from the gorge, the tranquil waters of Dewey's Mill Pond are another lovely spot; bordered by a pretty expanse of reeds and grasses. The pond is named for AG Dewey, who set up a prosperous woolen mill here in 1869.

Virginia

Beautiful Virginia is a state steeped in history. It's the birthplace of America, where English settlers established the first permanent colony in the New World in 1607. From then on, the Commonwealth of Virginia has played a lead role in nearly every major American drama, from the Revolutionary and Civil Wars to the Civil Rights movement and the attacks of September 11, 2001.

Virginia's natural beauty is as diverse as its history and people. Chesapeake Bay and the wide sandy beaches kiss the Atlantic Ocean. Pine forests, marshes and rolling green hills form the soft curves of the central Piedmont region, while the rugged Appalachian Mountains and stunning Shenandoah Valley line its back.

A wonderland for history buffs, Virginia has an incredible past that's still on display. It's possible to visit the Virginia of George Washington or Thomas Jefferson (their historic homes are here), skip through Colonial times in Williamsburg, or absorb the power of the Civil War in Manassas. But don't miss the appeal of modern Virginia, from its wineries to its beaches.

Sights in Virginia

Shenandoah National Park

Price: one-week pass per car $20

Contact: http://www.nps.gov/shen, 540-999-3500

One of the most spectacular national parks in the country, Shenandoah is like a new smile from nature: in spring and summer the wildflowers explode, in fall the leaves burn bright red and orange, and in winter a cold, starkly beautiful hibernation period sets in. White-tailed deer are a common sight and, if you're lucky, you might spot a black bear, bobcat or wild turkey. The park lies just 75 miles west of Washington, DC.

Your first stop should be the Dickey Ridge Visitors Center at Mile 4.6, close to the northern end of Skyline Dr, or the Byrd Visitors Center at Mile 50. Both places have exhibits on flora and fauna, as well as maps and information about hiking trails and activities.

Shenandoah National Park is easy on the eyes, set against a backdrop of the dreamy Blue Ridge Mountains, ancient granite and metamorphic formations that are more than one billion years old. The park itself was founded in 1935 as a retreat for East Coast urban populations. It is an accessible day-trip destination from DC, but stay longer if you can. The 500 miles of hiking trails, 75 scenic overlooks, 30 fishing streams, seven picnic areas and four campgrounds are sure to keep you entertained.

Skyline Drive is the breathtaking road that follows the main ridge of the Blue Ridge Mountains and winds 105 miles through the center of the park. It begins in Front Royal near the western end of I-66, and ends in the southern part of the range near Rockfish Gap near I-64. Mile markers at the side of the road provide a reference. Miles and miles of blazed trails wander through the park.

The most famous trail in the park is the stretch of Appalachian Trail (AT), which travels 101 miles through Shenandoah from south to north, and is part of the 2175-mile Appalachian Trail crossing through 14 states. Access the trail from Skyline Dr, which roughly parallels the trail. Aside from the AT, Shenandoah has over 400 miles of hiking trails in the park. Options for shorter hikes include the following: Compton Peak (Mile 10.4; 2.4 miles; easy to moderate), Traces (Mile 22.2; 1.7 miles; easy), Overall Run (Mile 22.2; 6 miles; moderate) and White Oak Canyon (Mile 42.6; 4.6 miles; strenuous). Hawksbill Mountain Summit (Mile 46.7; 2.1 miles; moderate) is the park's highest peak.

Colonial Williamsburg

Price: adult/child one-day $41/21, multi-day $51/26

Hours: 9am-5pm

Contact: http://www.colonialwilliamsburg.org

The restored capital of England's largest colony in the New World is a must-see attraction for visitors of all ages. This is not some phony, fenced-in theme park: Colonial Williamsburg is a living, breathing, working history museum with a painstakingly researched environment that brilliantly captures America of the 1700s.

The 301-acre historic area contains 88 original 18th-century buildings and several hundred faithful reproductions. Costumed townsfolk and 'interpreters' in period dress go about their colonial jobs as blacksmiths, apothecaries, printers, barmaids, soldiers and patriots, breaking character only long enough to pose for a snapshot.

Costumed patriots like Patrick Henry and Thomas Jefferson still deliver impassioned speeches for freedom, but the park doesn't gloss over America's less glorious moments. Today's re-enactors debate and question slavery, women's suffrage, the rights of indigenous Americans and whether or not it is even moral to engage in revolution.

Walking around the historic district and patronizing the shops and taverns is free, but entry to building tours and most exhibits is restricted to ticketholders. Expect crowds, lines and petulant children, especially in summer.

To park and to purchase tickets, follow signs to the visitor center, found north of the historic district between Hwy 132 and Colonial Pkwy; kids can also hire out period costumes here for $25 per day. Start off with a 30-minute film about Williamsburg, and ask about the day's programs and events.

Parking is free; shuttle buses run frequently to and from the historic district, or you can walk along the tree-lined footpath. You can also buy tickets at the Merchants Square information booth.

Monticello

Price: adult/child $25/8

Hours: 9am-6pm Mar-Oct, 10am-5pm Nov-Feb

Contact: http://www.monticello.org, 434-984-9800

Location: 931 Thomas Jefferson Pkwy, Charlottesville, USA

Monticello is an architectural masterpiece designed and inhabited by Thomas Jefferson, Founding Father and third US president. 'I am as happy nowhere else and in no other society, and all my wishes end, where I hope my days will end, at Monticello,' wrote Jefferson, who spent 40 years building his dream home, finally completed in 1809. Today it is the only home in America designated a UN World Heritage site. Built in Roman neoclassical style, the house was the centerpiece of a 5000-acre plantation tended by 150 slaves. Monticello today does not gloss over the complicated past of the man who declared that 'all men are created equal' in the Declaration of Independence, while owning slaves and likely fathering children with slave Sally Hemings. Jefferson and his family are buried in a small wooded plot near the home.

Visits to the house are conducted by guided tours only; you can take self-guided tours of the plantation grounds, gardens and cemetery. A high-tech exhibition center delves deeper into Jefferson's world – including exhibits on architecture, enlightenment through education, and the complicated idea of liberty. Frequent shuttles run from the visitor center to the hilltop house, or you can take the wooded footpath.

Monticello is about 4.5 miles northwest of downtown Charlottesville.

Steven F Udvar-Hazy Center

Hours: 10am-5:30pm, to 6:30pm late May-early Sep

Contact: http://www.airandspace.si.edu/visit/udvar-hazy-center

Location: 14390 Air & Space Museum Parkway, Northern Virginia, USA

The National Air and Space Museum on the Mall is so awesome they made an attic for it: the Steven F Udvar-Hazy Center, in Chantilly, VA. It's three times the size of the DC museum and sprawls through massive hangars near Washington Dulles International Airport. Highlights include the SR-71 Blackbird (the fastest jet in the world), space shuttle Discovery (fresh from the clouds after its 2011 retirement) and the Enola Gay (the B-29 that dropped the atomic bomb on Hiroshima). Visitors can hang out in the observation tower and watch the planes take off and land at Dulles, go on a simulator (piloting a jet, taking a space walk), or catch shows at the on-site Airbus IMAX Theater.

Free 90-minute tours through the collection are offered at 10:30am and 1pm daily. To get out here, take the Metro Silver Line to Wiehle-Reston East station and transfer to the Fairfax Connector bus 983 one stop to the museum (you can pay $1.75 cash or use a SmarTrip card on the bus). If stopping in from Dulles airport, you can bus it (again the Fairfax Connector bus 983) or cab it (about $15). If you're driving, take I-66 West to VA 267 West, then VA 28 South, then follow the signs. Parking is $15 (free after 4pm).

Washington

Washington state is the heart of the Pacific Northwest. With that title comes everything you'd hope for from the lush, green Olympic Peninsula, to the white peaks of the Cascade Mountains and the crisp, whale-surrounded San Juan Islands. Head East and you'll see another side of the state that's more cowboy than boutique where the world gets much of its apples and skies go on forever. The biggest urban jolt is Seattle but other corners such as Spokane, Bellingham and Olympia are gaining sophistication by the day.

Whether you're looking for hip cities, beautiful hikes, or laid-back beaches, the diversity of Washington state means there's something here for every type of traveler. In Seattle, you can sample farm-to-table treats at Pike Place Market and get a glimpse of the city lights at the top of the Space Needle, while smaller cities like Tacoma and Olympia entertain with quirky museums and small-town charm. Outdoor adventurers can explore national parks like Olympic, North Cascades, and Mount Rainier, as well hike up to Mt. St. Helens and the Cascade Mountains. Beach bums will find their bliss here too, with the San Juan Islands and Long Beach Peninsula offering plenty of swimming, surfing, and whale-watching.

Sights in Washington

Pike Place Market

Hours: 9am-6pm Mon-Sat, 9am-5pm Sun

Contact: http://www.pikeplacemarket.org

Location: 85 Pike St, Seattle, USA

A cavalcade of noise, smells, personalities, banter and urban theater sprinkled liberally around a spatially challenged waterside strip, Pike Place Market is Seattle in a bottle. In operation since 1907 and still as soulful today as it was on day one, this wonderfully local experience highlights the city for what it really is: all-embracing, eclectic and proudly unique.

If you're coming from downtown, simply walk down Pike St toward the waterfront; you can't miss the huge Public Market sign etched against the horizon. Incidentally, the sign and clock, installed in 1927, constituted one of the first pieces of outdoor neon on the West Coast. From the top of Pike St and 1st Ave, stop and survey the bustle and vitality. Walk down the cobblestone street, past perpetually gridlocked cars (don't even think of driving down to Pike Pl) and, before walking into the market, stop and shake the bronze snout of Rachel the Market Pig, the de-facto mascot and presiding spirit of the market. This life-size piggy bank, carved by Whidbey Island artist Georgia Gerber and named after a real pig, collects about $10,000 each year. The funds are pumped back into market social services. Nearby is the information booth, which has maps of the market and information about Seattle in general. It also serves as a ticket booth, selling discount tickets to various shows throughout the city.

Hiram M Chittenden Locks

Location: 3015 NW 54th St, Seattle, USA

Seattle shimmers like an impressionist painting on sunny days at the Hiram M Chittenden Locks. Here, the fresh waters of Lake Washington and Lake Union drop 22ft into saltwater Puget Sound. Construction of the canal and locks began in 1911; today 100,000 boats pass through them annually. You can view fish-ladder activity through underwater glass panels, stroll through botanical gardens and visit a small museum.

Located on the southern side of the locks, the fish ladder was built in 1976 to allow salmon to fight their way to spawning grounds in the Cascade headwaters of the Sammamish River, which feeds Lake Washington. Keep an eye out for the migrating salmon; nets keep them from over-leaping and stranding themselves on the pavement. Meanwhile, sea lions chase the fish as they attempt to negotiate the ladder. The best time to visit is during spawning season, from mid-June to September.

On the northern entrance to the lock area is the Carl English Jr Botanical Gardens, a charming arboretum and specimen garden. Trails wind through beds filled with flowers and mature trees, each labeled. Flanking the gardens is a visitor center containing a small museum documenting the history of the locks.

Vancouver National Historic Reserve

Situated within easy walking distance of the city center is Vancouver's most important historical monument, and also one of the most important statewide. Comprising an archaeological site, the region's first military post, a waterfront trail and one of the nation's oldest operating airfields, the complex's highlight is the reconstructed Fort Vancouver Historic Site.

Travelers should also pop into the visitor center – with a small museum and a fascinating video on the Lewis and Clark expedition – and the nearby Pearson Air Museum, devoted to the history of Northwest aviation.

Along the northern side of E Evergreen Blvd are the historic homes of Officers Row. Built between 1850 and 1906 for US Army officers and their families, they are currently rented out as offices and apartments. Three of the homes are open for self-guided tours: Grant House, Marshall House and OO Howard House. Ask at the visitor center about guided walks. Elsewhere, the lovely open spaces of the historic reserve are great places to enjoy a picnic, fly a kite or take a stroll. A land bridge connects the reserve with the Columbia River waterfront.

Paradise

Aside from hiding numerous trailheads and being the starting point for most summit hikes, Paradise guards the iconic Paradise Inn (built in 1916) and the massive, informative Henry M Jackson Visitor Center, that holds a cutting-edge museum with hands-on exhibits on everything from flora to glacier formation and shows a must-see 21-minute film entitled Mount Rainier: Restless Giant.

Park naturalists lead free interpretive hikes from the visitor center daily in summer, and snowshoe walks on winter weekends.

The daughter of park pioneer James Longmire unintentionally named this high mountain nirvana, when she exclaimed what a paradise it was on visiting this spot for the first time in the 1880s. Suddenly, the high-mountain nirvana had a name, and a very apt one at that. One of the snowiest places on earth, 5400ft-high Paradise remains the park's most popular draw, with its famous flower meadows backed by dramatic Rainier views on the days (a clear minority annually) when the mountain decides to take its cloudy hat off.

Washington, D.C.

With its neoclassical government buildings and broad avenues, Washington, D.C., looks its part as America's capital. Majestic monuments and memorials pay tribute to notable leaders and great achievements, and merit a visit. But D.C. also lives firmly in the present, and not just politically; new restaurants and bars continually emerge, upping the hipness factor in neighborhoods from Capitol Hill to U Street. Fun museums and tree-shaded parks make it a terrific place for families. You may come for the official sites, but you'll remember D.C.'s local flavor, too.

Sights in Washington, DC

Lincoln Memorial

Hours: 24hr

Contact: http://www.nps.gov/linc

Location: 2 Lincoln Memorial Circle NW, Washington, DC, USA

Anchoring the Mall's west end is the hallowed shrine to Abraham Lincoln, who gazes peacefully across the reflecting pool beneath his neoclassical Doric-columned abode. To the left of Lincoln you can read the words of the

Gettysburg Address, and the hall below highlights other great Lincoln-isms; on the steps, Martin Luther King Jr delivered his famed 'I Have a Dream' speech.

Washington Monument

Hours: 9am-5pm, to 10pm Jun-Aug

Contact: http://www.nps.gov/wamo

Location: 2 15th St NW, Washington, DC, USA

Just peaking at 555ft (and 5in), the Washington Monument is the tallest building in the district. It took two phases of construction to complete; note the different hues of the stone. A 70-second elevator ride whisks you to the observation deck for the city's best views. Same-day tickets for a timed entrance are available at the kiosk by the monument. Arrive early.

During peak season it's a good idea to reserve tickets in advance by phone or online ($1.50 fee, plus additional $3 if you order more than 10 days prior).

Washington National Cathedral

Price: adult/child $10/$6, admission free Sun

Hours: 10am-5:30pm Mon-Fri, to 8pm some days May-Sep, 10am-4:30pm Sat, 8am-4pm Sun

Contact: http://www.nationalcathedral.org, 202-537-6200

Location: 3101 Wisconsin Ave NW, Washington, DC, USA

This Gothic cathedral, as dramatic as its European counterparts, blends both the spiritual and the profane in its architectural treasures. The stained-glass windows are stunning (check out the 'Space Window' with an imbedded lunar rock); you'll need binoculars to spy the Darth Vader gargoyle on the exterior. Specialized tours delve deeper into the esoteric; call or go online for the schedule. There's also an excellent cafe here.

The Episcopal diocese runs this house of worship, but it's open to all faiths and creeds. Presidents attend multi-faith services following their inauguration, state funerals are hosted inside and this was where Martin Luther King Jr gave his last Sunday sermon. It took 82 years to build the edifice – Teddy Roosevelt laid the cornerstone in 1908, and construction didn't technically stop until 1990. The cathedral provoked strong opposition early on, but the multi-faith character of worship helped mollify the arguments.

The building is neo-Gothic, but it's embellished by distinctive American accents. In the main sanctuary, chapels honor Martin Luther King Jr (in the Kellogg Bay) and Abe Lincoln. Helen Keller and Woodrow Wilson, among others, are buried in the crypt. Themed tours ($15 to $25 including admission) take in all of the above; it's a good idea to make advance bookings online in spring and summer.

Other highlights… Take the elevator to the tower overlook for expansive city views. Meander outside through the peaceful winding paths in the Bishop's Garden. The 11:15am Sunday service features lovely choral music and a 10-bell peal of the carillon afterwards. Choristers sing Evensong at 5:30pm Monday to Friday (and 4pm on Sundays) during the school year.

The 2011 earthquake took a heavy toll on the cathedral (causing an estimated $26 millions of damages). Repairs are underway, but visitors still have full access to the key areas of interest inside the cathedral.

Capitol

Hours: 8:30am-4:30pm Mon-Sat

Contact: http://www.visitthecapitol.gov

Location: First St NE & E Capitol St, Washington, DC, USA

Since 1800, this is where the legislative branch of American government – i.e. Congress – has met to write the country's laws. The lower House of

Representatives (435 members) and upper Senate (100) meet respectively in the south and north wings of the building. Enter via the underground visitor center below the East Plaza. Guided tours of the building are free, but you need a ticket. Get one at the information desk, or reserve online in advance (there's no fee).

The hour-long jaunt showcases the exhaustive background of a building that fairly sweats history. You'll watch a cheesy film first, then staff members lead you into the ornate halls and whispery chambers cluttered with the busts, statues and personal mementos of generations of Congress members.

To watch Congress in session, you need a separate visitor pass. US citizens must get one from their representative or senator; foreign visitors should take their passports to the House and Senate Appointment Desks on the upper level. Congressional committee hearings are actually more interesting (and substantive) if you care about what's being debated; check for a schedule, locations and to see if they're open to the public (they often are) at www.house.gov and www.senate.gov.

White House

Hours: tours 7:30-11:30am Tue-Thu, to 1:30pm Fri & Sat

Contact: http://www.whitehouse.gov, 202-456-7041

Location: Washington, DC, USA

The White House has survived both fire (the Brits torched it in 1814) and insults (Jefferson groused that it was 'big enough for two emperors, one Pope and the grand Lama'). Tours must be arranged in advance. Americans must apply via one of their state's members of Congress, and non-Americans must apply through either the US consulate in their home country or their country's consulate in DC. Applications are taken from 21 days to six months in advance; three months ahead is the recommended sweet spot.

If that sounds like too much work, pop into the spiffy, renovated White House Visitor Center. It's not the real deal, but hey, executive artifacts and paraphernalia are on display. Or get a view of the White House from the outside. Cars aren't allowed to pass the building on Pennsylvania Ave; you can get good photos across the North Lawn from here. Or move to E St NW and take pictures across the South Lawn.

West Virginia

Wild and wonderful West Virginia is often overlooked by both American and foreign travelers. It doesn't help that the state can't seem to shake its negative stereotypes. That's too bad, because West Virginia is one of the prettiest states in the Union. With its line of unbroken green mountains, raging white-water rivers and snowcapped ski resorts, this is an outdoor-lovers' paradise.

Created by secessionists from secession, the people here still think of themselves as hardscrabble sons of miners, and that perception isn't entirely off. But the Mountain State is also gentrifying and, occasionally, that's a good thing: the arts are flourishing in the valleys, where some towns offer a welcome break from the state's constantly evolving outdoor activities.

With more than 226,500 acres of state parks, forests, and recreation areas, and more than a million acres of federal lands, West Virginia offers a quick escape from the urban centers of Baltimore, Philadelphia, Pittsburgh, and Washington, DC. Historic towns, ski resorts, caverns, and unparalleled natural scenery draw visitors to the Mountain State. The Monongahela National Forest, popular with hikers, anglers, hunters, and rock climbers, covers more than 900,000 acres along the eastern border.

Dominated by the craggy peaks of the Allegheny Mountains, part of the Appalachian chain, West Virginia has a varied landscape: The gentle hills of the eastern Panhandle give way to the rugged mountains of the Potomac Highlands and Mountaineer Country, which then slope into the lush Greenbrier and New River valleys and the scenic Mountain Lakes region. Moving west toward the Ohio River, the rolling terrain fades into the populous swath of the Metro and Mid-Ohio valleys and the northern Panhandle.

Sights in West Virginia

John Brown Wax Museum

Price: adult/child $7/5

Hours: 9am-4:30pm Apr-May & Sep-Nov, 10am-5:30pm Jun-Aug, 9am-4:30pm Sat & Sun only Mar & Dec, closed Jan-Feb

Contact: http://www.johnbrownwaxmuseum.com, 304-535-6342

Location: 168 High St, Harpers Ferry, USA

Not to be confused with the National Park–run museum, this private wax museum is a kitschy (and rather overpriced) attraction that pays tribute to the man who led an ill-conceived slave rebellion here. The exhibits are laughably old-school; nothing says historical accuracy like scratchy vocals, jerky animatronics and dusty old dioramas.

Black Voices

Hours: 9am-5pm

Location: High St, Harpers Ferry, USA

This worthwhile, interactive exhibit has narrated stories of hardships and hard-won victories by African Americans from the times of enslavement through the Civil Rights era. Across the street is the Storer College exhibit, which gives an overview of the ground-breaking educational center and Niagara movement that formed in its wake.

Storer College Campus

Contact: http://www.nps.gov/hafe

Location: Fillmore St, Harpers Ferry, USA

Founded immediately after the Civil Long, Storer College grew from a one-room schoolhouse for freed slaves to a respected college open to all races and creeds. It closed in 1955. You can freely wander the historic campus, reachable by taking the path to upper town, past St Peter's church, Jefferson Rock and Harper Cemetery.

Beckley Exhibition Coal Mine

Price: adult/child $20/12

Hours: 10am-6pm Apr-Oct

Contact: http://www.beckley.org/exhibition_coal_mine, 304-256-1747

The Beckley Exhibition Coal Mine in Beckley is a museum to the region's coal heritage. Visitors can ride a train 1500ft into a former coal mine. Bring a jacket, as it's cold underground!

Wisconsin

Wisconsin is cheesy and proud of it. The state pumps out 2.5 billion pounds of cheddar, Gouda and other smelly goodness – a quarter of America's hunks – from its cow-speckled farmland per year. Local license plates read 'The Dairy State' with udder dignity. Folks here even refer to themselves as 'cheeseheads' and emphasize it by wearing novelty foam rubber cheese-wedge hats for special occasions (most notably during Green Bay Packers football games).

So embrace the cheese thing, because there's a good chance you'll be here for a while. Wisconsin has heaps to offer: exploring the craggy cliffs and lighthouses of Door County, kayaking through sea caves at Apostle Islands National Lakeshore, cow chip throwing along US 12 and soaking up beer, art and festivals in Milwaukee and Madison.

Most of Wisconsin's landscape was formed some 10,000 years ago by a great glacier that left in its wake 15,000 lakes, 12,624 rivers and streams, pristine prairies, and some of America's finest examples of glacial topography. Today this means endless opportunities for hiking, bicycling, canoeing, bird-watching, snowmobiling, skiing, and ice fishing.

Door County (a limestone peninsula with more than 200 miles of shoreline) and Kettle Moraine (a swath of glacial deposit that runs 100 miles from north to south) are two of the best areas to appreciate fall foliage. Wisconsin Dells'

glacially sculpted cliffs along the Wisconsin River, paired with some of the country's best indoor and outdoor water parks, are the state's prime tourist attraction.
Milwaukee, Wisconsin's largest city, is a city of neighborhoods. Milwaukee's zoo and museum are among the best in the country, and there are top-notch art centers and galleries. From spring to late summer, a constant stream of lakefront festivals celebrates immigrant heritage with lively entertainment and, of course, Wisconsin's famous cheeses and beers.

Madison, the state's capital, is a bustling college town that has unique boutique shopping, ethnic dining, and the continental United States' only authentic Thai pavilion at Olbrich Botanical Gardens.

Sights in Wisconsin

Harley-Davidson Museum

Price: adult/child $20/10

Hours: 9am-6pm Fri-Wed, to 8pm Thu May-Sep, from 10am Oct-Apr

Contact: http://www.h-dmuseum.com, 877-436-8738

Location: 400 W Canal St, Milwaukee, USA

Hundreds of motorcycles show the styles through the decades, including the flashy rides of Elvis and Evel Knievel. You can sit in the saddle of various bikes (on the bottom floor, in the Experience Gallery) and take badass photos. Even non-bikers will enjoy the interactive exhibits and tough, leather-clad crowds.

It all started in 1903, when Milwaukee schoolmates William Harley and Arthur Davidson built and sold their first motorcycle. A century later the big bikes are a symbol of American manufacturing pride. The museum is located in a sprawling industrial building just south of downtown.

Dr. Evermor's Sculpture Park

Hours: 11am-5pm Mon & Thu-Sat, from noon Sun

Contact: http://www.worldofdrevermor.com, 608-219-7830

The doc welds old pipes, carburetors and other salvaged metal into a hallucinatory world of futuristic birds, dragons and other bizarre structures. The crowning glory is the giant, egg-domed Forevertron, once cited by Guinness World Records as the globe's largest scrap-metal sculpture. Finding the park entrance is tricky. Look for the old Badger Army Ammunition Plant, and then a small sign leading you into a driveway across the street. Call to confirm it's open.

The doc is in poor health now and isn't around much, but his wife Lady Eleanor usually is. The park is 30 miles northwest of Madison on US 12.

House on the Rock

Price: adult/child $15/9

Hours: 9am-6pm May-Aug, to 5pm rest of year, closed mid-Nov–mid-Mar

Contact: http://www.thehouseontherock.com, 608-935-3639

Location: 5754 Hwy 23, Spring Green, USA

It's one of Wisconsin's busiest attractions. Alex Jordan built the structure atop a rock column in 1959 (some say as an 'up yours' to neighbor Frank Lloyd Wright). He then stuffed the house to mind-blowing proportions with wonderments, including the world's largest carousel, whirring music machines, freaky dolls and crazed folk art. The house is broken into three parts, each with its own tour. Visitors with stamina (and about four hours to kill) can experience the whole shebang for adult/child $30/16.

Miller Brewing Company

Hours: 10:30am-4:30pm Mon-Sat, to 3:30pm Sun Jun-Aug, to 3:30pm Mon-Sat Sep-May

Contact: http://www.millercoors.com, 414-931-2337

Location: 4251 W State St, Milwaukee, USA

Pabst and Schlitz have moved on, but Miller preserves Milwaukee's beer legacy. Join the legions lined up for the free tours. Though the mass-produced beer may not be your favorite, the factory impresses with its sheer scale: you'll visit the packaging plant where 2000 cans are filled each minute, and the warehouse where a half-million cases await shipment. And then there's the generous tasting session at the tour's end, where you can down three full-size samples. Don't forget your ID.

Wyoming

While the days of the Wild West seem like history to many of us, Wyoming is still a land of cowboys and ranches. Even in high-end Jackson Hole, western attire mixes with ski gear. True to that frontier spirit, it's a land perfect for exploration. The world's oldest national park, Yellowstone, brings scores of visitors to the state every year for the geothermal features and abundant wildlife. But don't miss out on the Grand Tetons, atmospheric towns like Cody and Jackson, and vast stretches of wide-open plains.

With wind, restless grasses and wide blue skies, the most sparsely populated state offers solitude to spare. Wyoming may be nuzzled in the bosom of America, but emptiness defines it.

Though steeped in ranching culture – just see the line of Stetsons at the local credit union – Wyoming is the number-one coal producer in the US, and is also big in natural gas, crude oil and diamonds. Deeply conservative, its propensity toward industry has sometimes made it an uneasy steward of the land.

But wilderness may be Wyoming's greatest bounty. Its northwestern corner is home to the magnificent national parks of Yellowstone and Grand Teton. Chic Jackson and sporty Lander make great bases for epic hiking, climbing and skiing. For a truer taste of Western life, check out the plain prairie towns of Laramie and Cheyenne.

Sights in Wyoming

Buffalo Bill Center of the West

Price: adult/child $19/11

Hours: 8am-6pm May–mid-Sep, 8am-5pm mid-Sep–Oct, 10am-5pm Nov, Mar & Apr, 10am-5pm Thu-Sun Dec-Feb

Contact: http://www.centerofthewest.org

Location: 720 Sheridan Ave, Cody, USA

Cody's major tourist attraction is the superb Buffalo Bill Historical Center. A sprawling complex of five museums, it showcases everything Western: from posters, grainy films and artifacts pertaining to Buffalo Bill's world-famous Wild West shows, to galleries showcasing frontier-oriented artwork, to museums dedicated to Native Americans. Its Draper Museum of Natural

History explores the Yellowstone region's ecosystem with excellent results. The galleries are given regular overhauls to keep presentations fresh. There's also a daily (1pm) raptor presentation.

Entry is valid for two consecutive days. Save a couple of bucks by booking online.

National Museum of Wildlife Art

Price: adult/child $14/6

Hours: 9am-5pm, from 11am Sun spring & fall

Contact: http://www.wildlifeart.org, 307-733-5771

Location: 2820 Rungius Rd, Jackson, USA

If you visit one area museum, make it this one, with major works by Bierstadt, Rungius, Remington and Russell. It's worth driving up just for the outdoor sculptures and the building itself (inspired by a ruined Scottish castle). The discovery gallery has a kids' studio for drawing and print rubbing that adults plainly envy. Check the website for summer film-series and art-class schedules.

Mammoth Hot Springs

Location: Yellowstone National Park, USA

The imposing Lower and Upper Terraces of Mammoth Hot Springs are the highlight of the Mammoth region. An hour's worth of boardwalks wend their way around the Lower Terraces and connect to the Upper Terraces Loop, which is also accessed by car. Surreal Palette Springs (accessed from the lower parking lot) and sulfur-yellow Canary Springs (accessed from the upper loop) are the most beautiful sites, but thermal activity is constantly in flux, so check the current state of play at the visitor center.

The famously ornate travertine formations that characterize the lower terraces of Minerva Spring have been dry since 2002 but are still beautiful. The terraces are the product of dissolved subterranean limestone (itself originally deposited by ancient seas), which is continuously deposited as the spring waters cool on contact with air. As guidebooks love to say, the mountain is in effect turning itself inside out, depositing over a ton of travertine (limestone deposits) here every year. The colored runoff from the naturally white terraces is due to the bacteria and algae that flourish in the warm waters.

At the bottom of the terraces, by the parking area, is the phallic, dormant 36ft-high hot-spring cone called Liberty Cap, apparently named after hats worn during the French Revolution. The former spring must have had particularly high water pressure to create such a tall cone over its estimated 2500-year life span.

Across the road, Opal Spring is slowly converging on a century-old residence designed by Robert Reamer (the architect of the Old Faithful Inn and Roosevelt Arch). Park strategists have to decide which to preserve – the architecture or the spring. The rutting Rocky Mountain elk that sometimes lounge on Opal Terrace in fall are a favorite photo opportunity.

A 1.5-mile paved one-way road loops counterclockwise around the Upper Terraces; vehicles longer than 25ft will have to park on the main Grand Loop Rd. The overlook affords impressive views of the Lower Terraces and Fort Yellowstone and offers access to Canary Springs and New Blue Spring. Highlights further around the loop include the sponge-like Orange Spring Mound and the perfectly named White Elephant Back Terrace. The loop joins the main road near the large Angel Terrace.

For an alternative perspective on foot walk the Howard Eaton Trail from Orange Spring Mound (unsigned) or from the Snow Pass trailhead.

Ninety-minute ranger walks leave from the Upper Terrace daily at 9am.

Back Basin

Location: Yellowstone National Park, USA

Two miles of boardwalks and gentle trails snake through Norris' forested Back Basin. The main show here is Steamboat Geyser, the world's tallest active geyser, which infrequently skyrockets up to an awesome 380ft (over twice as high as Old Faithful). The geyser was dormant for half a century until 1961 and quiet again for most of the 1990s, but erupted in 2013 and 2014. At the time of research the geyser was splashing with frequent but minor bursts only.

As you exit the museum from Porcelain Basin, take the right-hand path into Back Basin. Emerald Spring combines reflected blue light with yellow sulfur deposits to create a striking blue-green color. For a shorter loop take the right branch just past Steamboat Geyser; otherwise continue clockwise around the basin.

Near to Steamboat Geyser, yellow-and-green Cistern Spring is linked to Steamboat through underground channels and empties for a day or two following Steamboat's eruptions. The spring is slowly drowning its surroundings in geyserite deposits.

Dramatic Echinus Geyser (e-ki-nus), the park's largest acidic geyser, erupted every couple of hours until fairly recently, with spouts reaching up to 60ft and sometimes continuing for more than an hour, but these days it's pretty quiet. You can get closer to the action here than at almost any of the park's other geysers, and if you sit in the grandstand, you may well get wet during an eruption (kids love it). Furious bubbling signals an imminent eruption. Echinus is named for its spiny geyserite deposits (echinoderms include sea urchins), characteristic of acidic solutions.

After deposits sealed its tiny, 2in-wide vent, Porkchop Geyser exploded in 1989, blowing huge lumps of geyserite 200ft away (you can see a lump of Porkchop in the Old Faithful Visitor Center). Recent rises in the ground temperature forced the park service to reroute the boardwalk around the back of Porkchop Geyser for safety purposes.

Nearby Pearl Geyser is one of the park's prettiest. Punsters love the British pronunciation of Veteran Geyser – 'Veteran Geezer.' Minute Geyser is a victim of early visitor vandalism and sadly no longer erupts every 60 seconds, despite its constant bubbling.

Conclusion

Thank you for reading my travel guide to USA book. If you enjoyed it, make sure to check some of my other books (including more travel guides) at https://www.amazon.com/Alex-Pitt/e/B0184KH3EI.

CPSIA information can be obtained
at www.ICGtesting.com
Printed in the USA
BVHW040644250720
584655BV00015B/543